RADICAL
FOOTBALL

Steve Fleming

RADICAL FOOTBALL

Jürgen Griesbeck and the Story of Football for Good

Featuring a Radical XI on their vision for football

Foreword by
Lotte Wubben-Moy

First published by Pitch Publishing, 2022

Pitch Publishing
A2 Yeoman Gate
Yeoman Way
Worthing
Sussex
BN13 3QZ
www.pitchpublishing.co.uk
info@pitchpublishing.co.uk

A CIP catalogue record is available for this book
from the British Library.

ISBN 978 1 80150 114 9

Typesetting and origination by Pitch Publishing

Printed and bound in Great Britain by TJ Books, Padstow

Contents

Life doesn't end here. We have to go on. Life cannot end here. No matter how difficult, we must stand back up. We only have two options: either allow anger to paralyse us and the violence continues, or we overcome and try our best to help others. It's our choice.

Andrés Escobar, Wednesday, 29 June 1994

Acknowledgements

JÜRGEN AND Steve would like to thank everyone who has been a part of the story, and the many people who have contributed directly to the creation of this book; it has been a team effort, and it wouldn't exist without the time, energy and commitment of family, friends and colleagues around the world. The telling is one part, the sharing is another, so we also take this opportunity to ask for your help in spreading the word, and in taking the book and its message far and wide.

A special note of thanks to the thousands of Football for Good practitioners – the coaches and the educators – who are on the pitch every day, using their passion for football, and sometimes risking their lives, to tackle the world's most pressing challenges. We honour those colleagues and young people who have been killed for standing up for what they believe in, and we thank the people in the background – the friends and family members – who, like our own loved ones, have made great sacrifices along the way.

We also recognise that this is not the whole story of Football for Good, and there are many people not mentioned in the book who have contributed enormously to the mission. We acknowledge you all. And it is, of course, a story that continues to be written, in thousands of back yards, streets and classrooms, on concrete pitches and dusty fields, and, increasingly, in the stadiums and boardrooms of professional football. We are a growing team, playing together, for the game of our lives.

Foreword

I'VE LEARNT most about life with a ball at my feet.

Born and raised in London, I was immersed in street football from a young age. In football I found freedom and independence. On the concrete pitch where my love for the game began, anything was possible. And that is a feeling that years later, as I play week-in week-out professionally, I still fight to hold on to.

When I read Jürgen's story, I felt an energy that I can only liken to that which you share with team-mates in a huddle before a big game. Jürgen has managed to unite competing players, managers and brands in a unique huddle that is the Common Goal movement. Harnessing the power of football, Common Goal encourages all within the industry to pledge 1% back to a chosen cause. This book details the incredible journey that led to the establishment of the movement, going on to explore its growth from strength to strength in the years since.

I am proud to be a member of Common Goal.

At seven years old, I would get home from school and stuff down a snack. Then it was immediately out the door to play football on the housing estate at the end of my road. I wouldn't even pause to change my shoes, having worn my beloved astroturfs all day ready for lunchtime kick-arounds. I would get to the pitch and begin the match I had been waiting for. It didn't matter if there were nine others at the pitch when I got there, or no one, the number of girls playing would always be the same. One. That was me.

I rarely knew any of the boys I played football with. We would go from strangers to team-mates in the space of an evening. When we took to the pitch it was less about who was playing and more about *what* we were playing – that's the beauty of the game. The possibility that in a moment, nothing else matters. With the ball, I found self-expression through the language of football, and a world where everyone was accepted and could be understood.

It is astonishing to think that if I had been born in London 30 years earlier, I would not have been allowed to even play football; 2021 marked the 100th anniversary of the FA's ban of women's football. That ruling lasted for 50 years. Could I have even dreamed of playing for my country at Wembley during that time? It would have seemed absurd. But I was born in 1999, my generation could dream, and in 2021 I turned that dream into a reality.

What does the next 50 years hold for football? *Radical Football* puts forward an exciting vision for what might be possible if we approach the future as a team. It is a story with an important message for every football fan and player, about working together to put purpose at the heart of the game. I see my pledge to Common Goal as a piece of that future. I want to empower thousands more young people to dream of representing their country, to discover the language of football or to simply enjoy a kick-about. After all, I learned most about life with a ball at my feet.

Lotte Wubben-Moy
Arsenal, England and Common Goal

The First Half

1

Manrique, July 1995

THE TWO groups of young men pulled out guns from their jeans and leather jackets and put them in piles on the ground. One member of each gang was left to stand guard over the weapons while the others stepped on to the football pitch. In that moment everything changed; the two gangs became two teams, and with the tools of violence left on the touchline, a game of football commenced. The players were unaware that watching from outside of the wire mesh fence that surrounded the dusty pitch was a young German man. Nor could they have anticipated that this fleeting moment in their lives would trigger a change of direction in his, which would ultimately transform the landscape of football forever.

Jürgen Griesbeck was walking the hilly streets of Manrique, a district in the north-east of Medellín, Colombia's second-largest city, when he saw the rival gangs take out their revolvers and ritually place them on the ground. What followed was a competitive football match, with the two teams self-officiating and reaching agreements. Jürgen watched the game for ten minutes before continuing his walk, taking with him the genesis of an idea.

In previous months, Jürgen had been walking a lot. He wanted to explore the city, naïve to the danger that he faced every time he stepped out alone into the unfamiliar streets. The Medellín Cartel had collapsed 18 months earlier in December 1993 with the killing of its leader Pablo Escobar by the Colombian National Police, and in the aftermath, a fragmented collection of gangs emerged. The boys Jürgen saw on the pitch that afternoon, just a 20-minute walk from the rooftop where Escobar was shot dead, were a part of that chaotic legacy.

Jürgen's walks were more than just a desire to familiarise with his local community. A year earlier, the Colombian footballer Andrés Escobar (no relation to Pablo) had been murdered less than two weeks after scoring an own goal at the 1994 World Cup against the USA. The death of Andrés – 'the Gentleman of Football' – shook Jürgen to the core. He had met Andrés while attending matches of his home club Atlético Nacional, gaining insight into the personality of a man so beloved by Colombians. In the wake of Andrés's murder, the PhD that Jürgen had been studying in Public Health became meaningless, and he resigned his Doctorate to begin a Master's in Contemporary Social Problems. As he walked the streets of Medellín, Jürgen wanted to understand more about the underlying complexities that characterised the city, but he was also searching for something more specific, a positive way forward from the brutal killing of Andrés. Until now, it had not occurred to him that the solution could be found within football itself.

As the blue Medellín skies faded to dusk, Jürgen arrived on 66th Street. The blue and white 1954 Ford Crestline parked outside his small house indicated that his wife Elida and their baby daughter were already home. After putting four-month-old Sara to bed, over dinner he told Elida about his experience at the football match. She was less enthusiastic about Jürgen's ramblings and, having grown up in Medellín, was acutely aware of the city's inherent risks, later explaining, 'When Jürgen began to walk the neighbourhoods of Medellín, especially those of greatest conflict, they were times of confusion and instability in the city, with armed violence from urban guerrillas, drug-trafficking groups, paramilitaries, common criminals, police and the military.'

Yet while the dangers were ever-present, Elida knew that her husband was going through a process, and needed time to work things out. So, while the walks continued, she advised him on how to stay safe and avoid dangerous situations. 'I would also pray,' she recalls, 'asking his angel for protection.'

That night, as she listened to Jürgen's story, Elida reflected on the many football pitches that Pablo Escobar had built in an effort to gain public support, a strangely positive legacy of a man who had brought so much death and misery to Medellín, and the country as a whole. These fields provided dedicated spaces for playing football, alongside the hundreds of makeshift pitches that marked the streets, up and down steep hills, around corners and incorporating street furniture. As he recounted the events at the pitch that afternoon, it was evident to Elida that something was brewing in her husband's mind.

Indeed, in the weeks that followed, the experience in Manrique continued to dominate Jürgen's thoughts, and in witnessing the transition of the young men from armed rivals to two teams co-operating in a sporting encounter, he started to believe that football could be more than just a leisure activity. He began sharing with friends, and colleagues at the university, the idea that football could be a wider civic experience, used purposefully as a vehicle for promoting peaceful coexistence and conflict resolution.

At the age of 30, Jürgen's journey in Football for Good had begun.

2

Costa Rica, 1989–1990

Six years earlier

JÜRGEN SAT bolt upright. Something was different. He took a few seconds to adjust to the light before realising that he, and his bed, were on the other side of the room. He jumped up, threw on some clothes and went out to the kitchen where Doña Zeidy and Don Antonio were preparing breakfast. His hosts explained that earthquakes were a daily occurrence in Costa Rica, most of them unnoticeable at around three on the Richter scale, but some with sufficient magnitude and proximity to rearrange the furniture, along with any young Germans who happened to be sleeping on it.

Jürgen had recently arrived for a year in Latin America, starting with nine months in Costa Rica, to be followed by three months travelling. The opportunity had come about through his studies at the German Sport University in Cologne where he was taking a diploma in Sports Science. His department had links with the University of Costa Rica, and a series of academic internships had been arranged, along with sports journalism placements at a local radio station and newspaper. Three years earlier, in 1986, he had spent several months travelling through Mexico and Guatemala, where the experience of struggling to communicate had prompted him to study Roman Languages when he returned to Germany. He had subsequently developed a workable proficiency in Spanish, and over the coming year he would move towards fluency.

Doña Zeidy and Don Antonio were an elderly couple in their 70s. They had never travelled more than a few miles, and with no children of their own, they doted on Jürgen like an adopted son, taking care of his every need and ensuring that he was amply fed and watered. Their two-storey house was in Heredia, a district on the outskirts of the capital San José, and Jürgen had been both relieved and amazed when the 'address' – '250 metres past the Church of Fatima, turn left after the big tree, third house on the right' – had been sufficient for the taxi driver to easily navigate from the airport to his temporary home. Thankfully, the house was just a 30-minute walk to the sports campus at the university where he would be studying.

Soon after he arrived in Central America, dramatic events began to unfold in Germany and Eastern Europe, with the fall of the Berlin Wall on 9 November 1989. With rolling news and smartphones still a thing of the future, Jürgen relied on what snippets of information he could gather from the local newspapers, along with letters from his girlfriend that took three weeks to arrive from Germany. Phone calls were too expensive.

While he recognised their historic significance, for Jürgen the events in Germany were both physically and spiritually distant, and he focused instead on embracing his time in Costa Rica. With interesting assignments, an active social life and many new friends, it was an all-consuming introduction to the Latin American way of life, and radically different to what he knew. His previous travels had provided a brief insight, but through the experience of living and working in one place, and of building meaningful relationships, he was gradually able to relax his instinctive 'Germanic restraint' and immerse himself fully into Latin culture. He also fell in love with the natural beauty of the small country, with active volcanoes and rainforest dominating the slender strip of land that separates the Atlantic and Pacific oceans, just 170 miles across at the narrowest point.

Jürgen's final month in Costa Rica coincided with the 1990 World Cup in Italy, and it turned out to be a memorable conclusion to his stay. Costa Rica had qualified for the finals for the first time, and the team played with an attacking flair that saw them achieve two victories in the group stages, beating Scotland 1-0 and coming from behind to defeat Sweden 2-1. A 1-0 loss to Brazil could not stop them from coming second in their group and qualifying for the knockout stages, where the fairy tale run ended with a 4-1 loss to Czechoslovakia. It was a magical time for Jürgen, watching the games in small, crowded bars and at his friends' homes, celebrating the victories, dancing late into the night, and sharing in the joy and passion with which the Costa Ricans embraced football and their national team.

There was, of course, another team that Jürgen was supporting at the tournament, but he became increasingly embarrassed as West Germany progressed in a style and spirit that contrasted the Costa Rican side. Led imperiously by Lothar Matthäus, and with many talented players, the West German team was equally recognised for its hard-nosed approach, regular altercations with the opposition and, ultimately, a savage final that saw Jürgen Klinsmann infamously writhing on the floor, two Argentinians sent off and a controversially awarded penalty that secured victory. Jürgen soon realised, however, that the Costa Ricans saw it differently, 'They admired the tenacity and resilience of the West German team, and respected their ability to win, even when it seemed improbable.'

As his time in Costa Rica came to an end, Jürgen prepared to spend the next three months travelling with his girlfriend, who had arrived from Germany. Funds were running low, but they resisted the temptation to bring forward their return flight and shorten their travels. Instead, they would stick to the original timeframe, even if it meant scraping by. He bade an affectionate farewell to Doña Zeidy and Don Antonio, and with generously packed lunches, they boarded a train at the station in San José.

They were on their way to South America.

3

World Upside Down, 1990

THE POST boat chugged along the Amazon River, the big paddle wheel at the stern churning the water that, once boiled, also served as a drinking and cooking source for the passengers. Jürgen swung out of his hammock, taking care not to knock the adjacent sleepers and send a chain reaction of swinging beds through the lower deck. As he emerged into the morning light the boat began to move towards the portside bank, where Jürgen could see nothing but densely packed rainforest. Gradually, the forms and faces of indigenous people appeared, and there was a brief exchange of parcels and food stuffs. As the boat slowly moved again into the heart of the Amazon, accompanied as ever by the pink river dolphins, the tribespeople melted back into the vegetation, leaving no visible trace of their fleeting presence.

Jürgen and his girlfriend had been on the road for more than a month, travelling mainly on small and stifling jam-packed buses and eking out their dwindling budget on a diet predominantly consisting of banana sandwiches. The journey had taken them first to Colombia and along the coast to Venezuela before heading south on the Orinoco to Brazil and the Amazon. Armed only with an increasingly battered South American travel guide as a source of information, they slept on the floors of train stations and sometimes in empty brothel bedrooms, awakened in the night by strange noises that pervaded the building.

After ten days on the post boat, the pair arrived in Peru, making their way along the coast into Ecuador and back into Colombia. Late one evening, as they travelled between Cali and Santa Marta, they arrived on a night bus into Medellín, and as the vehicle wound its way downhill towards the centre, Jürgen had the impression that he was looking at the world upside down, with the lights of the city below resembling the stars in the sky. Medellín is located in a valley, with steep slopes rising to the east and west; the higher up you go the more marked the poverty becomes, and the less regulation there is in terms of land ownership and connection to utilities. The bus drove slowly down through these communities, and into the well-lit centre, where the young couple caught a connecting bus for the next stage of their journey. As they zigzagged back up into the mountains, Jürgen turned one final time to see the city lights, once again with the sensation that he was looking down into the Milky Way, and decided that one day he would return to Medellín.

Moving through the countryside, the two travellers naïvely and unwittingly passed through areas that were heavily populated by guerrillas and busy with the production of cocaine. Yet despite these risks, the greatest threat to Jürgen's life occurred in the historic coastal city of Santa Marta, which had been hit by unprecedented rainfall in the days before they arrived. Small wooden bridges had been erected so that people could move about, and with the streets indistinguishable from the pavement, on one occasion Jürgen disappeared suddenly down an open drain, totally submerged and only saved from being washed away in the sewers by his rucksack which floated back up to the surface with its owner still attached. Several local people hurried over to assist as the spluttering backpacker was pulled out of the drain to safety.

After making it to Ciudad Perdida, the 'Lost City' in Santa Marta, and coupled with visiting a Mayan graveyard in San Agustín, Jürgen was touched with a mix of wonder and sadness, 'The magic of these cultures was tangible, but even by the end of the 1980s the indigenous people that remained, and their way of life, had almost disappeared.'

At the same time, his own life in West Germany seemed increasingly remote, as the country moved towards reunification with the East. With their money almost exhausted Jürgen and his girlfriend arrived in Caracas, the Venezuelan capital, and exactly 365 days after he had arrived in Latin America, they flew home to a country markedly different to the one he had left. Jürgen too returned a changed man, a lifelong relationship established with Latin America, and though it remained distant and undefined, a growing sense that his future would be shaped by a greater purpose.

4

Cologne, 1990–1992

AFTER A year away, Jürgen threw himself back into academic life at the university, and reintegrated himself within the social networks that had continued to evolve in his absence. He had four semesters remaining in a seven-year academic journey in Cologne that would ultimately result in diplomas in Roman Languages and Sports Science, the equivalent of two Bachelor's Degrees. Academia was a convenience for Jürgen at this stage of his life. He liked the professional and intellectual environment, and with tertiary education free of charge (as it largely remains in Germany), there was little pressure to complete his courses quickly. Instead, Jürgen enjoyed the freedom and flexibility to stretch out his education and to shape the focus of his studies, without committing to a specific career direction. He also found that he was increasingly drawn to research, and having once aspired to be a teacher, he now instinctively saw his future elsewhere. 'It was perhaps an early clue to the leadership style that I would later adopt,' says Jürgen. 'Developing new ideas to inspire change, as opposed to supervising or managing.'

Yet while his experiences in Latin America had opened his eyes to the world, Jürgen's aspirations for the future were still rooted in what he calls 'industrial-age thinking'; the idea that, after completing education, people adopt a traditional profession which they pursue for the rest of their working lives. This was not driven by a desire for wealth, more a reflection of the societal parameters of ambition that were Jürgen's frame of reference. Concepts of global citizenship and social entrepreneurship barely existed, and the idea of pursuing a career driven by purpose, and in order to contribute to people and planet, was not yet in his field of vision.

Throughout his studies, Jürgen spent the summer months in various employment. This often involved driving, from his first job, aged 15, cutting grass on a ride-on lawnmower at the local hospital, to operating a 7.5-tonne lorry transporting tomato ketchup. One of his favourite summer jobs was delivering parcels for Hermes, 'We had to arrive very early and load more than 200 parcels in our vans as efficiently as possible. I enjoyed the logistics of planning my route using only hard-copy maps. There was no GPS or mobiles so it required careful organisation to ensure we delivered everything on time. We did not get paid for any parcels that came back.'

When he wasn't driving vehicles, Jürgen was helping to construct them, and spent several months making exhaust pipes on an Audi assembly line. On his first day, after three or four hours, one of the workers came over and nudged him. He removed his ear defenders and was informed that having reached the required daily quota agreed by the union, they would now be stopping work. Jürgen lifted his goggles and looked around to see that everyone else was now resting or sleeping behind their work stations. It was a strange concept, but at the same time it seemed pointless to keep making an excess of exhaust pipes, so the next day he brought in a book and spent the spare time reading. Despite the unused hours, the job at Audi was well paid, and Jürgen was surprised and intrigued that he could earn enough in two months to sustain a year of travel and living in Latin America. He didn't understand what made this possible, but he sensed that it reflected an underlying injustice.

Another summer was spent working as a waiter at a Mexican restaurant in Cologne's Belgian District, an area popular with tourists. He relished the camaraderie of working with other young people as part of a dynamic team in a fast-moving environment, and enjoyed talking with diners from other countries. 'It presented another opportunity to practise my Spanish,' says Jürgen, 'and to further understand the value of languages in intimately and effectively communicating, and building understanding, with others.' At the end of each shift, in the early hours of the morning, he cycled home through the empty streets with a well-earned 100 Deutsche Marks in his back pocket.

These jobs, among others, were a means to an end for Jürgen, and they enabled him to be financially independent from his parents by the age of 18. He also took from these diverse employments, subconsciously, a greater understanding of his character and of his strengths – an enjoyment of connecting and collaborating with others, and an ability for planning and logistics in achieving effective and efficient ways of operating.

In June 1992, Jürgen and his girlfriend decided to break up. They had been together for nine years, since high school, and over breakfast one morning, sitting on their balcony, there was a painful but amicable conversation about their relationship. Where was it headed? Were they consciously together? After so many years, and from such a young age, maybe they needed to know what it felt like being apart. They decided to separate, for a time, that 'ended up being forever'.

Less than a month later, while training for his football team, Jürgen fell awkwardly on the wet clay surface and tore his anterior cruciate ligament (ACL). He underwent surgery and began eight weeks of recovery, with a pair of crutches to help him up the stairs to his fourth-floor apartment.

In the midst of the emptiness that Jürgen initially felt after the break-up, and the frustrating aftermath of his football injury, there emerged from these challenging months an exciting opportunity. One of his tutors at the university, Professor Rittner, had been invited to Colombia for a series of lectures on somatic culture, which explores body movement in the context of culture and society. He needed a translator and asked Jürgen to join him for the ten-day trip. At first, it seemed that the injury would preclude him from travelling, especially on a long-haul flight, so he requested two weeks to assess the progress of his recovery before committing. Thankfully, there was a big improvement, and a fortnight later he walked into Professor Rittner's office, 'If the offer still stands, I would love to join you.'

5

The Return to Medellín, September 1992

ELIDA GARCÍA took her seat near the front of the lecture hall. As a sports teacher at the Colombian Polytechnic in Medellín, she had eagerly accepted the opportunity to attend a conference on Sports Science, and was interested to hear what Professor Rittner had to say. But as the talk progressed, she became more intrigued by the younger man beside him who was translating from German to Spanish. He was clearly concentrating hard, but she could have sworn that he had just caught her eye.

Jürgen looked out over the audience from the raised platform he shared with Professor Rittner. There must have been 500 people seated below, all looking up at him expectantly as he endeavoured to translate, as accurately as possible, the latest statement from his learned superior. As he did so, looking broadly across the audience, his eyes stopped at a young woman near the front, and for a split second their eyes fixed. He momentarily forgot who he was, and where he was, but after a brief pause, he regained his composure, looked back across the auditorium, and completed the translation of the latest passage.

There it was again! This time he had almost smiled.

Jürgen couldn't help it. There was something about her that kept attracting his attention. Professor Rittner, as serious as ever, was moving on to the final stages of his talk, and somehow Jürgen managed to stay focused on the translation while occasionally gazing dreamily into the eyes of the girl in the second row.

At the end of the talk, the enthusiastic audience surged forward to introduce themselves and to ask further questions. Jürgen found himself at the centre of the academic melee, and suddenly he was face to face with the one audience member who seemed to be more interested in him than Professor Rittner.

'Where did you learn to speak German?' she asked.

Jürgen was slightly taken aback. Was she taking the mickey? He didn't think so. They exchanged a few words before someone interrupted with a question, and when he turned around, she was gone.

* * *

The chance to return to Medellín had come about sooner than Jürgen might have expected, less than two years after his transitory visit, when upon seeing the city lights from above through the bus window, he had imagined that he was looking down at the night sky. This time he arrived in the light of day, by aeroplane, offering a very different perspective of the sprawling metropolis. The drive from the airport, down through the barrios to the centre, took the same route as before, but this time he could see vividly the diversity and the poverty of the city.

The first stage of the trip had been in Cali, Colombia's third-largest city, where Professor Rittner had conducted a series of talks at the university, in what proved to be an unexpectedly formal environment. Jürgen was relieved to have successfully executed his role; by now he was very competent in Spanish, although translating an academic lecture to a live audience was a new challenge that required all of his skill and concentration. He liked Cali, but he was particularly eager to return to Medellín, and in the coming days he would develop ties that would permanently connect him to the troubled city.

The atmosphere at the University of Antioquia in Medellín was considerably more relaxed, and the staff from the sports department were keen to welcome and embrace their German counterparts. The lectures were less formal and more engaging, and the local hosts were proud to show their guests the city. This included a busy schedule of evening activities, and on the second day of their visit, Jürgen and Professor Rittner were invited to a reggae bar.

* * *

The academic sports community in Medellín was close-knit, and Elida was pleased to accept an invitation to a social gathering after another busy day at the conference. She was chatting to friends when the translator from Professor Rittner's lecture walked into the bar. That evening, the two were inseparable. Jürgen and Elida spent hours talking over the music, before eventually joining everyone else on the dance floor, where the festivities continued late into the night.

As Jürgen was driven back to his hotel in one of the city's iconic yellow taxis, he happily reflected on the evening and went through everything Elida had told him. She was one of 13 siblings, and the family had grown up in the countryside before moving to Medellín in her early teens. Her father, like his, was a hospital administrator, and he worked hard to bring in enough money to feed and clothe the family, while her mother got up at 4am every day to prepare a breakfast for the hungry children that consisted of corn bread, with all of the ingredients grown in their small garden. Her parents had, unusually, encouraged the girls to pursue their academic and career ambitions, and as a keen sportsperson who loved athletics and gymnastics, Elida had become a sports teacher. She now had three jobs teaching and lecturing at different institutions in Medellín.

Elida had also provided Jürgen with insight into the problems that put Medellín in the international spotlight, seriously affecting the city's economy, as well as the everyday life of its citizens. It was a time of bloody confrontations between the regular army and the guerrilla groups, which also led to many massacres of the civilian population, especially among younger people. She told him that she lived in fear, that explosions were an everyday occurrence and that he should avoid walking near any police because they were a prime target of hitmen who received a million Pesos for each officer killed. At the school where she worked, the daughters of local political figures arrived in the morning with military escorts.

This was the life they lived. This is why they enjoyed dancing and partying so much, because life in Medellín was so fragile and could be snatched away in the blink of an eye.

* * *

The following evening, as the conference came to a close, one of the local professors invited a small collection of friends and colleagues to her house for dinner. Elida was delighted when Jürgen arrived, and once again they were drawn to each other. At the end of the night, he insisted on walking her home. It was a short distance to where she lived with her parents, but before turning the corner into her street, they stopped. Elida's parents were strict Catholics and she did not want to cause a scandal by being seen with an unfamiliar man.

'One day,' he said, 'I am going to marry you.'

Elida recalls, 'He sealed the words with a kiss and we exchanged the rings that we were each wearing.'

A few hours later, Jürgen was on a plane on his way back to Cologne.

6

A House in the Andes

'NOT AGAIN! We can't take any more,' cried Elida in exasperation.

'I'm sorry. I just couldn't leave it to die.' Once again, Jürgen had returned with a dog cradled in his arms.

'That's the third one this month!'

On his route home each day, Jürgen passed a busy market that sold a wide range of produce and a selection of live animals. This often included dogs, and Jürgen couldn't bear to see them suffering, tied up and with sad eyes that told of mistreatment. So one day he bought one, and took it home to join the dog they already owned which had been given to them by a friend. A week later, he returned home with another, and then another, until eventually there were ten dogs living with them at the small house in the Andes, along with 25 chickens which they had inherited when they purchased the property. A few of the dogs didn't live for long, such was their condition when Jürgen bought them, but having never had pets as a child, he enjoyed caring for the animals.

* * *

Jürgen had started writing his first letter to Elida at the airport in Medellín before boarding the plane home. It had been a whirlwind trip and he had fallen head over heels in love. More letters to Colombia soon followed, and then phone calls and parcels containing mix-tape cassettes, with carefully selected track lists featuring songs he loved, or that meant something to him, or which carried some deeper message about his feelings for her.

There was no internet or email, and calls from his home phone cost a small fortune, but in a stroke of luck, Jürgen was able to cycle across Cologne to the university where one of the public phone booths was miraculously allowing calls free of charge to anywhere in the world. An informally agreed schedule emerged which involved international students arriving to use the phone at times of day compatible with the time zones in their respective countries.

For Jürgen, it meant cycling an hour each way in the middle of the night for a ten-minute phone call. Eventually the university fixed the phone and Jürgen resorted to using his own rotary dial telephone. It wasn't cheap to call South America, and his monthly phone bill was more than 400 Deutsche Marks – four shifts at the Mexican restaurant. But it was a small price to pay for the chance to hear Elida's voice.

Back in Colombia, Elida had fallen as well for the man who had suddenly arrived in her life. She had only met him three times over a matter of days, but in December 1992 she flew to Germany for Christmas, leaving South America for the first time. 'Before taking the relationship further,' says Elida, 'I wanted to know about his environment and his life.'

After visiting Cologne, they spent the holidays with Jürgen's family before travelling to Paris, and enjoying a short road trip around Belgium and the Netherlands. They had a magical time together, but it was also extremely cold.

'It was one of the harshest winters in years,' remembers Jürgen, 'often down to minus 20.' For Elida, used to pleasant warmth for 12 months of the year in Medellín – 'the City of Eternal Spring' – it was a shock, and she decided that if they were going to live together in the future, Jürgen would have to move to Colombia.

Six months later, they arranged to meet again at a Pan-American Sports Science conference in Costa Rica where Elida was giving a talk. For Jürgen, it was a welcome return to the country where he had spent nine happy months just a few years before, but more importantly it offered another chance to spend time together. He told Elida that with his studies in Cologne coming to an end, there was an opportunity for him to move to Medellín on a scholarship to start a Doctorate in Sports and Public Health, and to reactivate the links between the universities in Colombia and Germany. She was thrilled, but also knew that starting a relationship with Jürgen, and living together before marriage, would cause a rift with her family, at least initially, 'That was the price I paid for betting on love.'

In the coming months Jürgen and Elida, still separated by thousands of miles and relying on letters and extortionate phone calls, consolidated their plans. Elida found a beautiful farmhouse at 3,000 metres up in the Andean mountains above Medellín where properties were considerably more affordable, and which matched the romantic ideal they envisaged for a self-sufficient life together. The house was small and had no heating, and it would be a long, winding drive to the city each morning with a descent of 1,500 metres, but the large rural plot was exactly what they were looking for, and after borrowing money from friends to supplement their own savings, the house was theirs. Jürgen had still not seen it.

On 27 December 1993, 14 months after they had first met, Jürgen landed in Medellín with all of his belongings in a small wooden box. Elida met him at the airport and they left immediately for the house in the Andes to start their new life together.

7

The Gentleman of Football

ANDRÉS ESCOBAR grew up in a middle-class district of Medellín. He was a studious child but his first love was football, a passion that he shared with millions of Colombians. There is no single agreed-upon moment when football was first played in the country, but in the early years of the 20th century there are numerous stories of the game being introduced. Some claim it arrived with English engineers and sailors; others cite a wealthy Colombian, Arturo de Castro, who attended university in England and returned with a ball, two kits and a rulebook. There was even a US colonel, Henry Rowan Lemly, who came from the Great Sioux Wars (where he had witnessed the death of Crazy Horse), and introduced the game at Colombia's National Military School. Regardless of who came first, all of these people, and others, undoubtedly contributed to the subsequent spread of football across Colombia, at first steadily and then rapidly until it became a national obsession. In 1948 the game turned professional, by which time the national team was already held up as a symbol of unity, with a unique ability to bring people together from across the divides of Colombia's violent political and social past and present.

From a young age it was obvious that Andrés was gifted. He possessed natural athleticism and technical ability, but what marked him out as different was a rare composure on the ball. He was soon spotted and taken into the youth system at Atlético Nacional, one of two big clubs in his home city, alongside Independiente Medellín, making his first-team debut for 'El Nacional' in 1986, aged 19. Andrés was also a leader, not by desire or through overt control, but via the qualities that he held and demonstrated on and off the pitch; he inspired others, brought calm in moments of stress, defused conflict and embodied an intelligent approach to life and football. With this special combination of attributes, Andrés developed into an exceptional central defender and in 1988 he was called up to the national squad for the first time, playing in a 3-0 win against Canada. Two years later he played in all four of Colombia's games at the 1990 World Cup in Italy.

It was a time of great change in Colombian football. The drug cartels were increasingly controlling the game, most evidently through the ownership of clubs, which presented an excellent opportunity for money laundering – declaring gate receipts far in excess of what was actually taken, and thus making clean vast sums of cash. Their involvement in the game became known as 'narco-soccer' and it exacerbated endemic corruption, with players and officials bribed and threatened in order for the drug lords to achieve desired results and to make large amounts of money through gambling.

This injection of finance into Colombian football also brought success, with top clubs able to hold on to their best players, who might otherwise have gone overseas, and to bring in foreign stars attracted by the large wages on offer. The most defining example of this combination of corruption and success was Pablo Escobar and his financing of Atlético Nacional, where Andrés was by now one of the club's most important players. The two Escobars shared a surname, but they had little else in common, and throughout the late 1970s and the 1980s, Pablo Escobar established himself as the 'King of Cocaine', amassing a multi-billion-dollar fortune via the Medellín Cartel which dominated the exploding Colombian drug trade, fuelled by demand from the United States. His empire was founded on violence, with murder, kidnappings, torture and intimidation a feature of daily life in Medellín, a city he effectively ruled by the late 1980s, as well as wielding terrifying power throughout Colombia, ordering the murder of rivals and politicians who opposed or defied him.

Yet he cast himself as a modern-day Robin Hood figure, using his enormous wealth to gain public and political support, particularly in Medellín, where he built homes for the poor and funded hospitals, as well as the many football pitches on which some of Colombia's emerging stars learned their craft. 'Only once did I see Pablo Escobar in person,' says Elida. 'I saw him from afar, he went to inaugurate a soccer field in a local neighbourhood where people received him with a festive atmosphere. I would say that people loved him when he started in politics; the feelings changed when the acts of violence intensified.'

Football was Pablo Escobar's great passion, and through a combination of investment, bribery, threats and murder (including the killing of a referee who had been bought by a rival cartel), he helped to elevate El Nacional to unprecedented success, becoming in 1989 the first Colombian club to win the Copa Libertadores, South America's leading club competition. Still only 22, Andrés was a key part of the team's success, and calmly slotted in the first penalty in an epic final shoot-out in which El Nacional prevailed over Paraguayan side Olimpia. Soon after the final whistle, as the celebrations ensued, and against the backdrop of the chaotic footballing environment in which he existed, Andrés cut a serene figure as he was interviewed on the touchline, 'Yes, our team has won this for the whole country. We had to beat the best teams on the continent, but we've won it all, fair and square.'

In moments such as this, Colombians took Andrés to their hearts, and he became known as 'El Caballero del Fútbol' – 'the Gentleman of Football'. Through his conduct on and off the pitch he became regarded as a beacon of morality, and he spoke, without judgement, of football becoming a vehicle that could bring an end to violence. A devout Catholic, he also wanted to use his status and wealth to help others, and he contributed to initiatives helping some of the many poor children in Medellín.

Elida had witnessed his gentle nature first-hand. When she was little, her father had often taken her on Sundays to watch her brothers playing for the local town, and she enjoyed the festive atmosphere of matches. When they moved to Medellín she started supporting Atlético Nacional, and admired the acrobatic skills of René Higuita, the goalkeeper who would amaze the world with his scorpion kick against England at Wembley in 1995.

Elida gradually became more involved with El Nacional, volunteering as a photographer for the club magazine, and it was in this capacity that she met Andrés, 'He was a very calm, quiet boy, but always with a smile on his lips and he was known for being a good, fair person.' Later, Jürgen sometimes accompanied Elida on photo shoots, and on several occasions, he spoke to Andrés. Like everyone who met the central defender, he was taken with his charming manner.

As the early 1990s progressed, things began to unravel for Pablo Escobar. The United States and Colombian governments resolved to eliminate the cartels, and the US Drug Enforcement Agency (DEA) along with the Colombian army and police force effectively declared war on Pablo Escobar and the Medellín Cartel. Fearing extradition to the US, and increasingly on the run, Pablo Escobar is alleged to have influenced members of the Constituent Assembly in banning extradition, and in agreement with the authorities he subsequently, and voluntarily, surrendered, incarcerating himself in La Catedral, a luxurious prison built to his own specifications, including an 11-a-side football pitch. His 'imprisonment' lasted little more than a year, and after being tipped off that forces were about to make a formal arrest, he made a dramatic escape.

Meanwhile, the Colombian national team was thriving with a generation of great players reaching their peak, including Carlos Valderrama, Freddy Rincón, Leonel Álvarez, Andrés Escobar and René Higuita, along with emerging young talents such as Iván Valenciano and Faustino Asprilla.

In 1993 the team was seemingly unstoppable, qualifying comfortably for the 1994 World Cup in the United States, with the qualification campaign culminating in a devastating 5-0 demolition of Argentina in Buenos Aires in September 1993. The team played with an exhilarating style and verve that delighted home fans, and the players became national heroes, along with their leader, coach Francisco Maturana.

Elida remembers, 'Never in my life have I seen so many Colombian flags, flying everywhere, for so long.' A growing number of people, including Brazilian legend Pelé, started to predict that Colombia could even win the World Cup.

Despite this exciting progress on the pitch, problems in Colombia were already negatively impacting the team. Higuita was imprisoned for his alleged involvement in a kidnapping plot linked to Pablo Escobar, with whom he had close ties, and upon release the flamboyant goalkeeper was unfit to play at the World Cup. The infant son of defender Chonto Herrera was also kidnapped in Medellín and held to ransom, just days after the famous victory in Argentina, before the capture of two accomplices ensured the child's swift return. Pablo Escobar continued his increasingly desperate bid to evade capture, and in December 1993 he was eventually tracked down and cornered by the Colombian National Police, who shot him dead on the rooftops of Medellín. But the death of Pablo Escobar – the wealthiest criminal in history – failed to bring stability. Instead, while power shifted to the Cali Cartel, a power vacuum was created in Medellín that led to more violence and more killing. As the World Cup approached, there was also increased pressure from betting syndicates who were placing large sums on the success of the Colombian team, and on the performance of individual players, as well as selection pressure on the coaches from regional drug lords who wanted to see their players gain exposure on the world stage.

Andrés continued to keep his cool, and after guiding El Nacional to the Colombian title in 1994, at the age of 27, he was a prime target of AC Milan, who wanted to bring the graceful yet tough defender to Serie A. He was excited by the prospect of signing for the Italian champions after the World Cup, and joining the likes of Franco Baresi, Jean-Pierre Papin and Marco van Basten. With the future looking bright for Andrés, expectations in Colombia were reaching fever pitch as the national squad departed Bogotá for their base in California, ahead of three group matches against Romania, hosts the USA and Switzerland. Based on their form and ability, Colombia were expected to comfortably qualify for the knockout stages.

8

The 1994 World Cup & the Murder of Andrés Escobar

Friday, 17 June
The 1994 FIFA World Cup in the USA kicked off as Germany faced Bolivia in Chicago. A second-half goal by Jürgen Klinsmann secured a 1-0 win for the holders.

Saturday, 18 June
The García family, along with friends and neighbours, crowded into the home of Elida's brother Vicente – more than 25 people physically and emotionally connected in a shared experience of joy. They were all focused on a small television set in the tiny living room, as the heroes of the Colombian team marched on to the pitch. The whole city was enveloped in the yellow, blue and red of the national flag, and the room in which Jürgen now found himself was awash with brightly coloured football shirts and painted faces. The sense of excitement and expectation was immense, and so too was the noise, with singing, shouting and animated conversation drowning out the barely audible match commentary.

Colombia started brightly against Romania in their opening Group A match at a packed Rose Bowl in

Pasadena, but despite the South Americans dominating early possession, the stylish Romanian team took the lead after 15 minutes through Florin Răducioiu. Their lead was doubled when talisman Gheorghe Hagi scored an extraordinary goal from near the touchline. Adolfo Valencia pulled one back just before half-time, but the Colombians were unable to find a second-half equaliser, and in the final minutes Răducioiu sealed a 3-1 win after a mistake by Óscar Córdoba who had replaced René Higuita as first-choice goalkeeper.

In Medellín there was disappointment, but certainly not despondency. How often a team starts slowly in a major tournament before finding their form and building momentum. This was the sentiment that Jürgen perceived as the Garcías departed for their respective homes.

Meanwhile, in Pasadena, immediately after leaving the pitch, Chonto Herrera was informed that his brother had been killed in a car crash in Medellín. That evening Andrés comforted his team-mate and persuaded him to remain with the squad.

Wednesday, 22 June
Ahead of their second game, against the USA, coach Francisco Maturana arrived at the pre-match team meeting in tears. In the days after the defeat to Romania there had been a backlash in Colombia, with anger from betting syndicates which had lost heavily after backing a Colombian victory. That morning things had reached a new level. A 'witch' had called the hotel cursing the squad, with death threats made against players and their families. Astonishingly, someone had managed to programme the televisions in the hotel so that the threats appeared on the screens when the players returned to their rooms. There was a specific demand that influential midfielder Barrabas

Gómez be left out of the starting line-up that afternoon, with the threat that the families of Gómez and Maturana would be killed if he played. Maturana understandably gave into the demand and Gómez was omitted from the side. Back home in Colombia, police officers were sent to the players' homes to protect their families, and in a state of confusion and fear, the Colombians took to the field against a pumped-up United States team, cheered on by a 93,000 home crowd.

The Colombians started strongly with a series of blistering attacks, but the woodwork and a resilient USA defence prevented an early lead, and gradually the hosts gained a foothold in the match. In the 35th minute the USA attacked on the left and John Harkes sent a dangerous low cross into the box towards Earnie Stewart. Andrés Escobar, in his customary number two jersey, realised the danger, but uncharacteristically misjudged his interception and sent the ball past Córdoba into his own net. It was the first and only own goal of his career.

For Jürgen, once again crammed into his brother-in-law's small house, it felt like 'a knife in the heart', as he watched Andrés pick himself up and prepare for the restart. The mood before this second game had been different, more tense, but still with belief that Colombia would beat the United States and progress to the knockout stages. Now the whole atmosphere shifted, and the living room was filled with anxiety and a sense of dismay.

The Colombian team tried to find a way back into the game, but they were ultimately a shadow of the side that had dismantled Argentina ten months before. Stewart extended the USA's lead after 52 minutes, and in response the Colombians could only manage a last-minute goal by Adolfo Valencia. It was too little, too late. United States 2 Colombia 1.

The bright yellow, red and blue merged into black, as tears ran down the painted faces of the García family. Across Colombia there was shock and disbelief. Their beautiful team had been all but knocked out of the World Cup after only two matches. Over the last two years they had lost just once in 40 games, now they had been defeated twice in five days.

There was a terrible feeling of loss throughout the country, much deeper than mere disappointment, and the Garcías and their friends and neighbours left the house in what reminded Jürgen of a funeral procession. But for the betting syndicates and drug lords which had staked a small fortune on success, the emotions were darker than the pain of heartache. For them, it was anger.

Thursday, 23 June
Media in Colombia reported of national humiliation after defeat by the USA.

In light of the circumstances surrounding his omission from the team, Barrabas Gómez announced his retirement as a player.

Sunday, 26 June
In their final group match, to have any chance of progressing to the knockout stages, Colombia would have to beat Switzerland and hope that the USA would defeat Romania. If this happened, there was the possibility of advancing as one of the best third-placed teams. With goals from Gaviria and Lozano, the South Americans secured a 2-0 win at the Stanford Stadium in Palo Alto, but it was to no avail as news from the Rose Bowl came through of a 1-0 win for Romania. Colombia were the first team to be eliminated from the 1994 World Cup.

Wednesday, 29 June

As the players returned home to Colombia, a short column taken out by Andrés appeared in several national newspapers. It read:

'Life doesn't end here. We have to go on. Life cannot end here. No matter how difficult, we must stand back up. We only have two options: either allow anger to paralyse us and the violence continues, or we overcome and try our best to help others. It's our choice. Let us please maintain respect. My warmest regards to everyone. It's been a most amazing and rare experience. We'll see each other again soon because life does not end here.'

Friday, 1 July–Saturday, 2 July

Against the advice of his coach and closest team-mates, Andrés decided to go out in Medellín with some friends. He told his girlfriend that he wanted to show his face and not hide away. The exact events of the night are unclear but at 3am on Saturday, 2 July, in the car park of El Indio nightclub, Andrés was shot six times. It is said that the gunman shouted 'Gol!' after each shot, mimicking the football commentator who had reported on the own goal. Andrés was rushed to hospital but bled to death soon after.

It is unknown whether the killing was pre-planned or the result of an altercation in the nightclub, in which some claim that Andrés defended himself after being rebuked for the own goal. Either way, it seems certain that the killing was ordered by the Gallón brothers, known drug traffickers, who were believed to have lost heavily on Colombia's performance at the World Cup. Their bodyguard and driver, Humberto Castro Muñoz, who later confessed to the killing, was subsequently jailed for 43 years, of which he served just 11.

At their house in the mountains above Medellín, Jürgen and Elida were up at 4am as usual, preparing to head down to the city to start work. Jürgen was in the shower when he heard Elida running up the stairs. The bathroom door flew open and she was sick into the toilet.

'Eli, what's wrong?'

In tears, Elida looked up at her fiancé, 'They killed him. They killed Andrés.'

Monday, 4 July

Jürgen was at his desk, unable to focus. The events of the last two weeks, culminating in the murder of Andrés, had seen the expectations of a nation slide from the highest of hopes to the depths of despair. The streets had been even quieter than normal as he arrived at the crack of dawn to start work, but from outside he could now hear what sounded like a football crowd slowly beginning a song for their team. He got up from his seat and walked over to the third-floor window overlooking the city. The streets were filled with green and white, the colours of El Nacional, as thousands of people gravitated towards the hillside cemetery where Andrés would be laid to rest. The singing had built into a rousing chorus, and Jürgen opened the window to make out the words. Across Medellín, more than 120,000 people were on the streets, and now he could hear what they cried, 'Andrés, amigo, Dios está contigo' – 'Andrés, friend, God is with you.'

Earlier, at a ceremony in one of the city's indoor sporting arenas, President César Gaviria, who had played such an integral role in the downfall of Pablo Escobar, spoke to a packed crowd, 'Andrés Escobar will remain in our hearts as our hero of moral integrity, as a family man and exemplary Colombian. We must not lose this match against violence. Colombia must not let its best children be expelled from life's playing field. Our country is shaken. We share this profound pain with Andrés's family. Together we will shoulder this burden.'

Sunday, 17 July
Following a goalless draw in the final at the Rose Bowl in Pasadena, Brazil won the World Cup, defeating Italy 3-2 on penalties.

Saturday, 23 July
The pain of recent events was put aside as Jürgen and Elida were married in Medellín. Jürgen's parents and younger sister had travelled from Germany, leaving Europe for the first time, along with some of his closest friends. Although the rift would soon be healed, Elida's mother was still upset about the relationship and did not attend, but many of the García family were present, and the event was a joyous fusion of Colombian and German culture. A local farmer offered up his house for the celebration, allowing half of the guests to sleep at his property. The salsa dancing, and beer drinking, continued well into the early hours.

Thursday, 25 August
Having resigned his Doctorate in the wake of the circumstances surrounding the murder of Andrés, Jürgen attended the first day of his new Master's course, in Contemporary Social Problems, at the University of Antioquia.

9

A Game of Three Halves, 1995–1997

IT IS no exaggeration to say that the killing of Andrés Escobar devastated Jürgen.

He remembered the incredible 5-0 win over Argentina, and on reflection now saw it as the moment when things started to fall apart. The style of that victory was so emphatic and so stunning, and it embodied everything good about Colombia – its beauty, its diversity and its vibrant culture. On that pinnacle the dreams of a nation had been pinned, a vision of a Colombia that was anathema to the drugs and violence that defined how the country was seen by the world.

But it turned out to be an unhealthy high. All of the expectations, and the hopes of a generation, were piled on to the backs of the national football team, and it was a pressure that would ultimately break them. Jürgen had seen football lift the country, and then, as the nation imploded, it brought the game crashing down with it. As such, the murder of Andrés was not just the death of a good man, it felt like the end of a dream for the country he now called home, and to which he had become inextricably tied through Elida and the child she was carrying.

A month before the birth, Jürgen and Elida sold their house in the mountains and moved into Medellín. With a baby on the way they wanted to be closer to the hospital. It had been a difficult pregnancy, and if something went wrong it was a long drive down into the valley. Two of the dogs came with them, the rest were given to families who could offer them a loving home. Jürgen had then started walking the streets of Medellín, which resulted in him witnessing the gangs placing down their weapons, which in turn instilled within him a conviction that football could provide a pathway out of the darkness.

It was this chain of events that led him to a meeting room at the Department for Peace and Reconciliation at the Mayor's Office, where Jhon Jairo Vahos Vasquez, a representative for the gangs of Medellín, had just put his feet up on the table, 'Women do not play football. My wife and daughter will never step on to a football pitch. It is a stupid idea.'

Jürgen had been expecting some resistance to his proposals, but this was a direct and aggressive rebuttal to one of the key principles of the methodology that he and fellow Master's student Alejandro Arenas Tobón had spent months creating. After his game-changing experience in Manrique, Jürgen had switched the focus of his Master's thesis to a study of sport as an environment for peace-building and reconciliation, and he and Alejandro had developed a concept for a new way of playing football, designed specifically to address the violence in Medellín. They called it 'Fútbol por la Paz' – Football for Peace.

Vahos was born and bred in Medellín. He was a fixer for the gangs, a big deal, and if it hadn't been for a cruciate ligament injury he might have made it to the top level. Still in his early 20s, he wanted to stay involved with football, and had decided to organise a street tournament, 'The final match was between the two most fearsome groups in the city. It was more than a soccer game; power was being played out, and 25 million Pesos had been staked on the outcome. The players walked out to a reception of gunfire in celebration of both teams, and the referee jumped into the street and ran away. So, I had to do it, and in the final minute I awarded a penalty to one of the teams. There was uproar. A boy approached me and hit me in the chest with a machine gun and the crowd were throwing eggs, avocados and tomatoes. Thankfully, some of my friends stood alongside me and a fight was avoided. Afterwards there was a feast that lasted until the next day.'

It was a baptism of fire, but he'd made it happen, and word of the tournament spread rapidly throughout Medellín, coming to the attention of the Department for Peace and Reconciliation. They had invited Vahos to this meeting, where a 'fantasy person with a crazy project' was proposing to bring women into the mix.

Despite his resistance to their plans, Jürgen and Alejandro realised that Fútbol por la Paz could not succeed without someone like Vahos, with his ability to secure the support and involvement of the city's underworld. He was respected by the gangs, and had already proven his ability to bring people together through football, even if it had nearly ended in a riot. Vahos was exactly what they needed, although it was clearly going to take some work to gain his acceptance for the more progressive features of the methodology.

Jürgen and Alejandro had met on the first day of their postgraduate course at the university. Alejandro was a football fanatic and a huge fan of El Nacional. 'He could recall the results and details of every match they had ever played,' remembers Jürgen.

For Alejandro, football was an escape. He had grown up in Medellín, and had lost more than 50 friends, neighbours and family members to the violence, 'Almost all of them young and without affiliation to the bosses, ordinary people who studied and worked hard, with no ties to the criminals.'

At first, he was unsure what to make of Jürgen, 'I wondered, who is this German, what is he doing here, in a city like this. It was inconceivable that he could be in Colombia.' Regardless, the two students immediately hit it off, and a friendship was forged. As a psychologist, Alejandro had previously worked with some of the most vulnerable people in the city, including victims of violence and abuse. He too was passionate about making a difference, and when Jürgen put forward the idea of a football-based project to promote peace, 'I accepted it immediately.'

The Fútbol por la Paz methodology had several unfamiliar rules, and there would be no referees. Instead, the players would be responsible for self-adjudicating, calling their own fouls and taking collective responsibility for ensuring that fair play was observed. In recognition that disagreements might sometimes occur, mediators would be on hand to help the teams mutually reach peaceful resolutions. All players, on every team, would also wear the same jersey. At first, this seemed like an alien concept, but Jürgen and Alejandro were adamant that it was essential for breaking down partisan loyalties and eliminating, at least on the pitch, the concept of opposing sides. There would also be an alternative scoring system, combining goals and fair play points (awarded by the opposition) into a cumulative total.

A framework of 'three halves' was created to support the effective implementation of these rules. The first half featured a pre-match conversation in which the teams would discuss expected behaviour, as well as agreeing on any precise rules that might be required as a result of the playing space available. The second half was the match, and the third half was a closing discussion in which the teams would come together to reflect on how well fair play and respect had been observed. This final half would include the awarding of fair play points, with teams encouraged to honestly appraise and reward the conduct of the other team, even if it meant tipping the balance of the score in favour of their opponents. This structure was designed to promote peaceful dialogue, encouraging players and teams to find collaborative solutions, instead of resorting to violence.

Given the social context, perhaps the most unconventional feature of the methodology was the inclusion of several gender-based rules. Teams would have an equal number of males and females, and the first goal for each side could only be scored by a girl or a woman. This ensured that the male players would have to think differently, and that greater value would be attached to the role of their female team-mates, who themselves would be empowered. Jürgen and Alejandro believed that this would help to challenge widely held negative gender stereotypes that pervaded Colombian society, as well as reducing acceptance of gender-based violence.

It was this final set of gender-based rules that Vahos was so vehemently opposed to. The world that he inhabited was run by men. Women had their place, and it was most definitely not on the football pitch. Now this German and his pal wanted him to propose mixed-gender matches to the gang bosses. Despite his protestations, Jürgen and Alejandro had done their groundwork, and while the department agreed that it was a strange idea, the situation in the city was so desperate, they were willing to give it a try. A three-month pilot was approved, and the methodology would be trialled in its purest form. Vahos was not impressed, but he reluctantly accepted the decision.

10

A Man on a Mission

ON 23 August 1541, conquistadors led by Marshal Jorge Robledo saw in the distance what appeared to be a deep valley. A detachment was sent to explore the terrain, and that night they reached the land that would one day become Medellín, naming it the Valley of St Bartholomew. A settlement did not appear until 2 March 1616, when another explorer, Francisco de Herrera Campuzano, established, by royal edict, the small village of San Lorenzo de Aburrá. A complex social structure, which characterised Spanish colonisation across the continent, was already forming, and a law in 1646 ordered the separation of castes without pure Spanish ancestry. This included Amerindians (indigenous people), mestizos (those with mixed European and indigenous ancestry) and mulattos (those with mixed European and Black African ancestry). The required segregation led to the construction of a new town in the valley, which in 1674 was renamed Villa de Nuestra Señora de Medellín. The name was chosen by settlers who had originated in the village of Medellín in Badajoz, a province in western Spain.

For centuries, it remained a relatively small agricultural town, until demand for food rapidly increased, spurred by a booming gold-mining industry in the north-east of the Antioquia region. Medellín was strategically positioned between several new cities and industries, and with increasing influence and importance, it soon replaced Santa Fé as the region's capital. When the gold-mining industry declined, coffee and textile exports surged and, between 1870 and 1940, the city's population grew from 20,000 to 170,000. It was a time of prosperity, and Medellín became widely regarded as an industrious and culturally sophisticated provincial city, self-sufficient with hydro-electrical power and long-established local agriculture.

The city's business and civic leaders had ambitious plans, and they initiated a swathe of urban development projects to drive forward Medellín's infrastructure and industrial expansion. These plans backfired, resulting in even more rapid and uncontrolled immigration from rural areas, at a rate which the city and its urban structures and services could simply not absorb. The population exploded from 275,000 in 1952 to 1.3 million in 1977, overwhelming the municipal government and resulting in the informal development of settlements on the valley slopes. With this lack of order came poverty, crime, corruption and violence, and a huge black economy. These conditions rendered Medellín particularly susceptible to the drug trade, and when the cocaine industry escalated in the 1970s and 1980s, Pablo Escobar was able to exploit the situation to devastating effect, establishing the wealthiest and most powerful narcotics cartel in the world.

After Escobar was killed in 1993, the situation further deteriorated with the creation of a power vacuum that saw hundreds of gangs and drug traffickers competing for territorial and market control of Medellín. This was exacerbated by politically motivated violence by paramilitary groups and 'social cleansing' of 'undesirables' by guerrilla militias, targeting beggars, prostitutes and homosexuals. High levels of petty crime also contributed to appalling levels of public insecurity. With all of these factors combined, Medellín came to be regarded as the most dangerous city in the world, averaging more than 20 violent killings per day by the early 1990s, close to 40 times greater than the UN's definition of endemic violence.

This had tragic consequences for the people of Medellín, most of whom were completely innocent victims, living in fear of violent murder, life-changing injury, kidnapping and the death and disappearance of friends and family. Community structures were destroyed and students were desperate to leave, further draining the city of hope and improvement.

For the civic leaders, it was a seemingly impossible task, yet at the height of the violence there emerged a network of civil society organisations, academics, community leaders and businesspeople who resolved to reclaim governance of Medellín, and to reconstruct the social and economic fabric of the city. These people and institutions collectively developed plans for urban transformation, with the modernisation of infrastructure, provision of social care, incentivisation of legal economic activity and a determination to bring the violence under control.

One of these people was Maria Eugenia, an experienced analyst and strategist at the Department for Peace and Reconciliation, who had lived through the city's descent into chaos. In various roles throughout her career, specialising in family consulting and social networks, she had been part of the efforts to save Medellín from further demise, and to work towards a better future for the city and its people. Maria had no interest in football whatsoever, but upon hearing Jürgen present his idea of Fútbol por la Paz, she instantly recognised the potential of the project, and was fascinated by the concept of 'using the game to recreate the social system and build new individual and collective identities'.

In Jürgen, she also quickly saw someone with enormous capacity for listening, observation and analysis, 'It was delightful to work with him, all of his ideas implied changes and required constructing new hypotheses and breaking the homogeneity of the established.'

Maria became a strong advocate of the project within the department, and it was the start of a lifelong friendship, through which she continues to act as a mentor for Jürgen, providing unconditional advice and acting as a sounding board for new ideas. 'She sees context more clearly than I do,' says Jürgen, 'and is always able to bring me back to purpose in my decision-making.'

* * *

On 17 May 1997, the first Fútbol por la Paz session took place on a field in Barrio Antioquia, a neighbourhood that had been carefully selected due to its relative neutrality. It was also one of the city's most impoverished areas. Sixteen teams had been invited, and as the games progressed, one of the department officials declared, 'I've never seen so much shit in one place.' He was referring to the unprecedented concentration of drug traffickers, contract killers, gang members and petty criminals, all in one place and without a single act of violence being committed. In that moment Jürgen realised that they had already succeeded in creating a space where partisan loyalties were temporarily set aside. The sanctity of the pitch was being observed.

In addition to teams that were directly associated with specific gangs, sides from other parts of society had been invited to participate, including university football teams, local sports clubs and community groups. This was very deliberate, with Jürgen and Alejandro strongly believing that real and lasting solutions, genuinely promoting community-wide understanding, empathy and tolerance, could only be found by collectively engaging all sections of society. Fútbol por la Paz would therefore bring together perpetrators, victims and everyone else somehow involved in, or affected by, the city's deep-rooted and endemic violence.

The first event was a success, and as the pilot progressed, the players continued to respond positively to the methodology. Initial concerns that the rules would be ignored or derided proved to be unfounded, and teams from across the social and territorial divides of Medellín accepted the new approach. Perhaps most notably, the gender-based adaptations were respected and, in some cases, even embraced.

Before the pilot came to an end, Jürgen knew that he could no longer return to his studies at the university. Instead, he wanted to exclusively pursue the development of Fútbol por la Paz, 'I was on a mission, and could see no alternative to it.'

Elida remembers, 'One day Jürgen returned home and expressed his desire to work full-time with young people in the barrios. There would be no salary. That was the situation. We had a baby and no other income, but I believed in him, and I was clear in my answer – follow your heart, if you have to quit your job to be happy, quit. We will find a way to survive.'

11

Fútbol por la Paz, 1997–2000

VAHOS LOOKED across the field to where his wife was celebrating a goal. His daughter was there too, smiling back at him. It had been quite a transformation. From being completely opposed to women playing football, he now enjoyed seeing his wife and daughter sharing the game that he loved. He was the first to admit that this radical change of attitude had been facilitated by the Fútbol por la Paz methodology, which according to Maria 'questioned the order of the street and the house, of the relations between men and women, of domination and patriarchal subordination'. When they had first met, Vahos had dismissed Jürgen and his plans as 'dreamy and fanciful', but he was now an ardent champion of the project.

Jürgen's gamble to pursue Fútbol por la Paz on a full-time basis had paid off. Having established a charitable entity under which to operate, the methodology continued to be well received, and there was growing evidence that the project was having a measurable impact. Mortality was down sharply among players, along with significant reductions in violence. At the same time, social mobility was up, with more young people progressing to further education, training and employment opportunities. The impact also extended beyond youth, with parents playing alongside their sons and daughters, as was the case with Vahos and his family, building generational understanding and resolving family disagreements.

This success had attracted more funding from the Department for Peace and Reconciliation, as well as from the Departments for Youth and Sport. There was also international support from the German FA and the International Olympic Committee, and in-kind contributions of kit and equipment from local companies. This growth had enabled Jürgen to take a salary, relieving some of the financial pressure on his young family, something which had become particularly pressing after Elida gave birth to their second daughter, Hanna.

At its peak, Fútbol por la Paz had more than 10,000 regular players from across every district of Medellín, and the number two shirt worn by all participants – in recognition of the jersey worn by Andrés – became accepted currency for travel across the city's bus network. As such, the shirts not only meant that players could afford to travel to matches, they also acted as a passport, enabling them to travel unharmed through rival territories, such was the respect with which Fútbol por la Paz came to be universally regarded. The jersey became something that young people were proud to be seen wearing, as a symbol of their courage and solidarity in the pursuit of peace.

An operation of this size required a significant team, and ten people were employed across various duties including the identification and engagement of teams, match-making fixtures in safe spaces, arranging tournaments and conducting monitoring and evaluation activities. It was a diverse and highly motivated group, from Vahos in his unique position as a bridge between the gangs and the project, to Maria, who left the security of her job at the department to join Fútbol por la Paz full-time, supporting strategy development and building partnerships with the many local institutions that were keen to get involved. There was also a huge team of over 200 volunteer community mediators, who were trained to facilitate sessions, and provide arbitration when this became necessary.

Jürgen remained focused on maximising the impact of Fútbol por la Paz. Maria recalls, 'He was kind, disciplined, organised and demanding with himself and with others for the fulfilment of commitments. Rigorous and methodical, he came to meetings with his proposals or with the results of the previous meeting written, always on double-sided paper, which was cheaper and more environmentally friendly.' Jürgen also became known for some of his quirks including his old car 'in a city where new, high-end vehicles were flaunted', and for the mug that he always carried with him to serve his coffee. 'He hated disposable cups,' says Maria. Due to some challenging local interpretations of his name, Jürgen also temporarily resorted to calling himself Jorge Grisales, but the pseudonym was soon abandoned after triggering 'a security incident' when he attempted to gain entry to a meeting venue.

By 1998, although still volatile, the situation in Medellín was improving. At its peak, in 1991, the death rate had been 381 homicides per 100,000 people; by 1998 this figure was down to 154. Backed up by a growing body of research, Alejandro was confident that Fútbol por la Paz was playing a part in this shift, 'The socio-political situation was still complicated, but there was a sense of change and optimism. Sports pitches and spaces in the city were being reclaimed for peace.'

Four years on from the murder of Andrés, 1998 would also see the next instalment of the men's World Cup, which was being staged in France. Jürgen and the team at Fútbol por la Paz decided that this was an important moment to project a positive image of Colombia, and to celebrate how the game was now being used in the country as a force for good. A delegation of young people – three boys and three girls – would be drawn from the six districts of the city, with the opportunity to travel to France and experience the tournament. Alejandro remembers, 'There was supreme expectation.'

The morning before the draw took place one Friday night at the Parque de Banderas, 18-year-old Nolbeiro turned up for his job as an ice cream vendor in the city centre, only to be told that his services were no longer required. It was a blow. Nolbeiro was the youngest of eight children. Both their parents had died in recent years, and the siblings relied on their collective income to get by. Before heading home to break the news, Nolbeiro attended the draw and was astonished when his name was called out. He ran home and told his brothers and sisters that he had lost his job, before casually adding that he was going to the World Cup. His siblings were upset about the job, and simply did not believe him about the trip to France. 'His brothers accused him of losing his mind,' says Alejandro. 'After a few days, he came to the office and was given a letter of confirmation which he took back to show them, proving to their amazement that he was indeed going to the World Cup.'

The Fútbol por la Paz delegation had no official role in France. Instead, they turned up at squares and outside grounds in Paris and Lens, setting up small-sided football pitches with transportable goals and equipment which had been brought over on the plane. The plan was to encourage fans from across the world to interact with them, to join in games, and to learn how the project was building a positive legacy from the killing of Andrés after Colombia's elimination from the tournament in 1994. 'We received a brilliant response,' says Jürgen, 'and for the young people it was an incredible, intense and eye-opening opportunity that exposed them to new cultures and broadened their horizons.' The power and lasting impact of their experience was profound, and the concept of using the World Cup as a platform to bring young people together from across the globe would feature heavily in Jürgen's future.

Despite these wonderful moments, and notwithstanding the significantly falling rate of violent deaths among participants, away from the pitch there were still losses. Alejandro says, 'A dramatic moment occurred when a nephew of Vahos, who was a Fútbol por la Paz mediator, went to visit his girlfriend and inadvertently strayed into enemy territory. He was recognised as a non-inhabitant of the area and was shot in the skull, dying in the arms of a friend. The next day was the wake and the funeral, and Vahos's friends had everything ready to take revenge that night. I reasoned with Vahos that, guilty or innocent, no one had the right to murder someone in the name of this good boy and his family.'

On that occasion, a cycle of violent revenge was averted, but such events ensured that Elida could never truly relax, 'Every time Jürgen left the house to go to the barrios, I would stay at home with our two girls, still very young, hoping that he would return. There were no public telephones in the area and we did not yet have mobile phones, so it was not possible to get in touch when he was out. After a while, he gained the confidence of the young people and I felt a little better because, in their own way, they protected him. But there was always the possibility of a surprise confrontation or a stray bullet. There were days when I asked him not to go, but I knew he must. Then I prayed, asking his angel to protect him.'

Alejandro reflects on how Jürgen managed to stay safe, 'For some he was regarded as a fool-hero, he took so many risks. But his ease at adapting to the environment, his German temperament and his charisma protected him, and he became a character who is still remembered in the city to this day.'

12

A Road Back to Germany, 1998–2000

THE LIMOUSINES left the German Consulate and headed through the streets of Medellín towards the private residence of the honorary consul, Hellmuth Lücker, where an evening reception was being hosted. Inside the cars were the vice-presidents of the main German political parties who were in Colombia as part of a diplomatic mission to strengthen ties between the two countries. Along with an entourage of political aides, security guards and local officials, Jürgen was also present. As a locally based German who was running an innovative social project, and with a track record of forging links between the universities in Medellín and Cologne, he was an excellent example of existing collaboration, and the consul was keen to show him off.

The convoy came to an abrupt halt.

'What's going on? Why have we stopped?' asked one of the vice-presidents.

One of the aides put their head out of the window, 'There is a football match.'

'Can't we go around it?'

'No, the game is being played in the road, and they are not stopping.'

Jürgen looked out of the window, and turned back to his fellow passengers with an expression of mock surprise, 'It is a Fútbol por la Paz match! Why don't you come and take a look?'

The vice-presidents, bedecked in dinner jackets and cocktail dresses, clambered out of the vehicles and walked over to where the game was taking place. Jürgen explained what was happening, and how the methodology encouraged dialogue and collaboration between those participating. All of the guests seemed interested, but Antje Vollmer, vice-president of the German Parliament for the Green Party, was particularly impressed, and insisted that Jürgen translate while she asked questions of the players, and learned about their experiences. Before returning to the cars, she announced, 'This is exactly what we need in Germany, to address growing far-right tendencies among young people in some parts of our country.'

As the convoy resumed its journey, Jürgen could scarcely conceal his delight. He had known which route the vehicles would take, and had deliberately planned the football match as an opportunity to expose Fútbol por la Paz to a group of influential people. It had worked brilliantly, but more than that, it had also been a light bulb moment for him. He had previously considered the possibility of introducing the methodology to other cities in Colombia and even to other Latin America countries, but never the idea that it could be adapted and exported to other parts of the world, including his home country. It was a revelation!

The consul's home was high up in the hills, in El Poblado, one of Medellín's most affluent districts, and as Lücker recounted the dramatic story of his abduction by the National Liberation Army in 1988, Jürgen looked down at the lights and remembered the first time he had arrived in the city, on the night bus, when he had made a personal commitment to return. He had done that, and more. Medellín was now his home, his family's home, and through the establishment and growth of Fútbol por la Paz, he had invested all of his creative energy and passion in serving the city. Until now, he had not contemplated moving away, but the words of vice-president Vollmer had awoken something, and for the first time since he had moved to Medellín, Jürgen could envisage the possibility of a future that lay elsewhere.

* * *

When she returned to Berlin, Antje immediately initiated conversations to explore the idea of introducing a football project in Germany. It would be based on the Fútbol por la Paz model, but adapted to address the spread of far-right thinking among young people that was feeding a growing presence of extreme factions within the political structures of the country's 16 federal states. Like Jürgen's epiphany when the gangs placed down their weapons before a game of football in Manrique, her enlightenment on the road to the consul's home had been 'positively electrifying'. She had guessed that Jürgen had staged the whole thing, but that didn't matter, the project was exceptional, and she was determined to see a modified version launched in Germany. And there was only one person she wanted to run it.

With Germany strongly positioned to be selected as hosts for the 2006 World Cup, Antje discovered that many others shared her enthusiasm for the concept. The timing was good, and as well as helping to extinguish a 'wildfire' of far-right ideas, a project of this nature could help to further strengthen the excellent tournament bid that was already taking shape. Officers at the Ministry for Family Affairs, Senior Citizens, Women and Youth expressed interest in funding a pilot phase in partnership with the youth section of the sports confederation in Brandenburg, a state surrounding Berlin, in the former East Germany.

As the concept took shape, Jürgen was invited to Berlin, and during 1999 he travelled to Europe on several occasions to discuss the possibility of a return to his home country. In Antje he had discovered a kindred spirit; a true visionary, a pacifist and a passionate supporter of disruptive art. She presented an incredibly exciting proposition for an initiative that would unlock the popularity of football in Germany to challenge intolerance and to create a platform for the promotion of social justice. Jürgen was offered a three-year contract to come and make it happen. It was a tantalising prospect, but he remained unsure whether he could bring himself to leave Fútbol por la Paz, when there was still so much more to achieve in Medellín. It hadn't occurred to him, until he met Antje, that the methodology could be used in Germany, but he increasingly realised that the relationship between the two countries wasn't a one-way flow of knowledge and ideas, and perhaps it was no surprise that solutions should emerge from where the situation was most desperate. Equally, the issues in South America did not exist in isolation, and while the problems in Medellín were extreme, young people in Germany and Colombia faced similar challenges, no matter how geographically and culturally separated they were.

Maria was already proving invaluable as a mentor. Through Fútbol por la Paz, she had seen Jürgen's ability to 'create new scenarios that transcend institutional frameworks', and combined with 'great imagination, perseverance and dedication, he had contributed enormously to Medellín, making it visible as a city of coexistence'. Although she would be immensely sorry to see him leave, she also recognised that 'as an entrepreneur and a leader with the ability to manage far-reaching transformations',

Jürgen had tremendous potential to take his ideas and leadership to a bigger stage, and so she advised him to seize the opportunity. Besides, it was not an abandonment of Medellín, rather an extension of the purpose-driven vision which had been incubated in the city.

Elida was torn. It would be terribly painful to leave her wider family and her beloved home city, but she was also conscious of the dangers that her daughters would face growing up in Medellín, 'Sara, our eldest daughter, was due to be enrolled in the German school and there was an increased risk of foreigners being kidnapped due to the extradition agreement with the United States.'

While she had previously been adamant that Germany was for 'holidays only', Elida also recognised that life in a high-income country would have many advantages, most notably a world-class education for the girls. She and Jürgen spent many hours discussing and deliberating the pros and cons of moving, before collectively making a conscious decision to go for it. Together with the girls, they saw in the new millennium with the García family in Medellín, and in the following weeks made final preparations for the move to Germany. On 25 January 2000, they bade an emotional farewell to their friends and loved ones, before boarding a plane, destined for a new life in Europe.

* * *

After Jürgen left Colombia, Alejandro continued to grow Fútbol por la Paz, and in 2001 he moved to Bogotá, the capital city, to oversee a national roll-out of the project. The approach has since been implemented in more than 70 cities across Colombia, and has been delivered in various forms throughout South America, including the widely used football3 methodology which later emerged. Throughout this journey, Vahos has remained by his side, achieving a career and a life that was previously unimaginable, 'I have served my neighbourhood, my city and my country.'

Years later, on a return visit to Medellín, Alejandro was walking through the back streets of Manrique when he saw a group of children using the Fútbol por la Paz methodology, without facilitation. He walked over and asked where they had learned it. The children briefly paused to look up from their game, and told him, 'It has been played like this forever.'

13

From the Black Forest to Cologne, 1965–1987

AS THE Second World War came to a close, a Moroccan cook in a unit of the French army was stationed in the Black Forest, close to the picturesque village of Schonach, where he met and fell in love with a young German woman called Rosa. They had a brief and passionate relationship which ended abruptly when the soldier's detachment was relocated. After he left, Rosa discovered that she was pregnant, and faced the scandal of having a dark-skinned child in a country that was only just emerging from one of the most racially prejudiced regimes in history.

The Moroccan had not forgotten about Rosa, and unaware of their child, for years he continued to write to her, perhaps in the hope that their relationship could be rekindled. It was a futile effort; every letter that he sent was intercepted by her family, and only many decades later did she learn of his attempts to stay in contact.

In 1946, Rosa gave birth to a boy, Harry, who would become Jürgen's father. Soon after the birth, Rosa met and married Hans, who adopted Harry as his own, and became a loving father. Although he grew up unaware of his Moroccan heritage, Harry stood out. His skin was darker, and his eyes were brown, something that was unusual in this part of Germany. But the main way in which Harry stood out from his peers was on the football pitch. He was naturally skilful and quick, and by his early teens he was recognised as a promising right-winger, something that Jürgen believes helped to ensure that he was accepted, regardless of any difference in his appearance, 'It was his talent as a footballer, more than anything, that defined him in the eyes of those around him.'

In 1963, a girl and her family moved into the house that backed on to Harry's garden, and it wasn't long before the two 17-year-olds were dating. Irene had spent her early years in Überlingen, a city on the northern shore of Lake Constance near the border with Switzerland. She had endured a tough childhood; in the aftermath of the war, her parents had separated, and her mother had to go to work, leaving Irene locked in the house alone from the age of four. When she and Harry started to see each other, Irene was made aware that people in the community were talking, saying that she was dating a foreigner. She did her best to ignore the gossip, and the relationship continued.

In 1964 Irene fell pregnant, and a new dilemma emerged. The law stated they could not marry unless the father could prove his ability to financially maintain a family. Harry was still trying to establish his career as a footballer, and his contract at local club FC Teutonia Schonach was not sufficient to convince the authorities that the marriage could go ahead. Furthermore, Harry's family was affiliated to the Catholic Church, while Irene had a Protestant background, and the local priest was reluctant to let such a union proceed. Instead it was decided that the two young parents must continue living with their respective families until such time as the church and the authorities granted them permission to marry.

On 25 April 1965 Irene gave birth to a boy, who they named Jürgen. The child had brown eyes and a skin tone that were a subtle legacy of his Moroccan grandfather, a heritage that would remain unknown to Jürgen until his 40s. Irene left her job as a legal assistant to look after the baby, while Harry pursued his career as a footballer, later that year securing a move to FC Villingen, just over 20km away. This was a step up, to the second tier of the German football pyramid, and combined with the arrival of a more lenient priest, who overlooked their different confessions, the extra money was sufficient for their marriage to be granted. It also meant they could now live together as a family.

Harry did well at FC Villingen and, after two seasons, offers started to come in from some of the top-tier Bundesliga clubs including Borussia Dortmund, 1860 Munich and Schalke 04. But he turned them all down. Today such a move to a top-flight team in Germany would be too good to refuse, with the opportunity to earn enough in a few seasons to set a family up for life, but at the time, the wages were still relatively modest and there was little job security once careers came to an end when players reached their mid-30s. So instead, he accepted a move to another second-tier club, VfL Bochum, which offered a significantly lower wage, but with the option to pursue another career alongside football. More than 500km to the north of Schonach, Bochum is a city of over 300,000 people, wedged between Essen and Dortmund, forming part of the large industrial region of the Ruhr. For Harry and Irene, it was a big change, from a small and friendly village to a metropolitan and socially colder environment. Jürgen says, 'They felt that they became adults when they moved to Bochum.'

Harry continued to thrive on the pitch, and secured additional employment as an administrator for the city authorities, but the poor quality of the air in the industrial heartland meant they would remain in Bochum for only three years, with Irene concerned that it was causing problems for five-year-old Jürgen. Harry switched clubs again, signing for another second-tier side, VfR Heilbronn, in a considerably smaller, less-industrialised city to the south. Soon after moving, he became a hospital administrator, eventually progressing to head of human resources at the city hospital. He spent five years with Heilbronn, scoring 44 league goals in 137 matches, before moving to VfB Eppingen, another local team, where he ended his playing days and moved into coaching.

The majority of Jürgen's childhood was therefore spent in Heilbronn, where the family lived on the fourth floor of a nine-storey apartment. He enjoyed walking four or five kilometres to school every morning with friends, and playing in the fields and on a small-sided pitch outside the apartment. Like his father, Jürgen was a good footballer, and was top scorer for the under-11s at VfR Heilbronn, when a falling-out between his dad and the club resulted in the youngster being benched. The dispute, which had nothing to do with Jürgen, became increasingly frustrating, and he eventually decided to walk away and take up another sport – table tennis.

Jürgen describes his childhood as, 'Average, normal, there was neither scarcity nor abundance, not many ups and downs, but also not many edges. There were no great political or religious forces, and we did not travel much. I was raised to follow the rules of society, pay taxes and be fair to everyone. I later learned that my father had always tried to help disadvantaged people in his job and as a coach, but there was no particular encouragement for me to make a social contribution.'

In school he was drawn mostly to the social sciences, such as History and Geography, and discovered an early propensity for languages, developing a solid base in French and English that he would later build on, 'I was not at the very top of the class, but I didn't push too hard either.' Although he didn't particularly stand out, Jürgen was often called upon by his peers, particularly in primary school, to act as a spokesperson for the class, 'To raise any issues with the teacher or to mediate if there was any conflict between children.'

A school trip to East Berlin in the early 1980s was a particularly eye-opening experience, 'We couldn't believe how cheap everything was and how much we could buy with the small amount of spending money we had. The people were also very different from us and gave short and consistent answers to everything. I came away feeling that I had much more in common with the French and the Italians in western Europe than I did with the Germans in the Democratic Republic.'

When he was 15, the family moved several miles to a village on the outskirts of town, which Jürgen says was 'a step up the social ladder, with a house, a garage and a garden'. The extra space was very welcome with the imminent arrival of Jürgen's sister Katrin, but it also meant a longer journey to school, and to the table tennis club which had become the centre of his social life. A motorbike solved the problem and also provided a means of travelling to compete in regional tournaments.

Despite his transition to a new sport, Jürgen remained a football fan, and during his teens he became a keen supporter of SC Freiburg. The club was located close to where he was born, but more importantly he aligned with their values, 'They invest in their coaches for the long term instead of hiring and firing after a few bad results or even after a relegation. This sustainable approach to team management helps the club to do consistently well, despite having only a small budget, as well as maintaining an attractive style of play.'

In 1984, when he was 18, Jürgen began 15 months of compulsory military service, which he extended to two years so that he could take a basic salary and become financially independent, with his own apartment in town. It involved a three-month boot camp followed by 15 months working as a bookkeeper in a local office, 'It meant that I didn't have to carry a gun.'

As his stint in the army came to a close, one of Jürgen's closest friends, Bernd, said he was planning to attend an entrance exam for the German Sports University in Cologne. Jürgen had no clear plans for his future after the army, so decided to go along too.

* * *

Fifteen years later, as Jürgen reflected on his childhood and youth in Germany, the plane began its descent towards Berlin. His life had been so very different; different from what he had come to know and love in Medellín, where he had found purpose and discovered his 'place in the world'. Germany had also changed – reunified, full of promise yet evidently still tied to problems of the past. Through his new job, Jürgen knew that he would have a chance to contribute towards building a bright and socially progressive future for his home country, with the opportunity to extend the entrepreneurial journey he was now on. But as he looked down at his daughters, asleep in the middle aisle, he wondered whether he had done the right thing, taking them away from the large family and happy life they had in Colombia. Only time would tell.

An hour later, as the four travellers emerged from the arrivals hall at Berlin-Tegel Airport, Jürgen heard his oldest daughter ask, 'Ma, where does the sun live in this country?'

14

A Cold Reception

THE CROWDS lining the streets of Leipzig roared as Uwe Koch rounded the final corner in the 1986 national marathon championships in East Germany. He looked back one last time and, with a broad smile on his face, raised his right arm and punched the air with a clenched fist. For the 25-year-old, who trained at the Potsdam Army Sports Club, it would be one of the highlights of his running career, alongside competing for his country multiple times in the European Cup Marathon and placing 18th at the IAAF World Cup marathon in 1989.

A few years earlier, Uwe had graduated in Sociology from the Humboldt University in East Berlin, before attending the University of Potsdam, where he studied Sports Science, combining his academic journey with a deep love of sports. A doctoral thesis followed, on somatics and body movement, before Uwe accepted a position at the Brandenburg Sports Confederation. Over the next decade he ran several sports participation and integration programmes ranging from football and basketball to inline skating and climbing. When he first heard about Street Football for Tolerance, a project that was being introduced by the Federal Ministry, Uwe was cynical. For months, he had been trying unsuccessfully to secure additional funding for his street sports programme, and now, all of a sudden, there was money available for this new idea. What's more, he was expected to co-lead the initiative alongside a former West German, who was parachuting in from Colombia.

* * *

The four Griesbecks were standing out in the cold, wet night, as Jürgen repeatedly, and fruitlessly, rang the bell for his friend's apartment in Schöneberg, in the former West Berlin. They had come directly by taxi from the airport, with only sparse belongings, the rest to follow in wooden crates that remained in customs. The friend did not answer, they had no mobile phones, and on the ground floor a domestic argument had broken out.

Elida recalls, 'It was cold, very cold, too cold. No matter how many times we tried, the door did not open.'

Jürgen thought about knocking on the window and asking the warring couple how to get in, but decided against it. He turned back and looked at his family, shivering in the unfamiliar temperature on the pavement, vulnerable and unprotected. It was not the most auspicious start to life in Germany.

Eventually, a neighbour emerged, brandishing a key, and the family gained entry to the building. They stayed at the friend's apartment for a week, before finding a temporary flat in the east of the city where they remained for a month. During that time, Jürgen located another apartment back in the western district of Charlottenburg which would become their home for the next few years. With Jürgen due to start work in March, he and Elida had six weeks to get settled. They spent the time familiarising with the new community, buying a car (a second-hand Skoda) and equipping their apartment with home essentials, quickly discovering that their purchasing power in Germany was considerably less than it had been in Colombia; the savings they had made from the sale of their house in Medellín soon evaporated.

They also enrolled the girls in Berlin's bilingual Spanish school where the children picked up German with remarkable speed. In Colombia, Jürgen had always spoken to them in German, which they understood, but until now they had always replied in Spanish. Elida found the move tough. She missed the climate of Medellín, and without speaking German it was difficult to make friends and to integrate, 'Trying to start a conversation was impossible, and it was the first time in my life that I didn't speak to anyone outside of my home. The most difficult thing was the darkness; to cope, I would put on salsa music and start dancing, with my girls or alone. Other times I would just cry.'

The week before he was due to start work, Jürgen called the office at the Brandenburg Sports Confederation to ask about details and directions for his first day. He received a short, sharp reply, 'Look it up on a map,' before the voice was replaced with a dialling tone.

On his first day, Jürgen made the half-hour commute to the offices in the state capital of Potsdam, which were located in a set of prefabricated buildings at an old Soviet-era military base. Just over ten years before, this journey would not have been possible. At the end of the Second World War in 1945, Germany was divided into four zones – American, British, French and Russian. The capital city, Berlin, which was located deep inside the Russian Zone was divided on the same basis, and as tensions between the United States and the Soviet Union escalated towards the Cold War, access to Berlin was made increasingly difficult for the western powers. In 1948, land access was completely blocked, as the Soviets attempted to force their rivals to abandon the western sectors of Berlin, which were totally isolated and running out of food.

In response, the Americans instigated the Berlin Airlift, a huge operation to fly in provisions for the starving population, with planes taking off every minute. It was a strategic victory for the west, and in May 1949 the Soviets admitted defeat in their bid to take control of the whole city. Subsequently, the first three zones of Germany, together with West Berlin, became the Federal Republic of Germany (West Germany), with Bonn as its capital city. A few months later, the Russian Zone was named the German Democratic Republic (East Germany), under the Soviet sphere of influence, with the capital East Berlin.

Over the coming decades, Germany and Berlin were at the frontline of the Cold War. Through the Marshall Plan, the Americans pumped money into western Europe, helping the countries and their economies to make a speedy recovery from the devastation of war. This was no more evident than in West Berlin, which the western powers were determined to develop as a showpiece of consumerism and capitalist success, and as a demonstration of western values of freedom and civil liberties. This was in stark contrast to what happened in East Germany and East Berlin where, under a communist regime, subservient to Moscow, the economy struggled to recover. Furthermore, East Germany became a police state with the Stasi agency infiltrating and controlling every aspect of life, intimidating and terrifying the population into conformity. As a result, many citizens of East Berlin risked death attempting to cross the border into the western half of the city to claim refuge and citizenship. This resulted in the construction of the Berlin Wall by the eastern powers, which became the most symbolic physical manifestation of the Cold War.

Towards the end of the 1980s, the USSR and its grip on Eastern Europe began to unravel, as demands for democracy grew among populations behind the Iron Curtain. On the night of 9 November 1989, while Jürgen was in Costa Rica, crowds of mostly young people in East Berlin dramatically began to take down the Wall. There was huge elation, and the fall of the Berlin Wall was a major step towards the reunification of Germany which followed in October 1990. Over the coming decade, progress was made in forging a united nation, but most of the former East Germany remained decades behind the West in terms of its economic and social development.

Although it had been dissolved as a state under the German Democratic Republic (GDR), the area that now comprises the Federal State of Brandenburg had been fully within East Germany. It also encircled both parts of Berlin and, as such, was adjacent to West Berlin, which, despite the removal of the physical and political boundaries in 1990, remained a symbol of separation. On reflection, Jürgen realised that the phone call he made before starting work had been an 'immediate meeting of east and west'.

Indeed, he soon discovered that most of the staff at the Brandenburg Sports Confederation, including his superiors, and his small team of three, resented his presence, 'They wanted the project funding, but they didn't want me.'

With all the historical baggage of the last 50 years, Jürgen, as a former West German, was regarded as an outsider, and the local team begrudged the imposition of a project leader who didn't understand them, and whom they felt they didn't need, 'I began to realise that the uneven relationship between east and west resulted in them viewing reunification more like an annexation, and there seemed to be a crisis of identity. They hated to be underestimated and wanted to prove themselves. There was also resentment about the association with Medellín – they did not want to learn from the world's most violent city, and did not want a solution that came from Colombia.'

There was one notable exception.

* * *

Uwe had mixed feelings about reunification. While he was pleased that the GDR and its oppressive regime had come to an end, he also felt a sense of loss, and in the following decade there was a collective erosion of self-confidence, and dissatisfaction with what had been achieved so far, 'I noticed how the structures around us were changing, even partially being destroyed, and how people from the west were shaping the east. It was hard to find universal values, and we had to catch up with the west and align with them, to modernise, and there were questions about democracy. Nowhere did the East Germans have any say in what the new Germany would look like. It does something to people, and if you think that through to the end, it results in second-class citizens.'

At the same time, Uwe recognised there was an urgent need to address the growth of right-wing extremism, especially among young people, which was beginning to shape Brandenburg's reputation, 'The loss of identity had left a gap and this was being filled by anti-democratic forces. Xenophobic and violent incidents were increasing.' While he remained sceptical about whether a model devised in Latin America could be picked up and reproduced in Germany, from what he had read, he did like the concept, 'I was very interested in the ideas and wanted to help shape them.'

Uwe greeted Jürgen on his first day and helped him to settle in. The relationship was aided by their level positioning within the organisation, which ensured they avoided some of the hierarchical sensitivities which so significantly complicated internal behaviour and communication. 'I was used to operating in a very flat structure,' says Jürgen, 'where interaction between people at different levels was normal. At the confederation, there were strict protocols related to hierarchy, as there had been within the whole system of the Democratic Republic.'

It is perhaps unsurprising that aspects of Jürgen's behaviour irritated and surprised some of his new colleagues. Uwe remembers that he ignored conventional hours that were kept rigidly by everyone else, 'He wasn't a morning person, and often only appeared around noon, and then worked late into the evening. Sometimes this blasé approach gave me the feeling that he was an "artist", but in terms of the scope and the content of his work he remained very focused and organised.'

Regardless of the unorthodox hours Jürgen kept, Uwe showed none of the bitterness displayed by some of his colleagues, and a friendship grew in parallel with their constructive professional relationship. 'We appreciated each other,' says Jürgen. 'I think that Uwe benefitted from my belief that things were possible outside of the normal and accepted paradigms, and I greatly valued his support as a cultural translator, helping me to interpret the actions of others, and to avoid behavioural pitfalls that might have further alienated those around me.'

But despite Uwe's support, it remained an exacting return to Germany for Jürgen, at least in terms of his career. In Medellín, he had been able to ignore the political dimensions that were at play, because he had been so far removed from them, but here in Brandenburg he was unwittingly thrust into an environment where he would have to deal with the organisational dynamics of the confederation on a daily basis. With the exception of Uwe, this included difficulty in building individual relationships, as well as facing institutional resistance to his ideas and influence. After six years in South America, he also found that Spanish words often came to him first, and he had to learn the professional jargon of his native language, 'Initially, I experienced difficulty giving presentations, and sometimes struggled to find the precise word that I needed to express myself.'

Faced with these challenges, and with the coldness of his new physical and social environment, Jürgen found himself inextricably pulled back to life in Medellín, 'Everything had Colombian faces, shapes, the smell of the street. The smallest thing could take me there in an instant.'

15

Street Football for Tolerance, 2000–2002

DESPITE THE professional difficulties that Jürgen encountered on his return to Germany, Street Football for Tolerance was successfully launched in September 2000 with an official kick-off event in Potsdam. A tournament was held, followed by a reception on the terrace of the iconic Minsk restaurant, built in the GDR modernist style, which overlooked the city on the banks of the Havel. Uwe remembers the 'many celebrities' who were present. In the preceding months, a series of coach training courses and a trial period had been held, and the project was now rolled out across the state of Brandenburg, utilising a well-established structure of sports clubs which exists throughout the country, with facilities and organised activities in every city, town and village.

The Fútbol por la Paz methodology was largely well received, and only minor adaptations were needed. Most notably, the rule that required a girl to score the first goal was dropped after causing frustration among some of the male participants, and negatively impacting the process. Instead, a requirement for at least one girl to score for each team during the match was adopted. In some games, this resulted in teams outscoring their opponents 5-1, but losing the match because their five goals were all scored by boys, while the opposition's single goal was scored by a girl. This occasionally caused uproar, but the rule was retained, and it remained a powerful statement about the contribution of women and girls on the pitch and in wider society. Uwe remembers that acceptance of mixed games was one of the most challenging aspects of the project, but that slowly these attitudes improved, 'There was a tournament in Jüterbog, and my daughter Anne, who sometimes volunteered, was managing a conflict between two boys, both older, and a lot taller than her. She was able to settle the dispute and gained their respect. We started to see such events more regularly.'

Jürgen recalls, 'It was harder than in Medellín to convince the participants that it was a societal project, and not a football tournament, and on a personal level I found it more difficult to connect with the youth in Germany. There were more layers between us. On reflection, some of these were of my own construction; because I always regarded my involvement in the project as temporary, unlike in Colombia, I kept more distance, and allowed others to be more directly involved in building relationships with the young people.'

Although it took longer to gain traction, enthusiasm for the initiative gradually developed, and as they became more comfortable with the concept of open dialogue the participants began to embrace the sessions. 'Many of the young people seemed to be disorientated in terms of their identity,' says Jürgen. 'The framing of the world by the adult population, such as parents and teachers, who had grown up in East Germany, no longer had the same relevance, and there was also reluctance to question things outside of their own reference. We were able to challenge this by exposing them to new ways of thinking, as well as providing a setting where they interacted with different types of people, with opinions that contrasted their own.'

The opportunity to experience different environments also proved valuable in breaking down barriers. Jürgen says, 'During the winter the temperature was often sub-zero, so we had to find indoor venues and were occasionally able to use camouflaged airplane hangars from the Soviet era. There was a certain magic to delivering a project of peaceful conflict resolution in such a place, and the players enjoyed the uniqueness of the location. We also used the hangars in the summer, and then it became very hot and after the games we arranged barbecues outside. In these moments, you could sense they finally let down their guard.'

Perhaps the most meaningful progress was made in building understanding between young people who had grown up locally, and those recently arrived from Germanic communities in other parts of eastern Europe, including Poland, Russia and Ukraine. Although both sets of young people identified as German, there were stark differences of language and culture, and in some cases, this had resulted in resentment and intolerance. The methodology was able to bridge the divides, helping the players to understand the respective challenges and perspectives of their peers. 'We worked with some youths who were already engaged by the far right,' recalls Jürgen, 'with tattoos that indicated their affiliation, but a lot of the time we were trying to promote understanding between different groups, and prevent young people from developing radical views.'

As delivery across Brandenburg expanded, Jürgen endeavoured to build trust with the local team, 'It was hard to engage my colleagues, but I did my best to listen, show empathy, and try to avoid being received as an intruder.' Over time, he was able to build constructive and friendly relationships with his immediate team, but at an institutional level he never felt welcome, 'Although we were all German, I never stopped being a stranger, and I was never truly accepted. The issues were also a little more abstract than the life or death situation in Medellín; it was more about prevention than intervention, and this was sometimes reflected in the level of urgency and enthusiasm.'

Again, Uwe proved to be the exception, 'Jürgen and I were sometimes ridiculed, and the football association was reluctant to be involved, but the more I collaborated, the more enthusiastic I got, and the more I believed in the approach of using football in this way against xenophobia, violence and right-wing extremism. Jürgen was also very driven and was able to inspire me. I liked his determination and fighting spirit, and I saw the meticulousness with which he planned and pursued his goals. He took my expertise seriously and he trusted me, and that became mutual.'

The professional relationship became a friendship and they spent time together outside of work, as Uwe explains, 'I still remember when Jürgen's family visited us in Saarmund and stayed with my family.' Yet as their partnership developed, Uwe also sensed that Jürgen would not be around for long, 'It was clear that he had a plan, and that his time at the confederation was a stepping stone to other developments.'

Eventually, the local team as a whole embraced the project. This was aided by an advisory group set up by Antje, labelled the 'Supporters' Club', which featured a roll call of influential dignitaries from her network, including, among others, the mayor of Potsdam, the Minister of Interior for Brandenburg, several well-regarded journalists and even the ex-president of Germany from 1990–1994, Richard von Weizsäcker. Their involvement added credibility to the initiative, and motivated the confederation to get behind her vision of trialling the methodology in Brandenburg, before rolling it out across other federal states. Jürgen recalls, 'The Supporters' Club, and Antje's vision, helped to build pride in Street Football for Tolerance, and gradually people began to see it as their project, no longer something imposed by an outsider.'

To strengthen the case for a national roll-out, Jürgen commissioned an independent evaluation of the Brandenburg pilot. A partnership with the University of Potsdam was established, and one afternoon in August 2000, Professor Baur at the Department for Sport Sociology introduced him to a tall young man, with long, auburn hair, who had been invited to conduct the study as part of a doctoral thesis. The most enduring professional relationship of Jürgen's career was about to begin.

16

Enter Borković

VLADIMIR BORKOVIĆ looked up at the sky as hundreds of missiles flew overhead. It was August 1995 and a major offensive was under way as the Croatian army attacked along Serbian lines. Vladimir, a 20-year-old from Belgrade, had travelled through Croatia to Bosnia for the funeral of his uncle. He and his family had stayed overnight in the small village of Turjak, and they now faced a perilous journey home. As Operation Storm progressed, more than 200,000 Serbians living in Croatia fled their homes, and when the Borković family reached the main highway back to Serbia they inadvertently joined a huge train of refugees heading slowly east. Among the cars were people on tractors, parents on foot carrying their children, belongings loaded on to carts and donkeys. When they reached the outskirts of Belgrade – hungry, frightened and exhausted – only those with homes or family already in the city were permitted to enter. Everyone else was sent south.

Since 1991, war had gripped the Balkans as the state of Yugoslavia collapsed. The country had not been part of the Soviet bloc but revolution in neighbouring countries had further destabilised the increasingly fragmented collection of federal states, triggering Europe's largest conflict in five decades. The underlying tensions that caused the conflict were, however, much deeper. After centuries of Ottoman and Austro-Hungarian rule in the region, Yugoslavia had been conceptualised at the Treaty of Versailles, as the victors of the First World War redrew the borders of Europe, unifying the southern Slavic peoples into one nation, encompassing the modern-day territories of Bosnia and Herzegovina, Croatia, Kosovo, Montenegro, North Macedonia, Serbia and Slovenia. Yugoslavia incorporated a great diversity of people, with many different ethnicities, languages, cultures and religions, living alongside and among each other.

In 1941, during the Second World War, German, Italian and Hungarian forces invaded and occupied the country, unleashing four years of devastation believed to have left more than one million people dead. Partisan forces fought furiously against the invading Axis powers, resulting in mass executions and reprisals committed by the Wehrmacht and occupying Italian authorities. As they had done across much of Europe, the SS rounded up 'undesirables' – Jews, Roma, communists, people with disabilities – and interned them in concentration camps, where many of them perished. Meanwhile, communities that had lived in peace for decades, sometimes centuries, turned on each other along ethnic and religious lines; neighbour killing neighbour, with genocide and ethnic cleansing committed by multiple sides. As the war came to an end there was a crescendo of killing, with reprisals, purges, forced marches and civilian massacres.

In the aftermath of the war, Marshal Tito, who had controlled the largest partisan force, was able to reform Yugoslavia, ostensibly as a communist state, but operating independently from Moscow. Tito was popular, a benevolent dictator, and with relative market freedom,

Yugoslavia prospered; the bitterness and rage caused by the terrible events of the Second World War were put on ice. When hostilities resumed in the 1990s, the hatred resurfaced with the same intensity as 50 years before, and as they returned home from the funeral, Vladimir and his family found themselves caught up in a mass displacement of people, the latest tragic consequence of the region's troubled history.

Back in Belgrade, Vladimir continued to lie low, quietly pursuing his studies in psychology at the University of Belgrade. Young men throughout the city, including many of his friends, had been picked up by the Serbian military police and forced into battle. He did not want to fight. He lived in Serbia, but his family was originally from Bosnia, and before the war he had regarded himself as a Yugoslav. To avoid being called up for a war he didn't believe in, to fight against people he didn't hate, Vladimir had registered his grandmother's address, instead of his parents' house, where he actually lived, making it more difficult for the authorities to track him down, 'When the war ended, and I applied for a passport, there were more than 40 unanswered letters and demands on my file.'

* * *

Born in Yugoslavia in 1974, Vladimir had grown up in the quiet village of Pancevo, 40km north of Belgrade. Football was a massive part of his life and the foremost passion of his childhood. His father almost named him 'Sever', which means 'North', after the fanatical ultra-supporters of Red Star Belgrade, who occupied the northern block of the stadium during games. Instead, they opted for Vladimir, after the founder of Communism and former Russian leader Vladimir Ilyich Ulyanov, better known as Lenin. Regardless of his name, the youngster was destined to support Red Star, and he was soon playing within the club's youth system.

In 1983, when he was nine, the family moved to Ludwigshafen, a city in the German Rhineland. 'It was for economic reasons,' says Vladimir. 'Germany offered more employment opportunities for my parents, and there was a better education available for my brother and I.' They returned to Yugoslavia in 1987, and Vladimir remembers that the tension was palpable, 'There was so much hatred. If you went to a football match, in the stands there was antagonism and negative energy.' In a domestic match between Dinamo Zagreb and Red Star Belgrade in May 1990, riots in the terraces spilled over on to the pitch, with Zagreb's star midfielder Zvonimir Boban infamously kicking a police officer in the chest. The match was abandoned, with many people later viewing the game as a notable milestone in the road to war.

'It felt inevitable,' says Vladimir. 'So many families were influenced by what had happened in the 1940s, and they wanted revenge. Even if the perpetrators were dead, somebody was guilty. It was time for payback.' This included another of Vladimir's uncles, whose father had been killed by Bosnian Muslims in the Second World War, 'After the war my uncle became a teacher and he spoke for unity and federalism, but we discovered he was just waiting for the next war to start, and when it happened, he took his revenge.'

Vladimir remembers the start of the conflict as a time of great confusion, 'The state was very controlling and there were people saying it was not Serbia's war, but young men were being picked up on the street to fight. There was great anxiety and it also affected us economically; sometimes there was no milk, no petrol, things we had taken for granted. The gangs took advantage of the chaos and there was a lot of crime and violence. People used to drive around with petrol canisters in their cars, topping up the tank every few miles so that overnight the car could be left empty, otherwise it would be stolen.'

As the conflict ensued, Vladimir remained focused on his studies at the university. He also continued to train and play semi-professionally, where he had gained a reputation as a solid and technical central defender, 'At the university I was known as "The Footballer" while at the club they called me "The Psychologist". I liked both identities, and it helped to shape who I am.'

Before the war ended in December 1995, Vladimir decided, 'I wanted to do something with my life that would help to stop the patterns of behaviour I had seen, where neighbour could turn on neighbour, and to educate people to lead a dignified life.' He had already started to participate in a theatre group, giving performances in schools and universities that challenged some of the negative messages purported by Slobodan Milošević's regime, actively encouraging people to pursue dialogue over weapons. It hadn't yet occurred to him that football could be used in a similar way.

In June 1998 Vladimir completed his Master's in Psychology at the university in Belgrade. By now the war in Kosovo was already under way, 'I felt the same tensions as before, and saw again that the situation was going to get worse. I was still on the doorstep of professional football, and alongside an academic scholarship in Sports Science at the Technical University of Darmstadt in Germany, there was an opportunity to join SV Darmstadt 98, who were in the country's third level, the Regionalliga.'

With a good command of the German language from his years spent in the country as a child, it seemed like the perfect opportunity. The only thing holding him back was

Ana, a young woman he had met on his course at university. It was a difficult decision, but with the looming threat of conscription, he decided to go.

Vladimir quickly settled into life in Darmstadt, but as he had predicted, events at home continued to deteriorate. In March 1999, NATO began air strikes throughout Serbia, with Belgrade heavily targeted, and he considered trying to return, 'I felt that I should be there too, with Ana and my family, but this time every man of military age was being taken into the army. It was a choice: I could go to see Ana, maybe for an hour and then go straight to the army, or I could wait. I decided to wait. Even today I wonder if I did the right thing.'

The conflict ended on 10 June, and Vladimir made immediate plans to return. He and Ana married ten days later, with their marriage the first entry on the register after the war in Kosovo. Days later, they flew to Germany.

As he and Ana started their new life together, Vladimir found himself in the second team at Darmstadt, and it felt like his career as a footballer was not blossoming as he had once dreamed, 'Looking back, I was probably a bit lazy and I didn't train hard enough. It was a life lesson – if you don't invest in something completely, you don't get the rewards.' He asked his tutor at the university for advice.

'Do you see yourself making it to the Bundesliga?'

'No, I don't think so,' replied Vladimir.

'In that case, you should focus on your academic career. I actually have an opportunity that might be perfect for you. There is a project in Brandenburg, using football to challenge radicalism and promote dialogue. They want to conduct a scientific evaluation.'

It sounded fascinating. As a footballer and as a psychologist, it was immediately of interest, although from an academic perspective Vladimir 'remained sceptical'.

After discussing it with Ana, they made the decision to move to Potsdam where Vladimir also joined a new club, SV Babelsberg 03, who had just been promoted to the second tier, 'It soon became clear that I could not play at that level.'

One afternoon, not long after the move, Vladimir was at the university, when he saw Professor Baur leading 'a fast-moving, energetic' man across the office floor towards his desk, 'Vladimir, I'd like you to meet Jürgen, Jürgen Griesbeck. He's the founder of Street Football for Tolerance.'

17

The World Beyond

EVEN BEFORE leaving Colombia, Jürgen had started to wonder if there were people in other parts of the world who, like him, were utilising the popularity of football, and other sports, to address social issues in their communities. It was still the very early days of the internet, but every so often he was able to access a computer at the university and spend time researching what was happening elsewhere. Very few organisations had websites, and there was no social media, but he discovered articles and references to a small number of projects that had already been running since the late 1980s and early 1990s, with Africa emerging as a particular hub of activity.

Perhaps the most well-established example was MYSA – the Mathare Youth Sports Association, set up in 1987 in the huge slum district of Mathare in Nairobi, Kenya. The project had been founded by a UN Advisor for sustainable development, Bob Munro, a Canadian who had witnessed kids playing on a football field covered in waste. After getting the pitch cleared, he ran a youth football tournament, which then grew into a range of structured football-based programmes around health, education, personal development and creative arts. Environmental protection had remained a core theme, with regular clean-ups and initiatives to promote sustainable waste management.

Another interesting project, Altus Sport, had been launched in 1994 in the townships surrounding Pretoria in South Africa. Set up by Gert Potgieter, it supported disadvantaged kids with academic and life-skills development, as well as delivering health education, particularly around HIV prevention. As a junior athlete, Gert had competed in the 440 yards hurdles at the Melbourne Olympics in 1956, hitting the final hurdle to finish sixth when a medal had seemed certain. He subsequently broke several world records and won Commonwealth golds before a serious car crash in Germany in 1960, ahead of the Rome Olympics, meant he watched the final from a hospital bed in Heidelberg.

Gert's injuries, combined with South Africa's exclusion from the next seven Games due to the apartheid regime, meant he would never again compete at the Olympics, but despite significant damage to his eyesight sustained in the crash he moved across to the decathlon, winning the national title in 1966. His incredible career, which included two seasons of elite rugby for Northern Transvaal, was founded in a deep love of sport, and a belief in its inherent social value. Gert fought over many decades for the desegregation of sport in South Africa, and in 1988, six years before the end of apartheid, he helped to found the country's first Olympic Academy, as a fully non-racial body. Now, through Altus Sport, he was striving to empower some of the country's poorest children, with football at the heart of the programme.

Beyond Africa, Jürgen found projects being implemented in various parts of the world. Soccer in the Streets, launched in 1989 by Carolyn McKenzie in the US state of Georgia, aimed to increase social mobility among disenfranchised youth, while in Argentina, Asociación Civil Andar had been using football to promote inclusion for people with physical and learning disabilities since 1991. Another Argentinian project, Defensores del Chaco, was working with hundreds of young people in a sophisticated programme of civic engagement and personal development, with structured support into employment. The project had been established by Fabián Ferraro who had spent several years homeless on the streets of Buenos Aires from the age of seven, before he was adopted by a railway worker who supported his education and introduced him to organised football. After competing at a high level, he was now using the sport to help other young people build a better future – a journey which had started when he approached a group of 12 young men drinking beer in a park, and asked them to form a team.

Meanwhile, in Peru, Sara Diestro had set up the School for Sport and Life. Growing up in Lima she had volunteered with some of the city's most vulnerable people, at homeless shelters and providing physical therapy for disabled children. Inspired by these experiences, and seeing football's ability to bring joy in even the most impoverished communities, she created a programme of holistic support for disadvantaged adolescents. There was a strong focus on educational attainment, as well as medical and nutritional support, psychosocial counselling, opportunities to participate in creative arts and promotion of life skills. Through the project, Sara was helping many young people to pursue education, employment and peace, and to reject the drugs, gangs and violence, which were ruining so many lives.

Spirit of Soccer, initiated by Scotty Lee, was another powerful example. As a British aid relief worker during

103

the Bosnian War, he was delivering food and medicine to frontline villages and towns, when he first saw the devastating impact of landmines on civilian populations. Three years later in 1996, he returned to Bosnia as part of a coaching trip sponsored by Arsenal FC, when a group of children inadvertently set off a mine while playing football. Three were killed. Four were maimed. All were under ten years of age. Appalled by the incident, Scotty started using football to educate children in conflict zones about the danger of landmines and explosives.

These people and projects were all doing important, and sometimes life-saving, work, using football as the primary tool, yet despite their commonalities they were most likely unaware that each other existed. Jürgen also noticed a trend – these organisations were invariably set up by individuals who had used sport to overcome adversity in their own lives, such as Gert and Fabián, or who had witnessed football in desperate circumstances: Scotty and the children blown apart while playing football in Bosnia, Sara witnessing the joy of kids kicking a ball in the poorest districts of Lima, Bob and the children continuing to play surrounded by waste in the Kenyan slums. It resonated with Jürgen's own experiences in Colombia – the death of Andrés and the gangs placing down their guns. Football at its worst and at its best, football prevailing in the most hostile of environments. He would love to meet some of these people who shared a story similar to his own.

After he arrived in Germany, Jürgen began to think more deeply about the international dimension of his work, and the possibility of building connections with other projects around the globe, 'We could communicate remotely on an individual basis, but we were all doing our own thing, largely in isolation. There were no frameworks for sharing best practice or for exploring collaboration.'

There was added impetus, with a rapid growth of projects occurring between 1998 and 2001. More people were discovering that football could be an effective vehicle for promoting social change and, when he looked on the internet now, Jürgen found many more football projects, addressing an increasing range of issues, in a much greater diversity of places and social contexts. There was Magic Bus working with impoverished children in Mumbai, Bola Pra Frente tackling youth unemployment in Rio de Janeiro, and Play Soccer delivering health education in Ghana. In the UK, an English doctor, Damian Hatton, had encountered widespread destitution and desperation on the wards, and left his medical career to launch Street League, designed to help homeless people rebuild their lives and work towards independent living. Another Englishman, Tom Vernon, had set up a football academy in Ghana called Right to Dream. It was different from the others, in that footballing ability and development were core components, but education and holistic wellbeing were also central to the model.

There were many more organisations focused predominantly around other sports, and which appeared to be doing excellent work, but, for Jürgen, football had a uniqueness that set it apart. It was indisputably the world's most popular sport, in terms of the number of players and fans, as well as its geographic reach. The purity and simplicity of the game was at the heart of this success. Football was accessible, affordable and contained moments of beauty, and Jürgen felt that these attributes gave it a particular potency as a means of engaging, educating and empowering people. Besides, he needed a degree of focus, and there was sufficient activity and potential surrounding football alone to occupy his attention.

Jürgen's disenchantment with some of the circumstances at the confederation accelerated his thinking around how to achieve greater communication and collaboration between the world's growing number of socially focused football projects. He believed that this could be of enormous benefit to them all, with the chance to share experiences, learn from each other and find ways of working together efficiently, 'If we spoke with one voice, we could achieve more and, most importantly of all, advance the speed of transformation.'

He started to invest more time and energy in developing the concept of a global network, and exploring ideas that could help to make it a reality, already resolved that this would be his next move. In July 2000, Germany had been confirmed as the host nation for the 2006 World Cup, and in the coming years, and especially during the month-long tournament, the country would be a focus of the world's attention. Maybe there was an opportunity to reflect back a different image of football to the world.

streetfootballworld is Born, July 2000–March 2002

Jürgen Griesbeck

Jürgen picked up the phone to call his namesake. Before dialling the number, he briefly recalled the final of the 1990 World Cup, which he had watched in Costa Rica, when Jürgen Klinsmann had thrashed about on the floor like a captured fish after being fouled by an Argentine defender. After picking up a World Cup winners' medal at the age of 25, Klinsmann's stellar career continued, with club success at Inter Milan, AS Monaco and Bayern Munich. He also spent a successful season at Tottenham Hotspur in the English Premier League, a brave move given his reputation in England as a diver. Yet he almost instantly endeared himself to fans across the country, showing his sense of humour by falling to the ground in celebration after scoring on his debut.

Throughout his career, Klinsmann had developed something of a cult personality, known for his intelligence, a sense of rebelliousness, eccentricity and optimism, and after retiring as a player in 1998, in keeping with his sunny disposition, he had moved to California with his American wife Debbie Chin. Back in Germany, late one Saturday night in 2001, Jürgen Griesbeck had been watching the popular sports show *Aktuelles Sport-Studio* when Klinsmann appeared as a guest from the USA, talking about what the upcoming World Cup would mean for Germany, and the possibilities for a positive social legacy beyond the tournament.

Everything that he said had resonated with Jürgen, who saw in Klinsmann a potential ally for his idea to use the tournament as a platform for building and showcasing a global network of social football projects. He had somehow managed to get hold of Klinsmann's email and was surprised when he received a reply agreeing to a call. A week later, as the international dialling tone for the United States resounded in prolonged beeps, he waited for the legendary striker to pick up.

Vladimir

After their first meeting at the University of Potsdam, Jürgen and Vladimir quickly developed an effective working relationship. 'He was respectful from the start,' says Vladimir, 'and I was impressed that he had commissioned a study of his own project, something that was unusual at the time. I liked the way that his mind worked quickly and inventively.'

Jürgen, meanwhile, appreciated Vladimir's rigorous academic approach to the evaluation, and the thoroughness with which he conducted his research. Outside of work they also struck up a strong friendship. Jürgen says, 'I didn't have much of a social network when we first arrived in Berlin and Vladi was one of the few people that I spent time with.'

Soon after starting his research, Vladimir realised that a longitudinal study would be impossible given the rapid progression of participants through the programme, 'There were so many opportunities for young people in Germany, socially and academically, and they tended to move on quickly to other things, meaning it was not feasible to track impact of the programme over an extensive timeframe.'

Instead, he focused on the short-term outcomes of the project, revealing a number of profoundly positive results related to increased awareness and self-efficacy, 'The participants embraced the opportunity to collectively define the rules at the start of each match, and they were very motivated to ensure that these agreements were adhered to. This provided a foundation for the hypothesis that the programme helped young people develop belief in their ability to influence positive change in their lives and communities, and over the course of the study, this was scientifically proven.'

While Jürgen was clearly pleased with the findings, how to achieve and demonstrate genuine impact would become one of the big questions that he would seek to answer in the years ahead. Vladimir says, 'It continues to drive him. How do we measure our impact, beyond outputs and outcomes, to prove the effectiveness and importance of our work?'

Vladimir also realised that Jürgen's focus had already moved beyond the project in Brandenburg. It was a pattern of behaviour that he would see repeatedly in the years ahead, 'When Jürgen sees that something is established, his mind quickly moves on to the next imagination. It is often to the detriment of what he leaves behind, at least initially, but of course he goes on to new and more expansive creations. I remember one day we were standing by the railings of a park while his girls played with my baby daughter, and he said that youth employability, and the chance to live in dignity, was at the heart of solving many problems in society. I would discover later, not for the last time, he was already thinking ten years ahead.'

Gradually, Vladimir learned more of what Jürgen was planning in the present, and he was keen to get involved. The concept of a global network of socially focused football projects sounded fascinating, with potential to extend and further combine his academic and sporting interests. Before long, it wasn't Jürgen alone trying to canvass the support of others; Vladimir was fully bought in, and with his enthusiasm and intellect there was added momentum, and a sense of fellowship that encouraged Jürgen to press on.

Antje

Antje waited for her guest to arrive. Jürgen wanted to talk about a new idea, and she sensed that he was already thinking beyond Street Football for Tolerance. She had always known that Jürgen would have a wider vision, but he was only halfway through his three-year contract with the confederation, and it would be a shame to jeopardise the progress being made. With a solid base of evidence, the national roll-out was under way, with the sports confederations in Hessen and Baden-Württemberg, Jürgen's home state, already implementing the methodology. Another four federal states were preparing to start.

Antje listened carefully as Jürgen explained his concept of a global network of social football projects, with the potential to bring teams of young people from around the world to Germany during the World Cup. There would be a tournament, a celebration of football as a tool for social change, and a lasting legacy through the continued collaboration of the network beyond 2006. Jürgen wanted to turn his attention to it full-time. He explained it would be an extension of Street Football for Tolerance rather than a desertion, and an opportunity to showcase Germany's commitment to global development. Besides, it was time for him to move on. The project in Brandenburg needed local leadership, and Uwe was motivated to take it forward. His own initial purpose of successfully introducing the project and instigating a national roll-out had been fulfilled.

It was clear that Jürgen was not only expressing a desire to move on – he wanted Antje's support in persuading the ministry to fund his new venture. The rationale was compelling, but the Ministry for Family Affairs, Senior Citizens, Women and Youth was a domestically focused body and didn't typically fund international projects. That said, during the tournament, Germany would be receiving the world, and they wanted to make the world feel at home. The idea merited further consideration.

Elida

As Jürgen's vision continued to advance, perhaps no one had sacrificed more than Elida, 'When we decided to move to Germany, I knew that we would probably never live in Colombia again, but I believed in what Jürgen was trying to accomplish. He showed a great ability to propose and implement new ideas, and acted without fear. I knew that he would continue to start new conversations and build alliances, and use his strength to make the invisible visible and to generate empathy.'

After a difficult start to life in Berlin, Elida had found happiness. She knew that being alone was not an option, and as the first cold winter had slowly thawed towards a pleasant, if unpredictable, summer, she had made some good friends. At first, these were people who shared her Latin background, but as her grasp of German improved, her social circle expanded to include Germans, Russians and people of many nationalities, 'I learned that my place in the world is anywhere that life can be shared with others, no matter how different we are.'

Their daughters were thriving too, 'The German-Spanish school reinforced their languages and cultures, and they met people from many backgrounds, giving them a broader view of life. They adapted better and faster than I expected; as a family we all grew up, and we were very happy in Germany.'

Jürgen Klinsmann

Klinsmann picked up his phone and heard a familiar accent at the end of the line. The two Jürgens discovered they were from the same part of Germany, and conversed in the regional dialect. Klinsmann had been intrigued by the email. He was always a little wary of unsolicited approaches, but the message had been genuinely interesting, and aligned with his philosophy about the wider societal role of football.

Jürgen explained to Klinsmann that with the support of vice-president Antje Vollmer, and after a series of meetings, he had secured a funding agreement with the ministry to create a global network, with the main deliverable of hosting a youth festival and tournament during the World Cup. With this arrangement already in place, it was not just an idea, it was going to happen. Klinsmann indicated that he was keen to be involved, and over the coming months they kept in touch, as well as meeting in person on several occasions during his periodic trips back to Germany.

Eventually it was agreed that Klinsmann would house the new project under an existing body – the Youth Football Foundation – which he had established with a number of former team-mates from the German squad, including Guido Buchwald and the Werder Bremen winger Marco Bode, who was still playing for the international side. The foundation had two main areas of focus: firstly, to develop youth football in Germany, and, secondly, to consider the social role of football more broadly. Jürgen's proposal fitted well with the latter, and although the foundation was not particularly active, the governance structures were already in place, and Jürgen was bringing funding to the table, not seeking investment. The new project would subsequently operate under the umbrella of the foundation for the next two and a half years.

Johannes

Before his time at Street Football for Tolerance came to an end, Jürgen was mandated by the ministry to actively initiate conversations with other projects beyond Germany, and in autumn 2001 he and Vladimir organised a Europe-wide gathering of organisations that were running football-based interventions. They were seeking a venue for the event, and settled upon a sports facility run by the German Academy for Leadership in Sport. Their contact at the centre, Gabi, mentioned that her boyfriend would be very interested in their new venture, and she put them in touch.

Johannes Axster was already active in the field of youth and sports. As well as working for the academy, where he delivered management workshops for staff and volunteers at sports clubs and federations, he had co-founded a small NGO (non-governmental organisation) which promoted the participation of children and young people in the design of safe spaces in Berlin. As Gabi had predicted, he was eager to learn more, and a few weeks later Johannes attended the event, along with representatives from more than 20 organisations from countries across Europe, including England, Norway, Finland and Poland. There were also attendees from other parts of Germany, including Steffi Biester, who was overseeing the successful implementation of the Street Football for Tolerance methodology in the state of Baden-Württemberg. Several years earlier, she had started researching ways to use football as a tool for social change, and had come across Jürgen during his time at Fútbol por la Paz. She was excited to 'connect with other like-minded people, and to become part of a wider conversation'.

Vladimir remembers, 'It was an opportunity to share best practice, and we made a commitment to keep in touch and strengthen our communication.' The event also helped to seal the involvement of Johannes. With his experience in youth and sport, as well as a Master's in Sports Sciences, he had a solid and relevant background, but more importantly, he brought additional energy and enthusiasm. Johannes was soon embraced as a core part of the team, and, alongside Jürgen and Vladimir, became one of the three official co-founders of the new initiative.

At this point they still didn't have a name for the project, and one lunchtime the trio were bouncing around ideas as they walked through the centre of Berlin in search of a Turkish döner bar. Jürgen suggested streetfootballworld, with 'street' relating to the urban spaces where projects typically took place, 'football' the principal activity, and 'world' reflecting the global scope of their endeavour. The name was adopted, a decision that Jürgen 'regretted many times afterwards'. It was clunky, and the 'street' element in particular would not accurately represent the diversity of projects that would soon join the network. But they would only realise this later. The name was settled.

They secured a lease on a small two-roomed caretaker's apartment at the Sports Academy where the event had taken place. It would serve as an office, and an official start date of 1 April 2002 was agreed, with Jürgen leaving his role at the confederation the week before. A full-time salary had been earmarked within the grant from the ministry, along with part-time allocations for Vladimir and Johannes, who would respectively continue temporarily with their roles at the university and the NGO. The initial funding partnership with the ministry was for 18 months, with a view to this being extended to four years, based on Jürgen and his team securing additional funding to support the planned festival in 2006.

Uwe

Two years after his arrival at the confederation, Jürgen was leaving, as he had done in Medellín, confident that the project would continue to thrive in his absence. Uwe was sorry to see him go, but he knew that Jürgen had a bigger vision to pursue, 'I fondly remember our project and our relationship. Even if it was not the biggest programme that I worked on, it was the one that changed my life most lastingly.'

Immediately after Jürgen departed in March 2002, Uwe took full control of the initiative in Brandenburg, as well as supporting the continued national roll-out, with more federal states adopting the methodology. He stayed at the confederation until December 2018, continuing to run Street Football for Tolerance throughout this time. 'There were many special moments' with international tournaments hosted in Brandenburg 'on bridges, ships and roads', as well as taking teams of local youth to participate in events throughout Europe. Uwe believes the project helped to strengthen Brandenburg's reputation, not only in Germany, but in other countries such as Russia and Poland, where the approach has been replicated by government departments and NGOs.

Reflecting on the challenge of lost identity in the former East Germany, Uwe says, 'The consequences are still being felt,' and, 30 years after reunification, he believes the coronavirus pandemic has brought the inequities between east and west strongly into focus once again, 'It is evident that the impact in western Germany is being perceived with greater concern. After all, their society has not had to change since 1945, whereas experience of change has remained deeply embedded in the collective consciousness of Germans in the east. The current dissatisfaction of many people and the new emergence of some extremist and undemocratic attitudes is likely rooted in the loss of self-confidence, and a lack of belonging.'

In Germany as a whole, the project may have played a small part in a wider fall of right-wing tendencies and political influence that was evident during the early 2000s, but as Uwe indicates, in recent years there has been a re-emergence of these sentiments following a huge rise in immigration. In 2015, Chancellor Angela Merkel opened German borders to refugees, and in that year alone, an estimated 1.1 million people arrived from Syria, other parts of the Middle East, Africa and Asia. With xenophobia resurfacing again, there has been a surge in demand for projects that promote integration, and Street Football for Tolerance was already in place to help meet this urgent need. More than 20 years after Jürgen arrived in Berlin, the project is now more important than ever, and many of the young people who fled their homes and trekked desperately across Europe are active in the programme.

All of this was in the future. For now, Uwe watched Jürgen leave the office for the last time and drive away in his Skoda. His time at the confederation was over, but his impact would live on. And streetfootballworld was born.

19

The Letter

ON 1 April 2002 Jürgen made his way to the new office at the Sports Academy. As he cycled through the bustling streets of Schöneberg, he reflected on everything that had happened since the assassination of Andrés nearly eight years before. He remembered the sound of Elida's footsteps as she ran up the stairs to tell him the news, and the sick feeling in his stomach that lasted for days. The cries from the street of 'Andrés, amigo, Dios está contigo'. The decision to change his course, the gangs placing down their weapons, meeting Alejandro and creating the methodology. Then came Vahos, Maria, Fútbol por la Paz and the World Cup in France, before the convoy and Antje sent everything in a new direction. On a personal level too, so much had changed: the wedding in the Andes, moving to Medellín, starting a family and the difficult decision to begin a new life in Germany. The last two years had been more difficult, with all the challenges at the confederation, but it hadn't tempered his determination to continue building a positive legacy from the senseless killing of Andrés, nor dimmed his belief that football was the key to realising this ambition.

How had it all happened? Each step had been calculated and taken carefully, but as a collection of steps his journey could not have been planned nor foreseen from the outset. When he spoke to Maria, she still reminded him of a saying that he often used back in Medellín, 'Y todo sin hacer nada' – and it all happens without planning anything. Of course, developing vision and strategy were central pillars of how Jürgen operated, but he had learned that growing organically and acting on gut instinct were equally important, and as the next exciting chapter was about to begin, he resolved to remain true to this notion. That said, for the next four years, the broad direction seemed clear – establish a global network and deliver on the festival during the World Cup, but this could lead Jürgen and his small team in a thousand different directions, and it was exciting to contemplate where streetfootballworld would take them next.

When he arrived in the office, Vladimir and Johannes were already there, standing in a bare room. There were no chairs or desks, no stationery, no computers or printer. Not even a wastepaper basket.

'Good morning,' said Vladimir. 'We need to go to Ikea.'

* * *

Once the office was furnished, the trio agreed titles. Jürgen would be managing director, responsible for the overall operation and for handling the relationship with the ministry. Johannes was named partnerships director, with a remit to generate and manage new opportunities for funding and support. Finally, Vladimir was assigned to discover what was happening around the world, and to start building connections for the future network; he became research director, a title which caused Professor Baur to laugh out loud when he was informed of the self-appointment. In reality, it was a very fluid arrangement, with all three working closely together, and collectively taking responsibility for securing the additional funding that was needed to trigger an extension from the ministry in 18 months' time.

A few weeks later, a letter arrived stamped by the Deutscher Fußball-Bund (DFB) – the German Football Association. Jürgen opened it with anticipation, but was disappointed to discover a demand, from one of the DFB's most senior officials, that streetfootballworld cease operations. 'The letter asked us to stop talking about what football is and should be,' says Jürgen, 'and claimed that the DFB had sole responsibility for communicating about the game.'

It was an astonishing request. The team at streetfootballworld were amazed that the DFB – the largest national sports association in the world with more than six million members – felt threatened by their small operation. But even more incredible was the idea that someone, or one institution, could claim ownership of football, and an exclusive authority for discussing its role in society. Vladimir says, 'Jürgen sent back a polite reply explaining that we would continue with our work.'

Nonetheless, the episode raised a pertinent question that Jürgen had been contemplating for some time, and which he now began discussing with Vladimir and Johannes in more depth: how closely should streetfootballworld be seeking to work with the existing structures of football?

* * *

Over 3,000 years ago, in the great cities of Mayan civilisation, in modern-day Mexico, Belize and Guatemala, the game of pok-ta-pok thrived. Depicted in paintings and sculptures, it involved two teams of up to six players knocking a rubber ball through a single raised hoop, using only their elbows, hips and knees. It was a popular pastime, but also served a wider societal purpose, with games used to settle disputes between warring parties. Pok-ta-pok was one of numerous activities to emerge independently in different parts of the world that bears a resemblance to football. A military manual from the Han Dynasty explains the rules of tsu'chu, a physical exercise which involved kicking a leather ball into a small net of bamboo, while, in Ancient Rome, Julius Caesar popularised harpastum, with two teams using extreme violence to cross their opposition's defensive line. To the north, in the Arctic, the Inuit played aqsaqtuk – football on ice – with a ball made from whalebone and animal hide. The game was immortalised in legend, with stories of the dead travelling to the Northern Lights to play an eternal game with the head of a walrus.

Football as we know it today can be traced to Britain, with records of 'mob football' dating from the early Middle Ages. The game typically involved two teams of unlimited number trying to force a ball through their opponent's goal by any possible means. Violence was a key feature and residents barricaded their doors as the mob did battle through the streets. The game flourished in London where it became an expression of social unrest for the overcrowded and impoverished populace. Apprentices from the various trades gathered to compete in roaring games, hundreds of men, one trade against another. This disgruntled and sometimes radical element of the community would often use football as a means of voicing their discontent, with games ending in riots and unruliness that threatened social order.

In fact, football was fast becoming a problem for the authorities, and had become so popular during the reign of Edward II that merchants, fearing its damaging impact on trade, petitioned the King to put a stop to it. He agreed, and the following proclamation was issued on 13 April 1314 forbidding the practice, 'Forasmuch as there is great noise in the city caused by hustling over large balls, from which many evils may arise, which God forbid; we command and forbid on behalf of the King, on pain of imprisonment, such games to be used in the city in future.' This was the first of many unsuccessful attempts to stamp out the practice, described by one objector as 'beastlike furie and extreme violence deserving only to be put in perpetual silence'.

Attempts to codify the game had been made in the past, but it wasn't until 26 October 1863 that standardised rules were agreed. Representatives from 11 clubs met in the Freemasons' Tavern in London, and after protracted negotiations, association football was born. The first game played under the new regulations took place on 9 January 1864 at Battersea Park, and afterwards the players and supporters adjourned for a smoking concert at the Grosvenor Hotel in Pimlico, with the evening's toast, 'Success to football irrespective of class or creed.'

In the following decades, many people were exposed to the sport through institutions such as schools and churches, with football regarded as a healthy way of combating the degeneracy of urban life. Local industries also produced numerous football teams, with Newton Heath, the forerunner of Manchester United, set up in 1880 by workmen of the Lancashire and Yorkshire Railway Company. Perhaps even more astonishing was the meteoric rise of football as a spectator sport. With a shift in the nation's attitude to leisure, Saturday afternoons were increasingly given as time off, and at the one o'clock whistle workers poured from the factories to support their local sides. The rise of football also coincided with the climax of Britain's economic and political domination of the globe, and the game became one of the Empire's most successful and enduring exports, as soldiers, sailors, merchants and missionaries left the shores of their homeland with leather balls and the laws of the game. It was quickly and fanatically adopted in many parts of the world.

In Germany, the first football match is believed to have taken place in Braunschweig in 1874, after a school teacher named August Hermann obtained a ball from England. In the same year, the Dresden English Football Club was founded by Englishmen living and working in the city. After a relatively slow start, in comparison to some other parts of the world, in part due to the persistent popularity of a traditional form of gymnastics, football started to spread rapidly. On 28 January 1900, 86 football clubs from across Germany met in the Mariengarten restaurant in Leipzig to found the country's football association – the DFB.

With an increasing number of countries embracing the game, and with more international fixtures taking place, it became evident that football required a global governing body. The British Home Nations initially rejected the idea, so, progressing without them, the Football Associations of seven nations – France, Belgium, Denmark, the Netherlands, Spain, Sweden and Switzerland – gathered in Paris, and on 21 May 1904, FIFA – the Fédération Internationale de Football Association – was established. Later that day, the DFB sent a telegram confirming they would like to join, although they missed out on becoming founding members. England joined the following year.

In 1930, the inaugural FIFA World Cup took place in Uruguay, with 13 teams, and despite a gap of 12 years caused by the Second World War, over the coming decades the tournament grew in size and popularity, becoming, behind the Olympics, the most prestigious sporting tournament in the world. By the 1970s, the vast majority of national football associations were members, and six continental federations – confederations – were also now in place under the umbrella of FIFA, with devolved responsibility for governing football and running national and club competitions in their regions. The first confederation was the South American Football Confederation (CONMEBOL), formed in 1916, with the others, including UEFA, founded considerably later in the 1950s and 1960s.

The widespread popularity of football meant its transition to a serious profit-making business was inevitable, and FIFA grew in parallel with the commercial success of the game, with an acceleration of turnover and staff numbers from the early 1990s. FIFA's growth was predominantly based on the colossal success of the quadrennial World Cups, which were already generating huge revenues from broadcasting and sponsorship deals. By 2003, with so much at stake financially, selection of host nations was becoming increasingly controversial, and it was already widely known that bribery and corruption were endemic within the structures of football, especially at FIFA – the very highest level of governance.

Given these disturbing realities, Jürgen, Vladimir and Johannes discussed whether they should try to distance streetfootballworld from the existing institutions of the game. They surmised, however, that the best way to fulfil their mission, of changing lives through football, was by working with, and trying to influence, the sport's official bodies. Jürgen says, 'In an ideal scenario, a concerted and coordinated effort to maximise football's social impact would have come from within the game itself. It hadn't, so we decided that we had to intervene and drive change from the outside, and we believed that this could be achieved most effectively through co-operation and collaboration.'

The approach was agreed, at least for now, but it was purely philosophical unless they were able to secure funding to continue operations. In August 2003, the 18-month deadline set by the ministry was fast approaching, and they were almost out of money. They had made important progress towards the creation of the network, but without an injection of funding towards the festival in the next few weeks, the dream was over.

'It was a crisis,' says Vladimir, 'but Jürgen worked his magic.'

One sunny afternoon, Jürgen walked into the office and casually announced that funding had been secured, and that the ministry had therefore agreed to extend their support until the World Cup in 2006.

'Wonderful news!' declared Johannes.

'Incredible,' added Vladimir. 'Who is the funder?'

Jürgen replied, 'The DFB.'

20

The Launch of the Global Network, April 2004

SOME 141 years after the official formation of association football, when 11 clubs had met at the Freemasons' Tavern in London, Jürgen stood up to address the 11 organisations that were about to become the founding members of the global streetfootballworld network. Representatives from around the world had travelled to the small town of Witzenhausen, in central Germany, for a week-long event at Berlepsch Castle, an ancestral home, which dated to the 14th century. Located in a beautiful rural setting in the state of Hessen, the venue had been organised by the local sports confederation, an early adopter of the Street Football for Tolerance methodology.

As the delegates awaited the welcome dinner, Jürgen looked down the table and saw some familiar faces. There was Alejandro from his days at Fútbol por la Paz, Uwe from the confederation, and Steffi, from the state of Baden-Württemberg, who had attended the European event in 2001.

There were also people he had first read about online – Fabián from Defensores del Chaco, and Damian from Street League. For Jürgen it was 'the start of a global dream', and after a short speech he raised a toast to 'the power of football for social change'.

* * *

It had been quite some feat to gain financial support from the DFB, little more than a year after they had sent a letter requesting that streetfootballworld disappear. The DFB had subsequently established a Culture Foundation as a vehicle for delivering projects related to the 2006 World Cup, and with the German government involved in decision-making, Jürgen had leveraged his relationship with the ministry, 'The political dimension came into play and we were able to navigate our way towards a partnership with the DFB.'

Although it went down to the wire, Jürgen had remained calm, 'The pressure was always the same. I did what needed to be done. Pursuing streetfootballworld was never a career decision, it was a life choice. I did it because I wanted to and because I believed in it.' After moving on from the confederation, he had been instantly happier. There was more accountability for success, and a higher chance of failure, but without the politics and the bureaucracy, he had the freedom to set his own agenda and operate as he wished.

For Vladimir, the way that Jürgen played football was a metaphor for his resilience off the pitch, 'He usually plays on the right, at the back, and when he gets the ball, he pushes forward, head down, towards the goal. He doesn't always make it, but next time he goes again, and again, until eventually there is a goal.' Jürgen had shown this same determination in pursuit of funding, which eventually materialised from the DFB, and Vladimir would see it again 'many times over the coming years'.

With funding now in place until 2006, they could start making more concrete plans for the festival, and the next key step was to arrange a physical gathering, bringing together a selection of organisations that would be sending delegations of young people to the event. Since 2002, Vladimir had established links with more than 30 projects worldwide that were using football for social change in some capacity, 'The research was rudimentary and there was still very little information available online. To contact MYSA in Kenya I had to write and post a physical letter and wait months for a reply.' The projects ranged from large NGOs such as the Peres Center for Peace in Israel, which had a football programme as part of its much wider operations, to tiny community-based organisations in Africa operating with zero budget.

In reaching out, Vladimir received a range of responses, with everything from enthusiasm and gratitude to scepticism and bewilderment. Although their organisations would both soon become founding and active members of the network, Bob Munro, the founder of MYSA, originally questioned what streetfootballworld could offer them, as a long-established project, while Phil Hill, a board member of Soccer in the Streets politely expressed confusion.

'There was a lack of understanding,' says Vladimir. 'Many of these organisations had been working in isolation for years, and the idea of sharing their expertise and social value with others was an alien concept. We had to explain that the network was designed for both contributing and getting something in return, of achieving efficiencies and of strengthening our voice by speaking collectively. We had to build trust, and this would take time, to prove the benefits of collaborating, and to work towards a point where they felt comfortable sharing with us their vulnerabilities and weaknesses. This process has never stopped.'

Jürgen adds, 'Building trust is not a one-off event, it must be gained repeatedly, not only with network members but throughout the whole football ecosystem. It has been the most important factor in pursuing a vision with real honesty, and time and time again we have been able to harvest the fruits of continually investing in personal and true relationships.'

Backed by the British Council in Germany, the event in Witzenhausen was arranged, and 11 organisations from the wider list were invited to attend. As well as providing an important opportunity to plan for the festival, the gathering would serve as an official launch of the global streetfootballworld network, with the selected projects offering both geographic spread and thematic diversity, covering health, education, the environment, employability and peace-building. The list of the 11 founding network members, and their representatives at the meeting, is shown below:

- Defensores del Chaco (Argentina): Fabián Ferraro
- Craques de Sempre (Brazil): Alexandre Machado Rosa
- Golombiao (Colombia): Alejandro Arenas Tobón
- Street League (England): Damian Hatton
- Peres Center for Peace (Israel/Palestine): Alon Beer
- Mathare Youth Sport Association (Kenya): Peter Karanja
- Diambars (Senegal): Bruno Meura
- Soccer in the Streets (USA): Jill Robbins
- ballance 2006, Hessen (Germany): Michael Glameyer, Carolina Guerrero
- kick forward, Baden-Württemberg (Germany): Jochen Föll, Steffi Biester
- Strassenfussball fuer Toleranz, Brandenburg (Germany): Uwe Koch, Guido Cools

In the years that followed, some of these organisations would drift or break away from the network, or would be unable to maintain involvement as formalities of membership increased. Others would remain core and active members. Jürgen says, 'It has been a theme throughout the whole journey that partnerships sometimes come and go, and that relationships can serve a specific purpose at a specific time. On occasions we have made a link where there is a strong synergy, but the connection remains dormant until an opportunity for collaboration emerges years later.'

The people too would go in different directions. Some would move on to completely different things or would start new initiatives in the same field. Others would remain in their roles to the present day.

* * *

The first five days at Berlepsch Castle featured a range of sessions including introductions to their respective football-based programmes, sharing best practice on topics such as monitoring and evaluation, and planning for the festival that was now just two years away. It was an inspiring and energising coming together of people, and there were passionate debates about what the role and priorities of the network should be, and how closely they should align with the football industry and the game's governing bodies.

Steffi Biester recalls, 'We were already back then fighting about where this whole thing should go. We shared the same vision and the same picture of where it could go, but on how to get there, we were often of different opinion. We discussed the role of football in society and questioned the role of our organisations, the role of football clubs and professional players, the role of governments, sponsors and funders. The conversation went beyond the streetfootballworld network; it was about a whole ecosystem, and I believe Jürgen was already back then developing the bigger picture for what would come later.'

Steffi had also started to recognise in Jürgen some of the 'high-capacity' leadership traits that he would continue to display over the coming years, 'He has the ability to bring together the right people at the right time, and at Witzenhausen, I learned that in working towards a common vision, Jürgen is someone that you can really fight with. I cannot express enough how much I have valued this. It is a very constructive process of fighting for the same goal.'

Jill Robbins, from Soccer in the Streets, adds, 'It was difficult to grasp the entire vision of streetfootballworld. At the beginning, it was a collection of individual organisations with some commonalities. Jürgen and the founders were so far ahead in their thinking. Thankfully, they persisted and stuck to their ideals.'

For Jürgen, the event was indeed another important milestone towards his evolving vision for a global and systemic collaboration, with the potential to transform the role of football in society as a force for social change. He was already thinking ahead, and contemplating how the work and purpose of the pioneering people and organisations in the network could be moved from the fringes of the game to the heart of the industry. Football was so successful, and becoming so incredibly wealthy and influential, all of which was built on its popularity with people, billions of them around the globe who loved and followed the game. Given the many urgent challenges facing both people and planet, surely there was an opportunity, a necessity, for football to play more than a fringe role.

Although this concept was still in the early stages of inception, Jürgen's ability and inclination to look and think beyond the present would both inspire and frustrate those around him in the years to come. He says, 'These were the early signs of "lonely leader syndrome", of often being out on my own and trying to drag people along with me, of trying to find the right balance between push and pull. I wasn't always right in the details, and the vision has never been static, but it has often been challenging to convince people that if we remain only thinking in the present, then we just accept the direction of change. The world around us is constantly moving, and if we are ahead of the curve then we are leading and defining the change, and we are ready to respond in the present when the world catches up.'

Vladimir says, 'Jürgen presents ideas that are ungraspable, and only later, when time and events have moved on, do you realise what he was envisaging.'

Steffi goes even further, 'He is always thinking beyond the visible, beyond the contemporary, beyond the current realities. Sometimes I feel like he is even thinking beyond the future.'

For the final two days of the event, the group travelled from Witzenhausen to Berlin, where a number of further workshops, an evening reception at the British Council and a sightseeing tour had been organised by the growing team at streetfootballworld. As the delegates left for the airport, Jürgen felt a new sense of solidarity, and a strengthened resolve to press on with his mission. The network was established, plans for the festival were progressing, and it was nearly time for a conversation with the most powerful organisation in football.

21

The Unofficial Co-Founders

'TODAY ON *World Football* we hear about an unusual project using the beautiful game to address the danger of landmines in the former Yugoslavia.'

At his apartment in Berlin, George Springborg turned up the volume. The young Australian never missed an episode of his favourite weekend radio show on the BBC World Service, which featured the social, political and economic dimensions of football. George had first visited Germany as part of a school exchange in November 1995 during which he attended a match between Hamburger SV and FC St Pauli, a fierce local derby, 'The atmosphere was incredible. I'd never seen anything like it. Harald Spörl scored a penalty to give Hamburg the win and at the end of the game it went crazy.'

The experience helped to consolidate George's growing interest in Germany, and after completing his studies in Australia he had returned at the first opportunity, where in early 2005 he was studying German Literature and Modern History at the Free University of Berlin, while also undertaking an internship at the British Council.

By now, the team at streetfootballworld had grown. The fourth person to join, as early as 2002, was Sarah Bagel, then came Simon Schneider, with a gradual increase in numbers towards a project team of approximately 20 people by the time of the World Cup in 2006. To accommodate the extra personnel, the caretaker's apartment at the Sports Academy in Schöneberg was switched in August 2004 for a larger space in Charlottenburg, another trendy district in the western part of Berlin. Many of the new recruits were paid interns, usually young people who were either studying or looking for a stepping stone in their careers, and, with only a limited budget in terms of size and timeframe, this proved to be an effective way for streetfootballworld to increase capacity. The motivation to join was often rooted in a personal love of sport, and the opportunity to utilise this for a positive cause was a compelling proposition. As a result, a young team emerged that was energised, motivated and hardworking.

George listened intently as the reporter provided background to Spirit of Soccer, and explained how a British guy, Scotty Lee, had started the charity after experiencing the appalling impact of landmines while driving ambulances during the Bosnian War. Next, the reporter interviewed someone from an organisation called streetfootballworld, which was based in Berlin. George sat up.

'Spirit of Soccer is just one of a growing number of projects around the world using football to address social challenges in their communities. Whether it's peace-building in Colombia, tackling poverty in India or delivering health education in Africa, at streetfootballworld we are building a network of initiatives, to help them share best practice and work together to maximise their impact and voice.'

'And Vladimir, you are planning an event in Berlin during the World Cup next year which will bring some of these projects together?'

'Yes, festival 06 will involve delegations of young people from organisations around the world coming to Germany for a tournament, and for a celebration of football for social change. It will be a platform to share and promote the power of football, and to encourage the creation of more projects that use the game as a tool for development and peace.'

It was a 'light-bulb moment' for George, who had never previously heard about football or sport being used in this structured way to achieve social transformation. He asked his colleagues at the British Council for an introduction, and a week later he arrived at the crowded office in Charlottenburg for an interview.

'We didn't know what to do with him,' remembers Vladimir. 'We had no specific role and he had no project management experience. But he was bright and enthusiastic, so we took him on board to help Simon, who was responsible for developing cultural elements for the festival. Before long, George was first in, and last out of, the office each day.'

George says, 'When I started, the office was an old Berlin apartment and we were all crammed in on makeshift desks. The atmosphere was great – a really fun group to be around and we were gearing up for an event that no one had ever attempted before, so it was both incredibly exciting and enormously daunting.'

'We took young people on and we trusted them,' says Vladimir. 'Although they came after the official launch, in those early days, the energy, the impulses and the passion of the interns helped to shape streetfootballworld, and in many ways they were unofficial co-founders of the organisation. Thomas Weidner also joined us in 2005. Again, no relevant experience, but he worked with me brilliantly for years to grow the network.'

It was a story that would be repeated many times over the coming years, with young people, inspired by the concept of Football for Good, taking up internships that offered both a small income and the chance to gain experience in a dynamic, socially focused and sports-based working environment. For Jürgen, one of the biggest positives has been the regular injection of new energy, diversity and imagination, 'Internships have ensured that fresh ideas and initiative continue to rejuvenate the organisation.'

Some interns would stay for just a few months or sign up for a specific event before moving on, others would progress to full-time roles with streetfootballworld. Sarah Bagel, the very first intern, joined to help with marketing, and eventually became head of communications, staying with the organisation for over ten years. Many would move on to other organisations within the same field, such as Madleen Noreisch, who joined as an intern in 2005, staying for a year before joining the Laureus Sport for Good Foundation, and subsequently establishing a successful career at FIFA. Vladimir says, 'In both roles she has made an important contribution to our sector, and remained a friend and advocate of streetfootballworld.'

In the coming years, the internship model continued to offer an affordable and flexible approach. 'Our HR needs are often changing,' says Vladimir, 'largely due to the grants-based nature of our income model, which means that funding is not always at a consistent level. In addition, the size of the team often follows the cycle of major football events, with increased staffing needs for large festivals held alongside the tournaments. Since 2002, we have had more than 300 interns, who have made an immense collective contribution. Everyone has helped to further the mission, and I hope that every person has also taken away something positive for their future lives and careers.'

Working at streetfootballworld would also influence the future direction of some who joined directly as full staff members, such as Naomi Ryland, who led online communications between 2011 and 2014. She left to establish tbd*, a digital hub which supports and connects people and organisations working in social development and entrepreneurship, 'Through my time at streetfootballworld, and the experience of building digital tools to help connect the Football for Good sector, I realised that there are so many organisations working on similar topics to each other that are not connected and which are struggling to make themselves visible. This was an important factor in pushing me to found my own social enterprise that is focused on connecting talented people to impact-driven organisations.'

As the team and scope of activity grew, so too did the need for operational management, an area of responsibility that did not come naturally to Jürgen, 'I don't like it. It doesn't make me happy and I'm not very good at it.'

Vladimir says, 'He is a leader, not a manager. In fact, he hates managing, and it is not his strength. He likes to be kept informed, but prefers to delegate project and operational tasks to other people. At first, we shared the duties, but despite having no experience, I gradually took on much of the HR, while Johannes picked up finance and administration.'

Jürgen says, 'Vladimir is a more grounded person and is good at working through a process, step by step, which made him more adept at operations.'

From May 2004, Vladimir had to conduct some of these tasks from a distance, after he and Ana moved back to Belgrade with their two young children, Jana and Leon. They wanted to be near family, and to enable Ana to practice as a psychologist, as well as providing a childhood that was 'more real and free' than was possible in

Germany. This meant frequent trips to Berlin for Vladimir, and to save money he temporarily slept in a small storage cupboard at the Sports Academy, 'Online communication had progressed significantly and it made the move possible, but I still needed to be present in Berlin with the team on a regular basis. Over the coming decades I would spend around half of my time abroad, away from my family, in Germany and elsewhere.'

To date, George remains at streetfootballworld where, among other things, he has successfully managed numerous large and complex global events, 'The radio interview kicked off an incredible adventure, with many amazing experiences, and in the years since, I have met thousands of inspirational and dedicated people from all over the world.'

There was another person moved by the content of the *World Football* report that Saturday morning, when the direction of George's life irrevocably changed. It was the reporter himself, who, after producing the series, would ultimately leave the BBC and pursue a career in Football for Good. As the report came to an end, it was a name that George would not forget, and in just a few years' time they would be working together as colleagues at streetfootballworld.

'This was Mike Geddes for the BBC World Service.'

22

A Hybrid Structure, September 2004

SINCE 2002, streetfootballworld had been operating as a project within the Youth Football Foundation, which had been established by Jürgen Klinsmann with members of the 1990 FIFA World Cup and 1996 European Championship-winning squads. The players had been part of a fast-track training course organised by the DFB to enable them to gain their professional coaching licences, and during the course the idea of the foundation had emerged.

Marco Bode, who also played and scored in the 2002 World Cup in South Korea and Japan, where Germany finished runners-up, remembers, 'I was pleased when streetfootballworld became a part of the foundation. From a young age I understood the importance of football in developing values that could be transferred to society such as leadership, respect, resilience and teamwork. Then when I became a player, with all the privilege that came with that, I also saw that there was a responsibility. My focus was very much local in Bremen, where I played throughout my career, but Jürgen's idea was radical and showed how we could be part of a bigger team.'

By 2004, streetfootballworld's budget was larger than the rest of the foundation, and it appeared to have outgrown its status as a project under the umbrella of another organisation. Instead, the three co-founders wanted to establish streetfootballworld as a separate legal entity, which would also give them greater control over its direction and future operations. As it was, the foundation had ultimate power over the project, and although it was extremely unlikely, they could abandon or change the focus of streetfootballworld, or even sack Jürgen and the others. Furthermore, there was a strategic misalignment, with the foundation focused predominantly on youth coach development in Germany, while streetfootballworld had a long-term ambition to transform the social dimension of the game globally. For these reasons, the co-founders were not comfortable continuing with the status quo, and approached the foundation to propose a new structure.

At the same time, Klinsmann's life was about to head in a new direction that would put him very much back in the limelight. On 26 July 2004, he was appointed head coach of Germany's national men's team by the DFB, with responsibility to lead the squad during the upcoming World Cup on home turf in 2006. The appointment would have a number of implications for his involvement and association with streetfootballworld. In the short term, it would help to raise the profile and credibility of the project at a crucial moment, helping to attract additional support and 'open doors' ahead of the festival, which by now had been branded 'festival 06'. In the longer term, and especially beyond 2006, Klinsmann's involvement would gradually dissipate. Jürgen says, 'He gave us a platform to get started and an important voice in the early days, and having played his part, he was then ready to move on. This seems to be the way he operates.'

With Klinsmann's focus now directed elsewhere, it was a good time to propose a new arrangement. Under German law, as in many countries, there are various different options for charitable and non-profit organisational structure. For streetfootballworld, the most appropriate model was to set up both a regular limited company (GmbH) and a tax-exempt, non-profit limited company (gGmbH). This hybrid model would enable them to function as a traditional charity, receiving grants, as well as conducting business activities and entering into contracts. This was seen as critical given the nature of many activities that streetfootballworld was already undertaking for festival 06. Both entities would have social purpose enshrined within their constitutions, and the two would be linked, with the regular company effectively 'owned' by the non-profit entity.

In order to set up and legally register the structure, the founders would be required to put up a nominal, and not insignificant, minimum capital of €25,000 (the Euro had replaced the Deutsche Mark in 2002), providing limited liability for any losses beyond that amount. The foundation agreed to the plan, and although their future involvement turned out to be minuscule, they contributed €6,250 as a 25 per cent shareholder. Jürgen, Vladimir and Johannes also each put up a quarter to reach the required total. These shares could not increase in value and the funds could only be redeemed upon dissolution, or by selling the nominal stake to another person or organisation who wished to take on responsibility for the entity.

In September 2004, the new structure came into being, and the three co-founders now had majority control over the operations of streetfootballworld. 'I remember the discussions with the other former players,' says Marco, 'and for me it was a success of the foundation that we were able to incubate the project, see it flourish and then become independent.'

Jürgen says, 'Still today, Germany does not have an ideal legal form for social entrepreneurs, but the hybrid structure was the best option, giving us the flexibility to maximise our impact and to ensure we remain focused on our purpose.'

It would, however, also become a point of contention in the years to come.

23

The Volleyball Player

FEDERICO ADDIECHI was born in Mar del Plata, an Argentinian city on the Atlantic Coast, with long golden beaches and tree-lined streets that make it a popular destination for tourists from Buenos Aires and further afield. Growing up in the 1970s and 1980s, the statuesque and naturally athletic Federico could often be found on the sand, and in the sports halls, honing his talent for volleyball, a game that he loved. It was, however, one of the darkest periods in Argentine history, with a military Junta ruling the country from 1976 to 1983, and conducting a 'Dirty War', with right-wing death squads hunting down political dissidents. During a reign of terror, up to 30,000 people were killed or subjected to forced disappearances.

'My father was abducted by mistake,' remembers Federico, 'and my mother, sister and I had to flee our home to look for a safer place. We were lucky that he did not become one of the "desaparecidos", which happened in the majority of these cases. A few weeks later he was released and we were able to stick together as a family.'

These human rights violations instilled in Federico 'a profound sense of disgust towards injustices, and shaped in me a certain sensitivity to social causes. I also came from a very humble background. My mother was a primary school teacher working in disadvantaged communities, and my father was a social worker, leading institutions that provided shelter to homeless adolescents. My parents raised me with important values such as respect, gratitude, responsibility and integrity, and these have stayed with me throughout my life.'

Federico was a good student and, from a young age, academics and sport went hand in hand, 'I started playing volleyball at school when I was 11. The public schools were of a good standard and I was able to progress both academically and on the volleyball court.'

After graduating in Chemical Engineering at the University of Mar del Plata, Federico moved to Europe, where he played volleyball professionally in the Italian and Swiss leagues, and was selected to represent the Argentine national team. He continued his academic journey simultaneously, first studying Modern Languages and Literature at the University of Catania in Italy before gaining a Master's in Business Administration from the University of Dallas, and completing a programme in Corporate Social Responsibility (CSR) at Harvard Business School.

Along the way Federico was collecting languages – Spanish, English, Italian, French, German and Portuguese, and after completing his career as a player in 1995, he was well-positioned for various roles in global sports management and administration. This included four years as development officer for Beach Volleyball in Latin America and the Caribbean for FIVB – the Fédération Internationale de Volleyball. In 2003, ready for a new challenge, Federico joined FIFA, 'I was recruited to lead a small team responsible for the federation's charitable efforts, but I soon realised that the work of the department was far away from a proper social responsibility endeavour, especially in light of FIFA's calibre, influence and resources.'

In 2003, the first International Conference on Sport and Development was held in Magglingen in Switzerland. It was the first time that participants from sports federations, governments, UN agencies, the media, athletes, business and civil society had come together as a sector, and it opened up Federico's eyes to what might be possible, 'Very soon it was clear to me that FIFA's engagement in this field was superficial, and that the federation only had a philanthropic approach in which football played no role. This hands-off approach had been in place for many years, and it was time to review it.'

* * *

From its first location in Paris, FIFA had moved to Amsterdam and then to Switzerland in 1932. The federation outgrew its original Zürich office on Bahnhofstrasse and moved across the city in 1954 to an old mansion, expanding into the adjoining Sonnenberg hotel in 1998. Poised for rapid growth of staff and turnover, a modern headquarters was being constructed across the city at a cost of over €200m. This would open in 2007 with the existing buildings retained as additional office space. But in November 2005, as Jürgen approached the entrance, they were the home of football's global governing body.

For some time, Jürgen had been trying, without success, to establish a link at FIFA. Vladimir says, 'He contacted the football development section, the events department, the legal team. They didn't know what to do with him. Eventually he was directed towards Federico, who invited him to Zürich for a meeting.'

After registering at the front desk, Jürgen was led by Federico up one of the grand staircases of the old mansion.

The Argentinian was surprised to discover that his German guest was fluent in Spanish. 'I felt that we immediately clicked,' says Jürgen, 'and I believe that the ability to communicate in Spanish played a major role. It was not just the language – we could have used German, French or English – it was the sentiment, and it helped to make a connection and to create trust.'

Vladimir says, 'Of all the things that Jürgen took from his time in Colombia, his ability to speak Spanish, not just fluently, but like a native, learned on the streets of Medellín, was the most valuable asset in his future career. It helped him to identify with the Spanish network members, to establish partnerships with institutions in Latin America and to build relationships with key people like Federico.'

In that first meeting, Jürgen explained his vision for the network, and for the creation of an ecosystem of Football for Good, not just in the build-up to the World Cup in eight months but to achieve long-term, sustainable and global impact. With just the occasional, barely perceptible nod, Federico did not give much away, but he seemed interested and was eager to continue the conversation in the new year.

Jürgen says, 'At the time, FIFA's approach to Corporate Social Responsibility [CSR] was very much rooted in a charity mentality, of making donations and aligning with an organisation and a logo that added value to the FIFA brand. We were proposing something very different, a strategic partnership and a deeper involvement. We had no brand value to bring to the table, and very little experience or track record, but Federico understood what we were trying to achieve, and saw the potential for FIFA to develop a purpose-driven approach to CSR. I believe that we were three or four years ahead of the curve, and that we were bringing a new way of thinking to FIFA. Thankfully, we had reached the person not only with the responsibility for

CSR, but with the foresight and mindset to share in our vision.'

The partnership developed quickly, and a further visit to Zürich took place on 16 February 2006. On this occasion Jürgen was accompanied by Vladimir, 'It was a big deal for me. I had seen a bit of the world, but not much, and I only had limited experience of liaising with people at this level of influence. It felt like a profound moment.'

Vladimir recognised in Federico someone with both humanity and intellect, 'Federico has an extreme poker face, he shows nothing, and I was unsure whether I should continue or stop talking. But at the end he showed a strong commitment and also understood how we should progress to secure support at FIFA more broadly. He is remarkably professional, grounded and astute, and these qualities would help him become the most influential external person in shaping the future of streetfootballworld, and of Football for Good as a whole, over the coming decades.'

'The approach they suggested for partnership was novel,' says Federico, 'and it aligned with the need for social responsibility that I had identified at FIFA. We could be more directly involved, financial resources could be more efficiently used, and football could be central. From a management theory perspective, this final point reflected a key learning from my Harvard programme, that CSR is more strategic and effective the more closely it is aligned to the essence of the organisation. It was very clear to me that irrespective of the size of their organisation, they had a clear vision of how football could and should contribute to global development, and a strong conviction that they could be key players in the football ecosystem.'

There were three key outcomes from the meeting. Firstly, in March, Jürgen and Federico would travel to MYSA in Kenya and to Altus Sport (set up by former

Olympic hurdler Gert Potgieter) in South Africa for an exploratory visit. It would be a chance to learn more about some of the projects in the field and to see their work in action. Secondly, in April, Federico would host a meeting in Zürich of leading Football for Good organisations and other development experts, with the aim of generating additional interest and enthusiasm internally. Finally, FIFA committed to supporting festival 06 with a modest financial investment of €100,000 (about five per cent of the overall budget) and, more significantly, to having a wider involvement in the event, including attendance of special guests and media coverage. This arrangement suited streetfootballworld, providing additional financing and credibility, while ensuring they retained independence over the running of the festival, while for FIFA, it was a low risk way of backing the event, which, given streetfootballworld's lack of experience, was deemed a sensible approach. If all went well, they could build from there. 'It was a solution that worked for both of us,' says Jürgen, 'and it all started with a conversation between two people who shared a common goal.'

The first part of the plan worked well, with the trip to Africa strengthening Jürgen's and Federico's growing friendship and further consolidating their mutual resolve to strategically collaborate in supporting the organisations within the growing network. The event in Zürich was also a success, with active participation by multiple stakeholders within FIFA, including president Joseph S. Blatter. It was also a chance to engage with some new network members, such as Grassroot Soccer, an organisation that was delivering a sophisticated health education curriculum to combat HIV/AIDS in South Africa. Having joined the network earlier in 2005, they were represented by Kirk Friedrich, one of the founders, who added valuable context to discussions looking ahead to the World Cup in 2010, with South Africa announced as hosts in May 2004. Federico opened the event by stating, 'FIFA has changed from a charity-oriented approach towards taking responsibility as a global actor ... Football can be a means, not only an end, and if we want to have an impact, we need you ... in order to promote the use of football to make a better world. Let's write history together.'

The third and most important part of the plan, festival 06, was still several months away.

24

Kreuzberg

IN APRIL 2005, eight months before Jürgen's first trip to FIFA, a second network gathering had been held over several days in London, hosted by Street League, with meeting rooms provided by both the English Football Association and the Premier League.

'This was the first time we had been so formally hosted by institutions of the football establishment,' says Vladimir, 'and it felt like a pivotal moment.' Representatives of 15 network members attended, including several new faces, such as Sara Diestro from the School of Sport and Life, who Jürgen had first read about while researching Football for Good organisations when he was still in Colombia.

At the meeting, a network board was elected to serve as an advisory body to the streetfootballworld executive team. The arrangement was relatively informal, but the board provided an official means for network members to inform decisions related to the festival, to the growth of the network and to strategy development more broadly. The first board included the following organisations and lead individuals:

- MYSA (Kenya): Peter Karanja
- Peres Center for Peace (Israel/Palestine): Roni Kresner
- Street League (England): Damian Hatton
- Defensores del Chaco (Argentina): Fabián Ferraro
- streetfootballworld: Jürgen Griesbeck and
  Vladimir Borković

Meanwhile, in Berlin, plans for the festival intensified. The Mariannenplatz, a large square in the central borough of Kreuzberg, was identified as a venue, providing a symbolic location in one of the city's most multi-cultural communities. During the Cold War, Kreuzberg had been among the poorest areas of West Berlin, and it had become a political base for left-wing and anarchistic protests, with violent May Day riots taking place in the late 1980s. While it remained a highly political borough, Kreuzberg was becoming more well known for its annual Carnival of Cultures, and as a lively hub of creative and artistic flair.

The area had attracted a large migrant population, with nearly a third of residents without German citizenship. This included a particularly significant Turkish community and a vibrant LGBTQ+ scene, all of which contributed to Kreuzberg's selection as a diverse and progressive place to stage an international youth festival. In May 2005 the site was officially announced at a press conference on the Mariannenplatz attended by Otto Schily, the German Minister for the Interior, and Jürgen Klinsmann, who joined a kick-about after the formalities.

A close working relationship was established with the mayor's office and other local community bodies, creating a partnership approach to planning the festival. 'The event was not just taking place in Kreuzberg,' says Jürgen, 'it was taking place *with* Kreuzberg.'

The mayor's office granted permission for the temporary construction of a 2,200-capacity stadium at the Mariannenplatz, and provided space at the Bethanien, a large former hospital building next to the square. This would be used as a project base for the streetfootballworld team, and after just 18 months in Charlottenburg, the organisation relocated to Kreuzberg in February 2006, where they would remain for the foreseeable future. The building, which then housed a range of social and arts projects, was also intended to provide accommodation for the delegations, a cafeteria and a press centre during the festival.

After moving into the Bethanien, the team soon became aware that a large group of left-wing activists had taken occupancy of the floor below, and were squatting in the building. Each morning, as they walked up the staircase to the office on the third floor, the rich scent of marijuana hung in the air. Vladimir says, 'I remember when Federico first visited us at the office, immaculately presented as always. He had to step over the drunks and the vomit on his way up. But it didn't matter, he was one of the team, and it was part of the adventure that we were all sharing.'

The presence of the squatters did, however, make it unsafe to accommodate the visiting youths, and although they would still have their meals at the Bethanien, an unoccupied school building in the neighbouring borough of Mitte would house the delegations during their two-week stay in Germany.

Jürgen and the team wanted creative art and youth culture to infuse every aspect of festival 06, and architects were hired to work with young people from the local job training centre in Kreuzberg to design and refurbish the event locations. The stadium was constructed uniquely using scaffolding, with steep two-tiered stands on three sides, looking right down on to the small artificial five-a-side pitch, bounded by boards and measuring just 25m by 15m. On the final side, behind one of the goals, an enormous screen was planned for showing videos of the projects in between matches, and on the outside of the scaffolding, large plastic drapes would be hung, with gritty, urban designs in the festival colours of orange, black, yellow and white.

The use of scaffold extended to the school building, with classrooms divided into bedrooms and bathrooms. 'We were mostly from academic backgrounds, with no experience in event management,' says Vladimir, 'so we didn't have any parameters set on how we should go about organising the festival. As a result, we came up with crazy solutions, and instead of hiring a regular catering company we recruited disadvantaged young people who wanted to train as chefs and service staff. We also developed creative pro bono partnerships with lots of businesses in Berlin and engaged hundreds of community members as volunteers to help with different aspects of the event.'

Outside the stadium, a marketplace with stalls and exhibition spaces was created in the square, with six large murals painted on the ground expressing the international diversity of the 23 visiting delegations. These projects, drawn from five continents, were a representation of more than 80 organisations, from over 50 countries, that now belonged to the streetfootballworld network. In addition to some of the founding members that had been present at Witzenhausen in 2004, and at the London meeting in 2005, there were new organisations invited, such as Espérance, a peace-building project from Rwanda, and CHIGOL from Chile, which worked with homeless children. Some of the delegations would have participants from more than one country, such as the Peres Center for Peace which brought together players from Israel and Palestine, and Football Friends from the Balkans, with players from Serbia, Macedonia and Bosnia-Herzegovina, reflecting the organisation's work promoting reconciliation in the former Yugoslavia. One further delegation – fx united – would consist of players from both the host borough of Kreuzberg and neighbouring Friedrichshain, respectively within West and East Berlin during the Cold War.

In the months leading up to the event, the project team were in continuous communication with the delegation leaders as they prepared for the festival. This included helping to identify deserving candidates, as opposed to simply picking the best footballers, with the aim of offering the opportunity to participants in their late teens and early 20s who had shown commitment to the wider objectives of their organisation's programme. The most challenging task of all was securing visas for travel and entry to Germany.

George remembers, 'In some countries the young people were orphaned or from rural areas and had no documentation. We had to work with the network members to help them acquire birth certificates and other identification needed to even apply for passports, and had to familiarise with the visa and travel requirements of more than 30 countries. There were always new challenges to solve and we constantly had to be innovative and resourceful in coming up with solutions, all in a very tight period of time.'

In May 2006, a month before the festival, Jürgen was invited to the Laureus World Sport Awards, a glittering event in Barcelona, that recognised some of the greatest sportspeople and their achievements over the previous 12 months. Jürgen had been shortlisted for the Sport for Good Award, and he and Elida travelled to Spain for the ceremony. As the night progressed, they watched as numerous stars walked up to the stage to collect their trophies, including Roger Federer (Sportsman of the Year), Martina Hingis (Comeback of the Year), Janica Kostelić (Sportswoman of the Year) and Valentino Rossi (Spirit of Sport Award). Prior to the final accolade, which would see Johan Cruyff pick up the Lifetime Achievement Award, host Morgan Freeman opened the penultimate envelope, 'And the winner of the Laureus Sport for Good Award is …' The actor paused, and looked up at the audience, 'Jürgen Griesbeck.'

25

festival 06 and the 2006 World Cup

Monday, 5 June

The final vestiges of the former Yugoslavia came to an end as Serbia announced its independence from Montenegro, which two days earlier had made a similar proclamation. It followed an independence referendum in Montenegro two weeks earlier in which 55.5 per cent of the population had voted to dissolve their union with Serbia. Vladimir says, 'Serbia had tried to preserve Yugoslavia as a Serbian hegemony, but it had failed, totally, from the wars of the 1990s to this final rejection. It was more a declaration of being alone than of independence, and the subsequent feelings of failure and despair are still felt deeply.'

In the months leading up to the festival, Vladimir had temporarily moved to Berlin and rented a flat, but his family remained in Serbia, and he was relieved to see that events in his homeland were unfolding without violence. Having taken on the role of festival director it was not possible to oversee proceedings from afar, with occasional trips from Belgrade, so he made the difficult decision to be apart from his family for a prolonged period, 'Ana was left alone and it put a severe strain on our relationship. It was not like I was going away to work on an oil rig for six months to make a fortune. I was earning a small salary. But the importance of the moment was apparent to us all, and the intense investment of my time and distance was needed to help take streetfootballworld to the next stage. But it was tough, and there came a point when the children did not realise that I was a part of the family.'

Friday, 9 June
The 2006 FIFA World Cup in Germany kicked off with the host nation defeating Costa Rica 4-2 in the opening match in Munich. Jürgen remembers, 'Philipp Lahm's beautiful opening goal was the start of a very, very special few weeks in Germany. For the first time since the Second World War people started to feel comfortable waving and wearing the German flag, whereas previously this had always carried right-wing connotations. Football did that.'

After the game, Germany's head coach Jürgen Klinsmann said, 'We were a little bit nervous. We made some mistakes, but they happen. We can draw a lot of positives from this game. We are happy to come away with our first three points.'

As the tournament started, Europe was in the grip of a heatwave, and Germany was already experiencing one of the hottest summers since records began.

Thursday, 22 June
Two days before they were due to fly to Germany, it was confirmed that the delegations from Ghana and Nigeria would not be granted visas for travel. It was a devastating blow for the project team who had tried everything to secure the documentation, including a last-minute plea to the German Ministry for Foreign Affairs. The minister, Frank-Walter Steinmeier (later elected president of Germany in

2017, and still in post at time of writing), was due to attend the opening ceremony in ten days' time, but it was to no avail, and despite flights being booked and the young people being ready to travel, there would be two delegations missing from the festival. Jürgen reflects, 'The Ghanaian and Nigerian players were young people on a mission, without the ambition to abuse their invite to the festival and stay on in Germany illegally. Refusing the visas denied them the chance to take a wealth of experience back to their communities, with the opportunity to inspire others.'

Despite the disappointment, the final preparations continued. 'It was frantic,' says Jürgen. 'We had to build the scaffolding accommodation ourselves and everything went down to the last minute, with everybody helping out with everything, including last-minute guerrilla marketing with leaflets and posters put up all over Kreuzberg directing people to the festival. We all pulled together to make it happen.'

Saturday, 24 June–Tuesday, 27 June
Over several days, 21 delegations of young people from around the world arrived in Berlin ahead of festival 06. The players, along with coaches and delegation leaders, were greeted at one of Berlin's three airports at the time – Tegel, Tempelhof and Schönefeld – and transferred to their accommodation at the refurbished school.

Wednesday, 28 June
With all of the participating delegations now present in Berlin, the first collective moment took place as over 300 players and coaches gathered in the Mariannenplatz. The 22 different-coloured kits and flags reflected the cultural diversity of the participants, with an unprecedented coming together of disadvantaged youth from the slums of Nairobi,

the shanties of Buenos Aires, the villages of Rwanda, the tower blocks of London, the disputed territories of Palestine, the post-conflict communities of the former Yugoslavia, and the diverse streets of Atlanta, Kabul, Lagos, Poznan and São Paulo. They formed a procession and then marched through the streets of Kreuzberg in a show of international solidarity, receiving, says Jürgen, 'a spontaneous carnival of celebration, applause and music' from the residents of the borough.

Thursday, 29 June–Saturday, 1 July
Prior to the start of the tournament, the participants, many of whom had never previously left their own villages, cities or districts, had the opportunity to see and experience Berlin, with sightseeing tours, museum trips and organised visits to the embassies of their own countries. Intercultural sessions between the delegations were also held to build understanding, with opportunities to share and learn about each other's lives.

By now, the World Cup had reached the knockout stages, and remaining matches were shown live on the scaffold screen at the festival stadium, with the delegations sitting together on the pitch. This included the quarter-final between Germany and Argentina on 30 June, played several miles across Berlin at the Olympiastadion. After a tight 1-1 draw, Germany defeated Argentina on penalties, and as the home crowd celebrated, violence erupted on the pitch, with a confused melee involving players, officials and coaching staff.

In a post-match interview, Klinsmann said, 'I'd like to remind people that there are so many emotions running when you go all the way down to a penalty shoot-out. It's easy to lose control for a second and maybe some words that were not the nicest were said. Things happen in football because it is so emotional but we have to forget about that. For us it is no problem, no big deal at all.'

It was an unsightly episode at the Olympiastadion, and Jürgen was determined that festival 06 would set a better example.

Sunday, 2 July

Twelve years to the day since the killing of Andrés Escobar, Jürgen woke early and cycled from his apartment in Charlottenburg through the deserted streets of Berlin to the Bethanien. It was already warm, with the promise of another day of blazing sunshine. The project team were busy, as ever, making preparations ahead of the grand opening of festival 06 in the early afternoon, with the coordination of the tournament and cultural elements, technical logistics, security arrangements and the imminent arrival of thousands of guests, including multiple dignitaries. George remembers, of the whole festival, 'The commitment and collaboration of the team was exceptional and got us through what was an incredibly enjoyable, enriching, emotional and exhausting time.'

At 1.30pm, with the stadium full to capacity and with the flags of every competing nation hanging from the scaffolds, there was, says George, 'a booming entrance' as musicians and dancers from the South American delegations arrived on the pitch. They were performing the Murga, a carnival of music, theatre and contorted dance, once used by slaves to mock their owners, and now a popular street dance in many Latin countries. As the noise temporarily subsided, the Fútbol por la Paz delegation entered the arena, presenting the Copa Andrés Escobar to the crowd, for which the teams would be competing over the coming days. They were proudly led by Francisco Maturana, who had been head coach of the Colombian team in 1994 when threats of violence had forced him to change his line-up before their match against the USA. That day, he had been reduced to tears, as events spiralled tragically towards the murder of Andrés. Today, there were only smiles, as he accompanied a team of young people from the barrios of Medellín on to the pitch as part of a celebration of football for development and peace.

Federico had pulled out all the stops to ensure that FIFA president Sepp Blatter was in attendance for the opening. Jürgen says, 'He arrived by chauffeured car but moments later he was in the scaffold stadium, among the fans. There was no executive box and I don't believe he had experienced anything like it before.'

Blatter was introduced to the crowd, and with allegations of corruption already well known, he was roundly booed. But the greatest derision was reserved for Steinmeier, the Minister of Foreign Affairs, who had failed to intervene on behalf of the delegations from Ghana and Nigeria. Jürgen says, 'Blatter was happy and affable, and was chuffed that the minister received the most boos. It could have been worse – not for the first time, we had to negotiate in advance with the squatters not to water or paint bomb the officials, which we achieved by explaining the nature of our work and the backgrounds of the young people who would be attending the festival.'

Despite Steinmeier's unpopularity on the day, he and the ministry had played a vital role in making the event happen. Jürgen says, 'His assistant once told me they were supporting the festival because they were convinced that we were promoting a kind of humanity that could be radical enough to inspire politics to follow, but that it would never be the other way around.'

With the booing over, festival 06 was declared open, and the crowd reverted to a celebratory mood. Players from fx United and the Turkish delegation, Sokak Ligi, warmed up ahead of the opening match, as project videos were played on the colossal screen behind one of the goals. On the other three sides of the stadium, in two steep tiers, 2,200 spectators looked on, with entertainment by live DJs and commentary that would be provided in six languages during the tournament. Jürgen thought back to the makeshift games of football in the parks and plazas of Paris and Lens in 1998, when he and Elida had tied a single banner of Fútbol por la Paz to the nearest available railing, hoping that fans might join in. Now, eight years later, they were here in Germany, with 250 young people from 31 countries, along with thousands of spectators and journalists, attending a festival of Football for Good that was an official part of the German government's event programme for the World Cup. Jürgen's reverie was interrupted by Blatter, who was expressing disbelief and postulating in jest that the fair play on show in the first game could not possibly be authentic. 'Again, he had not seen anything like it,' says Jürgen, 'with players holding up their hands to admit a foul and resolving disagreements through dialogue. They did us proud.'

Monday, 3 July–Friday, 7 July

Over the next five days, a sun-drenched festival of football and culture progressed. Each day there were up to 20 matches, 12 minutes each, using adapted rules from the Fútbol por la Paz methodology. Games were competitive and intense, but, with no referees, fouls continued to be called by the players themselves, with contentious situations resolved through dialogue, with mediation by a group of 'teamers' as required.

Jürgen says, 'Each match was a celebration of intercultural exchange, with videos before kick-off showcasing the work of the organisations and promoting the social dimension of football. We wanted to show the person first, before the player, and to build understanding and appreciation before each match started.'

The games that were due to feature the teams from Ghana and Nigeria were kept in the schedule, with the clock ticking and a ball in the centre circle. Vladimir says, 'It was a show of solidarity with our friends who were unable to travel.'

Outside the stadium, on the Mariannenplatz, there was a profusion of art and culture as 32,000 fans from across the globe visited the festival as an official World Cup destination. There were stalls offering spray-on tattoos of the delegation logos, beat-boxers, football freestylers from Norway, ball-weaving workshops offered by the African teams, football memorabilia on sale, and numerous food outlets offering themed cuisine from around the world. On the grass, people sunbathed and had picnics, and one afternoon the delegation leaders came together for an informal gathering of the network to discuss next steps beyond the World Cup. An exhibition match was also held with members of the Laureus Sports Academy, including, among others, former England World Cup-winner Sir Bobby Charlton, three-time Wimbledon champion Boris Becker, 400m Olympic gold medallist Ed Moses, and heavyweight boxing champions Wladimir and Vitali Klitschko. For Jürgen, never a fan of celebrity culture, it was nonetheless another opportunity to raise awareness, 'Their involvement attracted a packed crowd, along with additional interest from the global media, helping us to promote the message of the festival and show another side of football.'

Each night the delegations came together for evening meals at the cafeteria in the Bethanien, before returning exhausted and sun-kissed to their accommodation at the school, staying up to share stories, sing and chat into the early hours. 'The festival was a whirlwind experience with a jam-packed schedule and many new experiences for the young people,' says Jürgen, 'and always new challenges for the project team, who worked tirelessly to make it such a success.'

Jill Robbins, who led the Soccer in the Streets delegation, reflects, 'When a hundred different things could've gone wrong and derail the whole concept, it boggles the mind to think of all of the details that went into putting on that event. Everything went the way it was supposed to go.

'Whether it was luck, good fortune or sheer determination, all of the different cultural influences came together in a beautiful realisation of the vision of a global network of Football for Good. Cynicism was replaced with belief, distrust with friendship, conflict with fair play. The vision that a tragic event could be parlayed into a movement that would be a worldwide positive force for change was birthed in 2004 and came to fruition in 2006. The Andrés Escobar Cup set into motion Jürgen's vision and changed us all.'

On 4 July, Germany were eliminated from the World Cup in the semi-finals, losing 2-0 to Italy after a dramatic extra-time period in Dortmund. Eight days later, Klinsmann would resign as head coach, stating, 'The World Cup has been a huge success for the team and for the country and has shown a whole new German face to the world and that is something we can all be proud of.' After a break from management, Klinsmann would briefly lead Bayern Munich before a five-year spell in charge of the USA national men's team, leading the side to the knockout stages of the 2014 World Cup in Brazil.

Saturday, 8 July

More than 2,000 spectators crammed into the scaffold stadium. Tomorrow would be the World Cup Final at the Olympiastadion, and 715 million people around the world would watch Italy beat France on penalties, with the world's best player, Zinedine Zidane, sent off for headbutting Italian defender Marco Materazzi in the chest. Jürgen, Vladimir, Johannes and members of their families would be there, as special guests of Federico, but for them, the true pinnacle of an extraordinary month was happening today.

As the final of festival 06 approached, the knockout games had become increasingly competitive, and there had been a growing need for mediation. Jürgen says, 'There was a cultural dimension, with the Latin American delegations prioritising the implementation of the methodology, while the African teams were more focused on winning the tournament.' The teams that had reached the final – MYSA from Kenya, and Altus Sport from South Africa – were both very physical sides, and with the pressure of a packed stadium, and with heightened stakes, the project team were concerned that the spirit of fair play would be set aside when it mattered most. The rules of the methodology had been so well observed throughout the tournament, and it would be a terrible shame if this was abandoned with hundreds of dignitaries, partner organisations and media representatives looking on.

The two teams were warming up on the grass outside the stadium, and coming from inside, they could hear a cacophony of noise as the remaining delegations entered the arena in a Murga of wild celebration, with whistles, drums and trumpets, accompanying the singing and dancing. This time it was not just the South American players, but a truly international entrance of young people from five continents. The costumed dancers took their places in the stands, and the crowd was further whipped up into a frenzy of excitement and anticipation by the DJs and commentators. The sun, which had been relentless for the entirety of the festival, seemed to take on a new intensity as the players prepared to enter the tunnel.

Vladimir pulled both teams into a collective huddle and shouted over the noise, 'What you are doing here, and what you will do now, in this final, is not only representing you and your organisations and your countries, it is representing all of us, and all of our work globally. So, play fair, be kind to each other, and let it be the best final that was ever played.'

As the teams walked out on to the pitch, Vladimir ran up into the stands and embraced Ana and his daughter Jana, who had flown over from Serbia for the final. After months of separation, it was a wonderful feeling to have them with him, as the most intense, challenging and uplifting period of his life reached a climax. Over the coming 12 minutes he watched as the teams put on an exemplary performance of fair play, 'It was an incredible match. These two tough teams, still trying their best and playing competitively, but calling fouls, helping each other up, acknowledging the skills of their opponents and congratulating each other.' The game ended 2-2, before MYSA won 4-3 on penalties.

The trophy was awarded to the captain of MYSA by Blatter's representative, Jérôme Champagne, and the crowd roared and hundreds of cameras clicked, as the raised effigy of Andrés Escobar sparkled in the Berlin sunshine. Federico, who had been present throughout the week, then awarded the FIFA Fair Play Trophy to the entire festival, and in that moment, it seemed that the whole stadium spilled on to the pitch. Jürgen saw them – Alejandro, Steffi, Uwe, Gert, Fabián, Jill – climbing over the boards and running to join hundreds of young people in a moment of unreserved emotion. And there was Johannes, and Vladimir, with Jana on his shoulders, and Ana by his side, and the rest of his amazing team – Sarah, Simon, Thomas, George and many others who had made it all possible.

Amid the scenes of joy, with Elida and the girls next to him, Jürgen was, for an instant, alone in his thoughts. Everything had been building up to the festival, practically over the last four years, and spiritually for 12, and he saw now with clarity that streetfootballworld was not just an organisation, and festival 06 was not just an event; it was a community of people with shared purpose and energy to change the world through football. He remembered what Andrés had written in the newspaper after his own goal, and before his murder, 'Life doesn't end here. We have to go on,' and Jürgen knew that the story was only just beginning.

The Second Half

26

Southampton, 1980s–1990s

I STILL remember the anticipation of those cold Sunday mornings in Southampton, with a frost on the grass as I looked out from my bedroom window and wondered, 'Will the game be on?' Today, I'm sure that, in similar conditions, a similar child would look from their window and conclude without hesitation 'the game is off', but in 1980s England, such was the appetite to play, that a rock-solid, frozen pitch was no guarantee of postponement.

Admittedly, some kids hated those icy conditions, but I loved them; there was a certain romance to the crisp, crunchy grass, every breath visible in the air, and an orange ball contrasting the pitch, still white from the early frost. Then it was back home for Sunday lunch, discussing the key moments of the game with my dad before sitting down to watch *The Big Match* – the only televised game of the week. At half-time my brother Pete and I would run into the garden to kick a ball around before dashing back in as the game resumed.

Football was a central component of my childhood and a common thread that bound many of my friendships, whether it was collecting and swapping football stickers, headers and volleys in the park or walking down to The

Dell on a Saturday afternoon to watch the Mighty Saints – £1.50 to get in and standing for three hours straight at the Milton Road End, waiting for a moment of magic from Matthew Le Tissier.

That said, my life was by no means one-dimensional, and I had many other hobbies and interests. I was a voracious reader with a passion for geography and history, a keen birdwatcher and angler, and avidly into music, recording the charts off the radio every weekend on a tape recorder, and buying my first singles on vinyl from Woolworths – Wham!, The Thompson Twins and Duran Duran among them. There were also multiple collections, some which to this day still occupy the most remote corners and alcoves of my parents' house: rocks and minerals, animal bones and pieces of glass and pottery dug up from the back garden. At one point I even had over 100 different empty drinks cans on a shelf in my bedroom, and in moments of incited rage Pete would angrily run his arm from one end to the other, knocking them all off and causing an appalling cacophony that resonated through every wall of our semi-detached house in Radway Road.

But of all these pursuits, at that moment in my life, football was the North Star, with its own calendar that marked the passing of the year. With their four-year cycle, the World Cups and European Championships were particularly special, and I can still vividly remember certain moments – where I was, who I was with, what people said and the feelings that came with it; staying up late with my dad, uncle and cousin to watch England beat Poland in 1986 with a brilliant hat-trick by Gary Lineker, David Platt converting Gazza's free kick against Belgium in 1990, pretty much everything about Euro '96. Even though all of these campaigns ended in defeat, those glorious moments, and others in the future, remain treasured shared memories, with my parents and siblings, my mates and later my own children.

There was one thing almost completely absent from this world of football – women and girls. This did not seem strange at the time, and it never occurred to me that it should be any other way. Football was for boys and men. That was the way it was, as I believed in my ignorance that it had always been, and always would be. In fact, until the early 1990s when I was well into my teens, I had never seen girls or women playing an organised football match. Although I'm not proud to have held these views, I was undoubtedly a product of the society in which I existed, and as women's football very slowly began to emerge, it was widely dismissed among my peers as a sideline, an irrelevance, a bit of a joke.

Alongside my love of football, and notwithstanding the gender inequity with which it was held, I also had a deep feeling that I wanted my life to have purpose. This was influenced by my parents and their strong sense of community, and fostered by my own interest in the world which was nurtured by a huge set of encyclopaedias kept in my bedroom. Along with my passion for football, which had been passed to my dad by his father, who as a boy had played barefoot on the streets of Glasgow in the early 20th century, the books were a treasured heirloom from my paternal grandparents, and I read them back-to-back before I was ten, often falling asleep with the pages still open. The world came to life in those encyclopaedias, and through reading them I developed a vague ambition to do something interesting and worthwhile in the future.

With this collection of passions and prejudices gathered in my childhood and youth, and imbued with a desire for purpose, I left Southampton in 1996 to attend the University of Sheffield, and although it was nearly a decade later, my love of football and my longing to achieve something meaningful would eventually come together, dismantling my preconceptions, and changing irrevocably the direction of my life.

27

Kick4Malawi to Kick4Life, September 2004–May 2006

AFTER LEAVING university I'd tried and failed to get a job working for an international development charity and I subsequently fell into various marketing roles in local government. It was a reasonably good fit with my skills, and by 2004 I found myself working in London for a government agency that existed to facilitate sharing of good practice and learning between local authorities. The job was decent, quite interesting and with a great set of colleagues, as well as making a social contribution.

The career prospects were also solid, something that was particularly important now that my wife Claire and I were trying for a baby. But underneath the surface, I knew that I was unhappy with my career, and while I recognised that I was fortunate to consider such questions from a position of secure employment, when I reflected on my younger self and remembered all of the excitement that I once held for the future, I felt like a failure.

I resolved to do something about it, not consciously with the intention of forging a new career direction but to add some more tangible and immediate purpose and creativity to my life. On reflection, I now recognise that this was also likely a response to the difficulty that Claire and I were experiencing getting pregnant. After many months without success, we had embarked on IVF treatment, and the plan that I was now concocting was probably, in part, subconsciously pursued as a distraction from the stress and anxiety of that situation.

I decided to undertake a unique challenge in order to raise funds for a good cause, and at some point the concept of dribbling a football over a vast distance was settled upon. I could find no previous record of such an endeavour, and when I called my younger brother Pete, who was just completing a Master's in Sports Performance at Brunel University in London, he jumped at the chance to join me. We devised a plan to dribble a ball for 250 miles across Malawi in Africa over ten days, from the national stadium in the capital Lilongwe to a community project in the northern city of Mzuzu, where many of the children had been orphaned by HIV/AIDS. Our fundraising efforts would be focused on supporting the project, via the international charity Action Aid.

Over the coming months we threw ourselves into Kick4Malawi, training and fundraising, recruiting a support crew of friends and family, recording a charity song, and making logistical arrangements for the challenge. This included finding and hiring a local guide and support vehicle, booking accommodation along the route, coordinating with the orphanage, and building connections with the Malawian FA to secure their support for a kick-off event and press conference. It was incredibly exciting; I had previously been on a package holiday to Tunisia, but otherwise we had never been to Africa, and we had very little clue as to how our bizarre expedition would be received.

One cold afternoon in February 2005, three months before our scheduled departure, I was in our small dining room in St Neots in Cambridgeshire waiting for the phone to ring. After a failed first round of IVF we had tried again, and the results of the second attempt were due. Claire was upstairs. She couldn't face the call. I was at the table flicking through a magazine, looking at the pictures and reading the captions, but taking nothing in. The phone rang and I nervously answered, trying to detect, as we exchanged pleasantries, any clue as to whether the news was good or bad.

'Well, Mr Fleming.'

I could feel my heart pounding.

'I'm pleased to say that Claire is pregnant, and by looking at the hCG levels I'd say there's a very good chance that there's more than one baby.'

The rest of the call was a blur, and after hanging up I remained staring momentarily at the magazine before looking up and out of the window, where snow had started to fall.

* * *

Five days into the challenge, exhausted and exhilarated, we reached our accommodation for the night, pleased to discover that the small and remote Kasungu Inn had a TV. It was 25 May 2005 and that night Milan and Liverpool would compete in the Champions League Final in Istanbul. We had a few hours before kick-off so went to our rooms to rest before dinner. The trip so far had been a whirlwind of new and emotional experiences. From a brilliant launch event at the stadium, we had set off through the capital city and over the coming days had worked our way through the Malawian countryside, passing through small towns and villages, and attracting delighted and bewildered responses.

The most incredible scenes occurred whenever we passed a school, and on one occasion hundreds of screaming children in blue and purple uniforms ran from their school field to join the dribble, some of them continuing barefoot for several miles.

After dinner, we walked through to the gloomy TV room, which was quickly filling up with local men, with a tiny television set high up on the wall, attached to a small stand. The line-ups appeared on the screen and I was struck by the superior quality of Milan's team: Cafu, Maldini, Pirlo, Seedorf, Kaká, Shevchenko and Crespo. I remembered thinking that it could be a long night for Liverpool, a sentiment that was reinforced when Maldini scored in the first minute, with Crespo adding two more before half-time. As the Liverpool players trudged off to the dressing room, their fans began a rousing chorus of 'You'll Never Walk Alone', which lasted for the full 15-minute interval.

We briefly discussed calling it a night. Having completed five back-to-back dribble marathons, some extra sleep would have been welcome, but my dad, who was part of the support crew, told his story about leaving The Dell early during a match between Southampton and Leicester City in 1967, and missing a goal by Leicester goalkeeper Peter Shilton. So we decided to see it through, which turned out to be a great decision, with Liverpool staging one of the most improbable comebacks of all time. Inspired by Steven Gerrard, they scored three goals in six minutes to end the game 3-3, with the stalemate continuing during extra time. As Andriy Shevchenko stepped up to take Milan's fifth penalty, which he had to score, silence descended over the Kasungu Inn. Liverpool's goalkeeper, Jerzy Dudek, dived to his right, and although Shevchenko went down the middle, Dudek managed to stick out his left hand and save the penalty, completing the Miracle of Istanbul. Four thousand miles away in Malawi, the small TV room erupted with an explosion of joyful disbelief. It was another of those football moments that I will never forget; our guide Henry, who had been so reserved throughout the challenge, on his feet and shaking his fists, my mate Dave Light wide-eyed and squiffy from the local brew, Pete filming the scenes on his camcorder and my dad accidentally declaring that Liverpool had just won the World Cup.

Over the coming days our life-changing adventure continued. There was a chilling encounter with a black mamba snake, an extraordinary exchange involving a battered football and a live chicken at a desperately impoverished village, and an overwhelming final day, as hundreds of young people joined us for the last few miles to the orphanage, where we were greeted by large crowds of people, singing, dancing and waving branches.

Even before we had flown to Malawi, we had a sense that this 'one-off' challenge was going to be the start of something bigger and more lasting, but the experience in Africa made it a certainty. As we flew back to the UK, I reflected on what we had achieved. We'd raised a good amount of money for the orphanage (about £15,000) and generated some awareness, but most of all we had gained momentum, and in the months and years that followed we came to realise that the lives most impacted by the trip were our own.

* * *

Five months later, on 13 October, Claire and I had been waiting nearly 15 hours for her scheduled caesarean section at Addenbrooke's Hospital in Cambridge. The operation kept being delayed until at 10pm we were taken down to theatre. At 11.15pm the first baby girl was delivered, the second just two minutes later. One of them was wrapped up and thrust into my arms; the other, smaller baby was being cared for by the midwives. On the operating table there was a problem. Claire was losing a lot of blood and she was whisked off to another room. A few minutes later a nurse came to fetch me, and said that I needed to be with Claire. I was oblivious to the seriousness of the situation until I saw her, grey and shivering, with hot air being pumped under a foil blanket and another nurse repeatedly saying, 'I can't get a vein.'

Although it probably took less than a minute, everything went into slow motion until a blood transfusion was successfully started, and over the coming hours the colour slowly returned to Claire's face as the five lost pints of blood were steadily replaced. She would live, and the baby girls were doing fine.

A few weeks later, as Claire and I adjusted to our new reality, Kick4Life formally came into being as a registered charity in the UK. Pete and I had quickly settled on the name, with 'Kick' a legacy of the challenge in Malawi, and a clear reference to our planned use of football as a principal delivery tool. 'Life' reflected our planned focus on health, but it also kept things open, and would fit nicely when we subsequently moved into additional areas such as life skills, education, livelihoods, gender equality and climate action.

* * *

Early in 2006, Pete and Dave Light, now a founding trustee, worked intensively for several weeks, along with producer Phil le Cheminant, to create a Kick4Malawi documentary. It was intended as a statement that we had arrived on the scene, and DVDs were produced and sent out with introductory letters explaining our plans to every relevant contact that we could find. Among them was streetfootballworld, an organisation based in Berlin, that was building a global network of projects using football for social change, something that immediately resonated with us. We wanted to be a part of something bigger, so a DVD was dispatched, along with a naïve request that we be permitted to the network.

A few days later, I received an email from the network manager, Thomas Weidner, politely explaining that we must 'wait until programmes have actually started on the ground'. At the time I remember feeling slightly miffed by the refusal, convinced that our epic dribble, along with our good intentions, should suffice for entry to the network. Later, I realised that it was, of course, the correct decision. Network membership was a seal of quality and credibility, and to gain entry organisations had to provide a range of documentation and evidence such as financial reports, a child-protection policy, and reporting outcomes from ongoing football-based programmes, none of which we had or were doing. It would be another 18 months before we were accepted into the network, but the documentary served its purpose, and years later Thomas told me that after receiving the DVD one morning, the whole team at the Bethanien, including Jürgen, took a break from festival preparations to watch it.

On 2 May 2006 at Southampton FC's new St Mary's Stadium, Kick4Life was publicly launched. By this point Pete and I, along with the founding trustees, had identified Lesotho, a small country in Southern Africa, as a focus for our work. With a passion for football and with the world's second-highest prevalence of HIV, we saw an opportunity to leverage Lesotho's love of the game to engage young people in health education and testing.

We had also contacted five or six African FAs, and Lesotho was the only one to reply; they had never heard of the concept of Football for Good, but said they would like us to come. We still had no significant funding, and had not yet even been to Lesotho, but we were single-minded in pursuing our plans. On reflection, we were undoubtedly naïve, but there was never any sense that we were parachuting in to rescue people on an aid mission. We were in it for the long haul, and always saw empowerment of young people as our goal. By coincidence, on the day of the launch, Prince Harry and Prince Seeiso of Lesotho unveiled their own new charity, Sentebale, which would also be focused on the Mountain Kingdom. We emailed the chief executive, Geoffrey Matthews, and the next day he replied, 'Let's talk.'

28

A Strategic Alliance, 2007

THE FESTIVAL had been a huge success, even beyond the high expectations of Jürgen and the team, and it provided an excellent platform for streetfootballworld to expand its mission. 'There were two key partnerships that we immediately sought to extend,' says Jürgen, 'the ministry and FIFA.'

Antje had now retired, but there was broad support within the ministry, including from the minister Ursula von der Leyen (later elected president of the European Commission in 2019, and still in post at time of writing). A new four-year funding partnership was agreed, with a focus on supporting the continued growth of the global network, and the ministry would also help to open doors to other government opportunities. This included the German Agency for International Cooperation (GIZ), an enterprise commissioned by the Federal Ministry for Economic Cooperation and Development. Through this link, streetfootballworld would soon introduce the concept of Football for Good to GIZ, who have subsequently embedded it within their ongoing approach, funding projects across the world for over a decade.

'When it came to FIFA,' says Jürgen, 'it was now a question of how we should continue working together, not if.' Federico had experienced the festival first-hand and was eager to build upon the success. Jürgen adds, 'We had to prove three things: firstly, that we could stage and manage a great event; secondly, that we could mobilise a global network behind a shared vision; and thirdly, that we could operate in harmony with the established structures of football. Through the festival, we had achieved all of these things, without compromising our values.'

In October 2006, Jürgen, Vladimir and Federico flew to South Africa on a fact-finding mission ahead of the next World Cup. 'It was another opportunity to strengthen our connection,' says Vladimir. 'Jürgen and I were acutely aware of the importance of individual relationships, and we saw that Federico was pivotal to the partnership with FIFA.' The trip was successful, but not without incident, 'During our free time we went on a whale-watching trip where Federico was drastically sea sick, and there was a flight on a tiny plane, where he and I, both over six foot, were extremely uncomfortable. But it was all part of bonding and getting to know each other.'

On 1 January 2007, a strategic alliance, under the banner of Football for Hope, was launched. The exact details were still being worked out but several components had already been agreed, including plans for a programmatic fund, with exclusive access for streetfootballworld network members. Via an annual Call for Proposals, the organisations would be able to apply for funding to support their community-based activities. Jürgen says, 'It immediately took our impact well beyond a one-off event. In the first year there was a funding pot of around US$3m, and in the following years this became a core part of the funding for numerous organisations in the network. In total we have since leveraged over US$50m for Football for Good activities via this programmatic fund.'

Vladimir says, 'It was not all plain sailing. Federico and Jürgen are both strong characters and there were times when they clashed and had to work through disagreements. With the programmatic fund, FIFA wanted to disburse the funds to streetfootballworld as a sub-granting body, but we believed a direct relationship between FIFA and the network members would be a stronger commitment to the movement. This would mean more work for FIFA in terms of contracting, and more risk through funding multiple organisations, but Jürgen was insistent.'

Federico adds, 'Never before had a large sports organisation like FIFA partnered with small NGOs [non-governmental organisations], but through streetfootballworld we realised that we could make it happen, and that the collaboration could have a huge impact on the lives of hundreds of thousands of children around the world. We also decided that the relationship with streetfootballworld would not be a donor-beneficiary one, but a strategic alliance between two partners, who, despite big differences in size, reach and resources, would have equally important contributions to make.'

The alliance also included plans for a forum of experts that would be held during the FIFA Confederations Cup, held in South Africa in 2009 as a trial run for the World Cup the following year. The forum would bring together practitioners and academics from within and outside of the network to further guide the development of the sector, as well as looking ahead to another key part of the alliance – festival 2010.

'festival 06 had been so successful,' says Jürgen, 'and we started working together towards a repeat event in Johannesburg with 32 delegations of young people from around the world coming together during the 2010 tournament. The festival model was an intellectual asset that we brought to the table as part of the alliance, and it would now be included as an official part of the World Cup programme, with participants and delegations invited in the same way as players and teams in the main tournament.'

The alliance was sealed with a new composite Football for Hope logo that featured the FIFA and streetfootballworld logos next to each other. Jürgen says, 'It was the first and, to my knowledge, only time that FIFA has permitted a combined logo that the other party has not had to pay for, or which hasn't brought equity as a well-known global brand.'

Vladimir adds, 'The strategic alliance was a quantum leap for the Football for Good sector through which we co-created a CSR strategy in partnership with the most powerful organisation in football. It was more than just a programme – we embedded a social movement at the heart of the football ecosystem.'

Jürgen's personal relationship with Federico had been central to this progress, and a field trip to Asia during September 2007 further strengthened their growing friendship. 'We visited Spirit of Soccer,' says Jürgen, 'which had expanded its landmine education programme from the Balkans to Cambodia, a country littered with mines after wars in the 1970s and 1980s.' Scotty introduced them to the project and offered to lead them safely through a minefield as part of the learning experience.

Federico says, 'I remember the moment that we had to sign the form, releasing the camp from any liability in case of an explosion. Jürgen was very scared, but we both did it.' The pair subsequently travelled on to China for the 2007 FIFA Women's World Cup, attending the final in Shanghai where Germany defeated Brazil 2-0.

'I have the highest possible respect for Jürgen,' says Federico, 'as a human being, as a professional, as a man of good values, as a global leader who early in his life decided to work for a better world and never deviated from that path, as a change maker like few, as a friend. He is committed to the right causes, tireless, stubborn and compassionate. He has a big heart and is good at thinking big and systemically.

'We also had strong disagreements and loud arguments from time to time, as well as a few setbacks. In all moments, however, every encounter with Jürgen has been enriching, and not just from a professional perspective but also from a personal one.'

Vladimir had also developed a strong connection with Federico, and Jürgen couldn't help to notice the stark difference in appearance between the two, 'Federico was always pristinely turned out in a nice suit, while Vladimir was casual, and by now had a huge set of unkempt dreadlocks that extended for several feet down his back. I started to wonder what impact this might have on our perception as a professional outfit, and I raised it with him. He didn't take it well, and said that people would have to accept who he is. In principle, I agreed with him, but I was also aware of the realities. Anyway, he kept the dreadlocks for several more years, and I think perhaps longer than he wanted as a show of resistance.'

Federico adds, 'Through the passion and commitment that transpired through both of their words and deeds, and the trust that I felt for them, I believed that we could be successful, and in the years that followed they would both massively influence the development of FIFA's social commitment.'

With the management of the programmatic fund, the forum and the festival, alongside numerous other new partnerships and initiatives, and the continued growth of the network, the next four years was set to be an intensive period of activity. There was, however, one more project to come, and it was the biggest of them all.

* * *

A few days before the draw for the qualifying stages of the 2010 World Cup, Blatter told Federico that he wanted a legacy project to announce at the event. The world would be watching and they needed something big to launch as a social legacy of the first tournament in Africa.

'It was sudden,' remembers Vladimir. 'Federico asked for our thoughts and Jürgen recycled an idea for an infrastructure project, something that he had pushed for alongside the festival in Germany but which hadn't gained traction. In Germany we had envisioned a community pitch in every host city, but for 2010 the idea was to build a continental legacy. The World Cup would happen in South Africa, but across the continent it was seen as Africa's tournament. The idea was also expanded from a pitch to a centre, with a building at each site for health and education programming, alongside a five-a-side artificial field.'

Federico liked the idea, and without much time to explore the practicalities and costs, there was a discussion around how many centres they should commit to. 'It was very abstract,' says Jürgen. 'We considered ten centres, but ended up going for double that – 20 centres for 2010.'

Vladimir adds, 'This was a decisive moment, and we urgently needed some solid commitments from organisations in the network so that Blatter could announce the first centre sites at the draw. We contacted some of the most established African projects and asked for them to come on board. They only had two hours to think about it and had almost no details, so it was a real show of the trust we had built that they all committed.'

There was also a battle with FIFA, firstly to ensure that the centres would be run and hosted by network members, not by the national football associations in each country. Jürgen says, 'The local FAs ultimately had primary interest in football development, not Football for Good, and we fought hard on that point.'

FIFA also refused to take on the contractual liability for the centres. 'On this occasion we saw that Federico was not able to budge,' says Vladimir. 'There were intense internal discussions and some people were firmly against streetfootballworld assuming all of the risk. It would mean contracts, not only with the network members, but with the municipal authorities where the centres would be based, and in some cases landowners and even energy companies. After many hours I remember Jürgen stood up and said, "We have to do this." I have only seen him assert his leadership like this on a handful of occasions, but he saw the impact and the lasting legacy that would be lost if we didn't.'

On 25 November 2007 in Durban, Blatter announced 20 centres for 2010, the official legacy scheme of the first African World Cup, along with the first five sites and the network member hosts:

- Grassroot Soccer, South Africa
- Espérance, Rwanda
- MYSA, Kenya
- Play Soccer Ghana, Ghana
- AMPJF (Malian Association for the Promotion of Young Girls and Women), Mali

Vladimir says, 'In the space of a few days we were committed to running what remains the largest single project in the history of Football for Good with a budget of US$14m. We had no architects, no engineers, no relevant experience. It felt like we had been here before, only this time the challenge was much greater.'

29

Lesotho, 2007–2008

PETE AND I approached the guarded entrance of
Clarence House, the official London residence of Prince
Charles. Geoffrey Matthews, the CEO of Sentebale and
also Prince Harry's private secretary, was hosting a meeting
which he had facilitated between us and Andrew Dunnett,
the director of the Vodafone Foundation. We were admitted
and taken to an ornate room, populated with royal portraits,
where we pitched our plan for a football project to tackle
HIV/AIDS in Lesotho. During the meeting, Geoffrey's
phone rang, and he left the room, returning minutes
later explaining that it was Elton John, calling about his
participation in the upcoming Concert for Diana.

Twenty minutes later, Pete and I left, cock-a-hoop and
laughing as we walked through Green Park, with news that
the Vodafone Foundation would give us a start-up grant to
get going in Lesotho, enough to last six months. We had
been relentless in our pursuit to get Kick4Life started, and
now Pete and his wife Susie would mobilise their plans
to move to Lesotho in July 2007. During a research trip
in 2006, Pete had established an excellent foundation on
which to get started, building links with local organisations
such as the Lesotho FA and the Ministry of Health. He

was also unexpectedly invited to appear on Lesotho TV as a pundit for the channel's coverage of the 2006 World Cup Final, where he was seen by King Letsie and subsequently summoned for an audience at the palace.

We were quickly learning about the past and present of Lesotho, a nation fully landlocked by South Africa, making it, along with San Marino and the Vatican City, one of only three countries in the world entirely surrounded by one other. This was a consequence of its formation during the 19th century when the Basotho, a tribe of humble origins, subordinate, ill-defined and relatively small, succeeded where many others failed, securing a nation of their own, against the greatest of odds. Guided by the brilliant military and diplomatic leadership of King Moshoeshoe, they resisted the warring armies of Shaka and the Zulus before repelling first British and then Boer invasions. Eventually, under the protection of Queen Victoria, Lesotho was founded as a territorial nation. The result, however, was a kingdom much reduced in size, short on arable land and characterised by the remote mountains that had been the Basotho's greatest defensive weapon during successive wars, but of limited use in peacetime. During the apartheid era, the country became increasingly isolated and dependent on South Africa, and with poor infrastructure, limited health services and an underdeveloped economy, Lesotho was ill-equipped to cope as the HIV virus began sweeping the continent from the 1970s. Today, Lesotho has the second-highest HIV prevalence in the world (23.6 per cent), a health crisis which has had a devastating impact on family and community structures, and which has dramatically held back the nation's economic development.

One of the key factors behind Lesotho's tragedy is a male-dominated culture, with long-standing and harmful gender roles which render women and girls as inferior to men, with high levels and widespread acceptance of gender-based and sexual violence. Women are marginalised in all areas of society – in relationships, in school, at home and in the workplace, and we soon discovered that this extended to the football pitch. 'There were very few opportunities for girls to play organised football,' says Pete, 'but when given the opportunity to join in, they embraced the game as enthusiastically as boys, and we decided that gender equality must be an underpinning principle of our programming.'

As we researched more about the challenges facing Lesotho and the wider sub-Saharan region of Africa, another important link was made, with Grassroot Soccer, an existing network member of streetfootballworld, which was delivering a well-regarded HIV prevention curriculum in South Africa. Their co-founder, Kirk Friedrich, who had recently attended the gathering in Zürich organised by Federico, told Pete that they were seeking an implementing partner for Lesotho. It was a perfect fit.

* * *

A few months earlier, the life of Maphoka 'Puky' Ramokoatsi had taken a devastating turn.

Puky was raised by her mother in Mafateng, a district in the west of Lesotho. She was a good student and a keen football player, although she was careful not to be too overt with her love of the game, 'I had seen girls receive abuse because they played football. People said they are trying to be a man or playing a man's game, and that they needed correcting.'

Puky was aware of HIV, but had only heard degrading comments and untruths which stigmatised the virus. As a result, when her aunt confided her HIV positive status, Puky was ashamed, 'I only knew that people who had it were being called names for sleeping around. My aunt had not even told her own kids. She trusted me and thought I would understand and provide emotional support, but instead I discriminated against her.' Puky's aunt grew increasingly ill and eventually passed away, 'It is very sad to say this, but due to the stigma that came with having an HIV positive relative, I was relieved when she died.'

When Puky turned 16, her mother informed her about the whereabouts of her father, whom she had never met. 'I went to visit him for four or five days, and he introduced me to his friends. The next day, my father went to work, and unfortunately one of the friends knew I would be at my father's place alone. He came to the house and raped me. I was a virgin at the time.' As Puky tried to leave, he shot her in the back.

When her father returned, he found Puky lying on the floor and immediately took her to the hospital where she spent the next five days in a coma on the brink of death. When she awoke, she realised that no one knew she had been raped, and she wanted to keep it that way, 'I didn't want to tell anyone. It was very hard for me to mention it. I didn't tell my mother or dad or friends, I just kept it to myself.'

It would be three years before she could speak to anyone about her ordeal.

* * *

After moving to Lesotho in July 2007, along with his right-hand man Refiloe Maphallela, Pete had made remarkable progress establishing a health education and HIV testing programme, building a large network of volunteer coaches and peer educators, with a number moving into full-time paid positions. The Grassroot Soccer curriculum, which included a range of fun, interactive and football-based games, along with the enthusiasm and energy of the coaches, was proving extremely effective in engaging young people in health education, as well as breaking down widespread stigma and discrimination related to HIV/AIDS. We had also pioneered a new initiative called Test Your Team, which consisted of large-scale events combining football matches, education sessions and voluntary HIV testing and counselling. Through the programme we were referring unprecedented numbers of HIV positive youth to ongoing medical treatment and support.

In November 2007, after only four months on the ground, we hosted a royal visit from Prince Harry. Pete was responsible for staging a Test Your Team event for 500 children, and the day before, he and David Cape from the Baylor Clinic drove past the field for a final check, 'There was a huge school event taking place which the local village chief hadn't mentioned, and we saw some children defecating in the open air due to lack of toilet facilities. There was also litter everywhere over the five-acre field. It looked like a landfill site. We mobilised an army of Kick4Life volunteers, and along with Kirk from Grassroot Soccer, who had flown in for the event, we worked late into the night, clearing up the mess.'

The next morning, Harry and Geoffrey arrived by helicopter and, as they disembarked, the kids ran straight past them and stood looking up in awe at the propellors. On another visit, Harry and his regiment were building an orphanage in a rural district. Pete says, 'Each day I put together a different team of players to drive up and play Harry and his mates. They loved it, and it was surreal playing and bonding through football with one of the world's most famous people, in such a remote place.'

In the same way that Jürgen had invested in the relationship with Federico, we recognised the importance of the individual bond that we had developed with Geoffrey, and it led to further opportunities including a link to the English FA, who arranged a visit to Lesotho for new England manager Fabio Capello, along with goalkeeping coach Ray Clemence. As Capello worked towards the 2010 World Cup in South Africa, the trip was designed as an opportunity for him to start building a positive relationship with the UK media, and he was joined in Lesotho by hordes of senior football writers and broadcasters. They attended a Test Your Team event where Capello witnessed a boy being tested for HIV, something that he described as the most emotional moment of his life. The Italian's words triggered a sensational media reaction, and the story appeared in every national newspaper in the UK, along with rolling coverage on Sky Sports News. The astonishing exposure, achieved after only nine months of operation, along with strong programmatic evidence, resulted in the Vodafone Foundation committing to a larger three-year grant. This gave us an excellent platform to firmly establish Kick4Life in Lesotho, although we also recognised that for longer-term sustainability, we needed to diversify our income streams, and we started to build partnerships with other funding bodies such as UNICEF, the Laureus Sport for Good Foundation and GIZ – the German international development agency which Jürgen had steered towards Football for Good.

From the start, we had dreamed of having our own centre where we could deliver Football for Good programmes to vulnerable children and young people, in a dedicated safe space. By now, we had a team of around 20 staff, and we rented an office on a hill in central Maseru, Lesotho's capital, which overlooked a dusty and rocky piece of land, including an unkempt 11-a-side football pitch. Pete asked around to find out who owned the plot, 'The landlord of our office block told me it belonged to the

Lesotho Police and she offered to make an introduction to the commissioner. It was a positive step but we still had no idea how we would fund a centre. Many donors dislike construction projects, but we felt a facility would contribute so much to our mission.'

A few months later, recently admitted to the global network, we heard about a scheme called 20 Centres for 2010, through which streetfootballworld was working with FIFA to create a legacy of the World Cup in South Africa. I fired off an email to Vladimir Borković.

30

Remaining Independent

IN APRIL 2007, streetfootballworld moved from the Bethanien to its current office in Moabit, a former industrial and working-class neighbourhood in western Berlin, which, like Kreuzberg, has a large immigrant population. Over the next few years there would only be a skeleton staff, as the centre of gravity shifted to South Africa, with a project team of over 30 in Johannesburg by the time of the 2010 World Cup. The festival was taking place in Alexandra, a township in the north of the city and close to the wealthy district of Sandton, and a temporary 3,000-seat stadium was being constructed. One of the 20 centres would also be built in Alexandra as a lasting legacy of the event.

In early 2008, Jürgen, Elida and the girls travelled to South Africa with a view to relocating ahead of the World Cup. 'We looked at properties and schools,' says Jürgen, 'and we loved the country, but we decided not to go through with it. We were concerned about the violence and unpredictability, and about what it could mean, especially for the girls, who were now in their early teens. We had moved from Medellín because we wanted them to grow up without fear, and South Africa would be taking them back into a similar environment.' Instead, Oliver Noe was hired to lead the local team in Alexandra, and Jürgen travelled to South Africa more than 20 times over the next three years.

As plans for the World Cup intensified, the CSR department at FIFA was growing, including the appointment of Madleen Noreisch who had started out as an intern with streetfootballworld. With increasingly close collaboration between the staff teams at streetfootballworld and the governing body, Federico suggested the possibility of bringing the operations, and the network, fully under the banner of FIFA's Football for Hope. It would essentially mean the dissolution of streetfootballworld and the network, which Jürgen and the team had spent years building.

'It was well intentioned,' says Jürgen. 'Federico saw that practically it would make things easier and more efficient, but for us it was a non-starter. The value of independence was sacrosanct, and we recognised that our ability to avoid political influence, to maintain our values and to remain focused on purpose and impact would ultimately be compromised if we handed over control.'

Vladimir adds, 'I felt in my gut that it was not the right thing to do, even if there were short-term benefits. We were unanimous in rejecting the proposal.'

Independence had been retained, but the discussion had once again raised questions about how closely streetfootballworld should align with the official bodies of the game. Jürgen says, 'Although we co-created the strategic alliance, and were an equal partner, such a close relationship with FIFA gave an impression that we had lost some of our independence, and the brand of Football for Hope made things increasingly blurry.'

Voices of discontent began to emerge, particularly among some of the Latin American network members, with claims that the relationship was reinforcing a post-colonial view of the world, with FIFA attempting to control the narrative of football and social change. Jürgen adds, 'There was concern that we were being dominated by FIFA, and that we were in danger of giving away our identity.'

These feelings were intensified at the Football for Hope Forum in Vaal, South Africa, in June 2009. 'The event was extremely positive and brought together many new network members,' says Vladimir, 'but it was also the first time we felt that streetfootballworld was not properly represented. There was dominant FIFA branding and a speech by Blatter that was not well received. We also knew that certain football ambassadors were being paid huge sums to attend some of our events, and that did become a moral and mental stretch for me.'

At the same time, the team at streetfootballworld remained convinced that a partnership with FIFA was in the best interests of the network and its beneficiaries. Jürgen says, 'We were unlocking opportunities and funding for our members to fulfil their mission, and we had positively influenced FIFA, introducing Football for Good and helping to instigate their first CSR strategy. We also regarded our relationship with Federico as personal, rather than institutional, and as such it was built on individual trust and respect.'

But with increasingly overt and chronic corruption at FIFA, a small section of the network began to feel that any links with the governing body were unacceptable. A storm was brewing.

31

Puky's Team

PUKY WAS at the new mall in Maseru with some friends when a group of young people in red t-shirts called them over. 'It was all to do with football so it immediately caught my interest,' says Puky. 'A guy called Swayi said we should come along to some sessions at Kick4Life.' They decided to try it, but initially Puky was frustrated by the HIV education and life-skills activities, 'I just waited for them to be over so we could play football.'

After a few weeks, the curriculum reached an activity called Coach's Story, when one of the peer educators talked about their personal experience of HIV/AIDS, and how the epidemic had affected them and their families. Puky says, 'Lerato told her story. She was HIV positive and she talked about the discrimination that she faced every day, and how Kick4Life was helping her.' It was a game-changing moment for Puky, who remembered when her aunt had privately disclosed her positive status, 'I immediately realised that by not supporting my aunt, I had made a very big mistake, and decided right then to support every person living with HIV that I met.'

Puky signed up to become a Kick4Life peer educator and was enrolled on a coach training course, where she found the one-on-one relationship between trainers and trainees to be reassuring, 'You could feel that they cared about us, and I was able to talk about what had happened. They advised us to get tested for HIV and I thought that since I had never had sex except for the time that I was raped, there was no point in me getting tested. But my counsellor, Palesa, was persistent and informed me of the risks of not testing. So, I did it. I ignored the pre-test counselling, but the result came back positive. I was in denial and I even tested a second time because I thought the first result was not accurate. That's when Kick4Life came to my rescue.'

The counsellors helped Puky to book an appointment at her local clinic and accompanied her when she first went to collect her medication, 'They informed me of the importance of not only starting, but of adhering to, medication far beyond the first few months. I was afraid to tell people. I knew that I had discriminated against people with HIV, and I was afraid to be stigmatised and discriminated against myself.'

Despite her fears, Puky remained true to her personal promise to defend those living with HIV, and in the coming years she supported hundreds of young people as one of Kick4Life's inspiring coaches.

* * *

By mid-2009, plans for our centre in Lesotho were progressing nicely. Pete had managed to secure a long-term lease on the land below the office, 'The commissioner of the police was very positive about the concept of both Football for Good, and the idea of a legacy from the 2010 World Cup.'

With the lease confirmed, we were in a good position to be selected to host one of the 20 centres, and we continued our communications with the team at streetfootballworld. We had already started to think about how we could leverage the anticipated support of Football for Hope to secure additional funding for an expanded centre, and led by our country director, Daniela Gusman, we structured a campaign around social enterprise, with the potential to generate some of our own income through business activities. We envisaged that this could further strengthen and diversify our funding model, giving us greater flexibility and independence, while retaining the accountability, credibility and expertise that came with our grant and foundation partnerships.

Through living in Lesotho, Pete and Daniela had seen a growing demand for high-quality hospitality offerings, and we started to explore the idea of opening a restaurant and a small hotel and conference facility at the centre. We envisaged that these social enterprises would improve our financial sustainability, with all profits reinvested in Football for Good activities, as well as providing structured training and employment opportunities for young people coming through our programmes – something that was desperately needed, with high levels of youth unemployment. It was an ambitious idea, and we had very little experience in the hospitality sector, but with growing excitement around the first World Cup in Africa, Daniela initiated conversations with a number of potential corporate sponsors in Maseru.

In late 2009, another, seemingly inconsequential, development occurred which would later significantly shape the direction of the organisation. A group of staff and volunteers wanted to form a men's football team, and, under the banner of Kick4Life, started to play in the lower leagues. We had been careful to avoid any association with elite development or competitive football, conscious that it might compromise our identity as a social-change organisation, but this seemed harmless enough and the team was started, immediately boosting morale and generating excitement. Watching from the sidelines, literally and figuratively, was Puky. She loved football, and while many other girls also enjoyed playing recreationally, there were only a handful who wanted to participate in structured matches, largely due to the stigma that was associated with doing so. These few occasionally joined in the men's friendly games and against visiting tour groups from the UK, but otherwise they didn't have a chance to play.

This story of women's marginalisation in football goes back to the early days of the game's formation in the UK, still 30 years before equal voting rights were granted. Women's clubs began emerging in the 1890s, in Lancashire and London, where the men's game was already very popular, with the first official women's match played between North London and South London on 23 March 1895. From the outset, there were voices which attempted to undermine women's football and to keep the game exclusively male, with the *Daily Sketch* reporting, 'The first few minutes were sufficient to show that football by women ... is totally out of the question. A footballer requires speed, judgement, skill, and pluck. Not one of these four qualities was apparent on Saturday. For the most part, the ladies wandered aimlessly over the field at an ungraceful jog-trot.'

Conversely, *The Sportsman* noted, 'True, young men would run harder and kick more strongly, but, beyond this, I cannot believe that they would show any greater knowledge of the game or skill in its execution. I don't think the lady footballer is to be snuffed out by a number of leading articles written by old men out of sympathy both with football as a game and the aspirations of the young new women. If the lady footballer dies, she will die hard.'

At the start of the 20th century women's football grew slowly, continuing to meet resistance from patriarchal governing bodies, until the extreme circumstances of the First World War presented an opportunity for it to gain a foothold. With many young men fighting overseas, millions of women went to work in the factories, and women's teams began emerging and competing. As investment and opportunities to participate increased, standards of play rapidly improved, and some fixtures attracted more than 50,000 spectators. It seemed that women's football had gained acceptance, and would continue to grow, but after the war, the FA saw it as an obstacle to the re-establishment and growth of the men's game, and it was quickly suffocated. A systematic campaign to stop women from playing was instigated by the governing body, with claims of financial impropriety related to women's fixtures, which often raised money for charity, arguing that 'an excessive proportion of the receipts are absorbed in expenses and an inadequate percentage devoted to Charitable objects'. Claims that the game was dangerous for females were also widely circulated, with the tennis player Eustace Miles stating, 'The kicking is too jerky a movement for women and the strain is likely to be severe.'

These developments culminated in a de facto ban of women's football, with an FA statement on 5 December 1921, 'Complaints having been made as to football being played by women, the Council feel impelled to express their strong opinion that the game of football is quite unsuitable for females and ought not to be encouraged ... For these reasons the Council requests the clubs belonging to the Association refuse the use of their grounds for such matches.' FA members were also prohibited from officiating at women's games.

A similar story of marginalisation existed throughout much of the world, and bans on women's football were also implemented in Germany, France and Brazil. These limitations ensured that football became synonymous with male identity, discouraging girls from participating, with those few who persevered often mocked and stereotyped as lesbians. After 50 years, the ban in England was finally lifted in 1971, with UEFA recommending that the women's game be taken under the control of the national associations in each country. This was the start of a slow revival, with the first UEFA Women's European Championship held in 1984 and the first FIFA Women's World Cup in 1991, but with the explosion of men's football as an entertainment industry, starting with the launch of the Premier League in 1992, the gap was arguably bigger than ever. Increasing investment in every aspect of the men's game ensured that standards continued to improve, while almost zero spending on women's football prevented significant progress in performance, further purporting mockery and a lack of interest. Former England player Kelly Smith writes about the start of the Women's Premier League in the mid-1990s, 'In fact we had to pay to play the game. At the start of each season, I had to hand over a fee, for referees, pitches and so on.'

There were some exceptions, such as the USA, where male preoccupation with baseball, American football and basketball created a window that allowed women's football to thrive. Globally, however, and despite exciting and rapid progress in recent years, football remains a bastion of male identity, and female footballers around the world face varying levels of structural resistance, unequal investment, discrimination and a lack of opportunities. In Lesotho, this extends to a threat of physical and sexual violence, and it was against this backdrop that Puky and four friends decided to set up a Kick4Life women's team, 'It was very informal. We managed to get a few more girls to join us and then we entered the Maseru District League. There was no national competition in the country, just a few small regional leagues with a handful of teams in each.'

One day the girls were preparing to leave on foot for a game when they bumped into Pete, who asked where they were going. 'We told him we had a match,' says Puky, 'but that we didn't have our transport covered, like the men's team. He took what money he had out of his pocket and gave it to us. After that, Kick4Life started to cover our small costs.' We soon saw that the women's team was challenging gender stereotypes within and beyond Kick4Life, as well as encouraging more of our female participants to play.

From the start we had ensured equal gender participation in our programmes, but with the football teams we had actively gone ahead with supporting a men's team, while it was left to Puky and her peers to initiate a women's side, with all of the risks that came with it. Setting up a men's team was easy – it was easy for the men's players to speak up and say they wanted a team, and it was easy to integrate them within well-established league structures. Most significantly, they were able to play without fear of abuse or violence. By going along with the status quo, and by conforming with the male dominance of football that we had known growing up in the UK, we had tacitly accepted the gender inequality that existed in Lesotho. It had taken the courage of Puky and her team to change that, and to change our way of thinking, and although there was still a long way to go towards achieving full gender equality in our approach to the football teams, we had taken the first step.

* * *

After a few years of trying to balance my job alongside the growing demands of Kick4Life, I had taken the plunge and gone full-time in February 2009, and was now fully focused on running the organisation alongside Pete. I remained based in the UK, leading our fundraising efforts, but was flying out to Africa increasingly often. In June 2009, Pete had attended the Football for Hope Forum – the first time that we had participated in a large gathering of the network, 'It was an incredibly exciting time with the World Cup approaching, and meeting Jürgen, Federico and many others in person helped to strengthen our case for having a centre in Lesotho.'

On the final day there was a football match between the delegates and a select local team. 'It was a curtain-raiser for a league match,' adds Pete, 'and there were several thousand people watching. It was a tight game and at half-time Vladimir came up to me and said, "We are the best players. We need to stick together."'

Six months later, in December 2009, the opening of the first Football for Hope Centre was taking place in Khayelitsha, the largest township in Cape Town, where it would be hosted by Grassroot Soccer. A two-day mini-festival and mixed-gender tournament were being staged, and a Kick4Life delegation had been invited. The team travelled by minibus for ten hours from Lesotho, and I flew out to join them. It would be my first time meeting Jürgen and most of the team at streetfootballworld.

On the day of the opening, I remember stepping off the air-conditioned coach, finding it hard to believe that somewhere nearby was a brand-new artificial football pitch, but after walking for several minutes it appeared, like an oasis in the desert, a tranquil patch of green, alone in the apparent endless beige, white and red disorder of the township. It was a searingly hot day and we sat in the temporary stand, watching first as Blatter declared the centre open, and then as Kick4Life took on the Khayelitsha team in front of a packed home crowd in the inaugural match. We lost 1-0 but played well and ended up reaching the semi-finals, with our star player, 15-year-old Senate Letsie, memorably scoring a hat-trick in a match where she could barely walk through injury. Beyond the event, Senate would go on to huge and continuing success with Kick4Life, representing the national Lesotho team and becoming the first woman in the country's history to secure a student-athlete scholarship in the United States.

For all of the young people in our delegation, the opening event was an incredible experience, and before leaving we squeezed in a trip to the stunning beach at Camps Bay. They had never previously left Lesotho, and had therefore never seen the ocean, and as soon as we stepped on to the sand, they sprinted directly towards the sea and into the icy waves.

On the final day, Pete and I were invited to a meeting where we were grilled by the Centre Operating Team from Football for Hope. As we had done with Sentebale and with the Vodafone Foundation, we gave it everything. We would learn in the years to come that in the not-for-profit sector, funding decisions are nearly always all or nothing, and that rejection is a huge part of the job. Sometimes we would work for months on a funding bid, building relationships and striving for strategic alignment as we attempted to meet all of the funder's expectations, only to be met with an abrupt dismissal. Those moments are hard to take, but when the decisions do fall in your favour it makes them all the sweeter. I landed at Heathrow, and switched on my data. There was an email from Pete with just three words, 'WE GOT IT!'

32

Eleven, March 2010

I WAS in a suite overlooking the pitch at Wembley for the launch of my first book, *Eleven: Stories of Development through Football*. Everything was ready: drinks, seats, a stage and screen, a step and repeat banner, and the event host Jonathan Pearce, a leading football commentator. Word came through that Fabio Capello, who had written the foreword, was on his way from his office elsewhere in the stadium. There was just one problem – there were no guests. The 150 invited people had gathered in reception, where vibrant socialising and networking were under way. I messaged Pete with an urgent plea to get everyone moving, anxious at the prospect of Capello arriving to an empty room.

Pete and I had thrown ourselves into the global streetfootballworld community, and during 2009 I had come up with the idea of writing a book that told the story of 11 individuals – the number of players in a football team – whose lives had been transformed by 11 different network members. In doing so, I also told the founding stories of the featured organisations. As well as our own story at Kick4Life, this included Soccer in the Streets, Spirit of Soccer, the Peres Center for Peace, Street League,

Magic Bus and Grassroot Soccer. Researching the book was a great way to learn more about the growing world of Football for Good, and was also the start of some lasting friendships with people who would become influential figures in the years to come: Anne Bunde-Birouste, who had set up Football United to promote social integration of migrant communities in Australia, and Ana Arizabaleta, director of Colombianitos, which was tackling poverty and violence in Colombia.

Jürgen had been immensely supportive of the book, writing the epilogue and securing the support of Adidas. He had also flown over from Berlin to speak at the launch, which was about to start in front of an empty room. I stepped out into the corridor, desperately hoping that someone, anyone, would arrive before the England coach, and that's when they appeared, coming towards me like a scene from *Grease*, Pete and Fabio, strutting and chatting, surrounded by a horde of buoyant, noisy guests.

* * *

Eleven was principally focused on telling stories of Football for Good, how and why people like Scotty and Kirk had created their organisations, the methodologies that underpinned their work and the young people whose lives had been positively impacted. But there was also a deeper message, which outlined a future where social development was not just happening on the fringes of the football industry, but 'a driving force of the game'. I outlined a theory that football had evolved in stages, firstly the disorganised beginnings and 'beast-like furie' which the British authorities had sought and failed to thwart, and secondly the emergence of a social phenomenon after the game was codified, with a dramatic rise in players, clubs and supporters, first in England and then throughout the world.

The third stage was the growth of football as a business, with several developments at the start of the 1990s catapulting the sport into a multi-billion-dollar entertainment industry. Even by the end of the 19th century, large attendances at matches in Britain had started to generate significant income, and the game's economic value had grown steadily in many countries during the majority of the 20th century, but the launch of the English Premier League in 1992, with a breakaway of the top tier from the Football League, enabled the clubs to negotiate much more lucrative broadcasting rights and sponsorship deals. These trends were mirrored across much of Europe, with the huge success of the UEFA Champions League helping to drive globalisation of the game, both in terms of player movement and audiences. With enormous, and growing, injections of investment into football, transfer fees rocketed, club valuations soared, and many new and existing businesses reaped the rewards, from stadium construction firms and advertising agencies to brands and hospitality providers. This outstanding commercial success appears to be unstoppable, with the recent failure of the European Super League unlikely to disrupt further growth in thriving new markets, with vast and largely untapped fan bases in China, India, the Middle East and the USA. The rapid growth of women's football in the 21st century, in terms of both player numbers and as a spectator sport, is also tearing down the game's male identity, creating a broader and more diverse following.

Yet despite this very positive growth of football among new audiences, cutting across social divides, the evolution of the game as a business has caused widespread discontent and criticism, particularly among supporters. This has focused on the high salaries of players and agents, lack of player loyalty to their clubs, rising ticket prices and grievances against boards and owners only interested in making money. The most controversial development is arguably the growing disparity between superclubs and those struggling to survive, with the same, wealthiest clubs repeatedly winning, reducing competitiveness and creating a risk that football will lose the unpredictability which makes it so compelling for spectators.

A common sentiment resulting from these changes is that football – the people's game – has lost its soul, with a chasm between the profit-focused industry and the billions of football fans around the world who ultimately sustain it through their love of the game. It was due to these continuing trends that I proposed, in *Eleven*, that this third stage was ultimately unsustainable and that a new fourth stage could emerge, with social development at its heart. Over the following decade at Kick4Life we would take some small steps towards this vision of football as a purpose-driven sport. Others within and outside of Football for Good would go further, and Jürgen, who was occupied with these ideas well before I put pen to paper, would perhaps do more than anyone. The seeds of Radical Football were being sown.

* * *

As we left Wembley, Fabio Capello warmly wished us well in our continued work. His involvement had been a huge help in getting Kick4Life off the ground, and following his visit to Lesotho, he had even invited two boys to the UK for a behind-closed-doors training session with the full England squad, including the lad he had seen tested for HIV. Pete, Geoffrey and I had watched as the boys, who had scarcely left their village before, let alone Lesotho, enjoyed a kick-about with David Beckham, Steven Gerrard and John Terry. As we departed the book launch, we also wished Capello good luck; in three months he was taking England to the World Cup in South Africa.

33

festival 2010 and the
2010 World Cup

One month to go

Jürgen and Vladimir were called to a meeting at the purpose-built FIFA HQ in Johannesburg. 'Federico and Madleen were there,' says Vladimir, 'and they broke the news. There would be no visible representation of streetfootballworld and the network members at the event. It was a part of the World Cup and as such had to be branded in FIFA colours. There was no room for negotiation. It was this way or no festival, and it felt like a punch in the stomach.'

'I believe it was a difficult meeting for Federico,' says Jürgen. 'The festival was an official part of the World Cup and there was a rationale that it should appear that way in order to demonstrate that Football for Good was truly embedded. FIFA were spending around US$4m on the event, but at the same time, we had invested our intellectual capital, and more importantly, the network members were investing their social capital. As with festival 06, the teams were also fundraising to cover their own travel to the event. It was a big commitment of their resources and identity, and the latter would now be hidden behind the FIFA brand.'

'We had seen it coming,' adds Vladimir. 'The strategic alliance gave us an excellent platform to work closely alongside FIFA, but with this decision, our hands were tied. Thirty-two delegations of young people were set to travel from around the world, and we could not let our pride deny them that opportunity. The festival would go ahead on FIFA's terms.'

Thursday, 20 May
Spain, the favourites for the tournament, announced their final 23-man squad, which included 22-year-old Juan Mata, an attacking midfielder who played for Valencia. He had scored three times in the World Cup qualifying campaign but remained a relatively fringe player in an exceptional squad. Mata says, 'When Vicente del Bosque made it public, I was at home with my dad and grandma. We started screaming and jumping … it was a dream fulfilled.'

Friday, 11 June
The 2010 World Cup kicked off at Soccer City in Johannesburg with Siphiwe Tshabalala scoring a superb opening goal for the host nation. As the stadium erupted, commentator Peter Drury shouted the now-iconic lines, 'Tshabalala. Goal Bafana Bafana. Goal for South Africa. Goal for all Africa.' Late in the second half, Rafael Márquez equalised for Mexico and the match ended 1-1. Throughout the game, the stadium was filled with the sound of vuvuzelas, brightly coloured horns whose monotonous drone became a defining noise of the tournament.

Wednesday, 16 June
Spain lost their opening match 1-0 against Switzerland in Durban.

Monday, 21 June
At Ellis Park Stadium in Johannesburg, where Nelson Mandela had watched South Africa beat New Zealand to win the Rugby World Cup in 1995, Spain won their second game 2-0 against Honduras. In the 70th minute, Juan Mata replaced Fernando Torres for his first and only action of the tournament.

Sunday, 27 June
A few rows behind Fabio Capello and the England bench, Pete was in the stands at Free State Stadium in Bloemfontein for the second-round match against Germany. After going 2-0 down, England fought back, and Frank Lampard was denied a perfectly legitimate equaliser. The officials incorrectly adjudged that the ball did not cross the line and Germany went on to dominate the second half, winning 4-1. England were knocked out of the World Cup. Capello said, 'We played well. Germany is a big team. They played a good game. We made some mistakes when they played on the counter-attack. The referee made bigger mistakes. Little things always decide the result.'

The following morning, Pete travelled back to Lesotho. We had successfully applied to participate in the festival, and he joined the Kick4Life delegation for the five-hour drive north to Alexandra.

Monday, 28 June–Friday, 2 July
Thirty-two delegations, with participants from 37 countries, arrived in Johannesburg and were transferred to the festival village, located at a school close to the stadium. Over the coming days they would take part in a range of cultural and learning activities, but while the young people embraced and enjoyed the experience with the same enthusiasm as their predecessors in Berlin, for

Jürgen it already felt different, 'On top of the frictions with FIFA, there was discontent among some of the delegation leaders, not only about the branding and representation, but about the quality of the accommodation. We were crammed in, sleeping in bunk beds, with limited and sometimes ineffective toilet facilities. It was also winter and we were desperately trying to find heaters to keep people warm. Some of the kids and staff got sick.'

After a relatively short journey, the Kick4Life delegation had settled in well. 'They loved the experience,' says Pete, 'and interacted positively with kids from many different countries. At times, some of them felt homesick, but at the end, when they had to leave their new friends, there were lots of tears.'

Saturday, 3 July

The delegations crowded into the school hall at the festival village where a large screen had been erected for showing World Cup matches. That afternoon in Cape Town, Germany and Argentina were playing in the quarter-finals, a repeat of the match in 2006 when violence had erupted on the pitch after Germany won on penalties. Four years on, Germany started well, scoring early through Thomas Müller, and despite a star-studded line-up which included Messi, Tevez and Di María, Argentina could not find a breakthrough. After several close chances for the South Americans, the Germans countered and extended the lead in the 67th minute through Klose. By the end of the game, it was a resounding 4-0 win for Germany.

Sunday, 4 July

I landed early at OR Tambo Airport in Johannesburg. Daniela and Pete were there to meet me, and we drove directly to Alexandra for the opening of festival 2010.

The young people had already arrived on a fleet of FIFA coaches; as official representatives of the World Cup, they were given a police escort from the school, something that would happen every day. 'The kids enjoyed the special treatment,' says Jürgen, 'but unlike in Kreuzberg, it added to a feeling that we were disconnected from the local community in Alexandra. This was further exacerbated by tight security into the stadium and a VIP section.'

After checking in with the Kick4Life team, led by Refiloe, we started to mix with friends and colleagues from across the network. Anne, from Football United, greeted us with her usual warmth before indignantly stating that network members were prohibited from the raised VIP area on one side of the stadium. Her disgruntlement was by no means isolated, and there were growing complaints that we were being denied opportunities to network on behalf of our organisations, while FIFA and their corporate guests were inside enjoying canapés and watching our delegations play football. In the meantime, the opening ceremony of the festival was under way, with Blatter and President Zuma of South Africa making speeches on the pitch, kicking off another packed week, with many elements retained from Berlin, from the football3 methodology and the project videos to a celebrity match, live acts and loud music.

Later that day, Jürgen and Vladimir spoke to Federico about the VIP area and the ruling was overturned. Delegation leaders would be allowed in for the remainder of the festival.

'We felt the strain,' says Vladimir. 'We were very stretched, coordinating a big event with many practical challenges and also managing the often conflicting expectations of FIFA and the network members.'

Monday, 5 July

Back at the school, after another busy day, a meeting was called for the delegation leaders. Pete had told me that most evenings there were lengthy discussions which centred on the dissatisfaction of some Latin American network members, but I was unprepared for both the duration and the intensity. We took our seats in the classroom with Vladimir and Jürgen at the front, and the meeting was soon being dominated by a small group of Latin American organisations – 'the Dissenters' – who were making long, impassioned speeches. Jürgen says, 'There were sociological factors at play. Many of them had grown up under brutal dictatorships, where democracy and freedom had been fought for and defended with great sacrifices. There was a fear of being exploited, and they felt that their identity and their rights were being taken by FIFA. They were not prepared to let that happen without a fight.'

Vladimir says, 'We agreed with many of the points. We had created the festival concept and it was painful for us to see the event unfold without the soul of festival 06. It was not what we had dreamed of, nor remembered. But in my opinion, some of the Dissenters were being destructive and it was becoming increasingly personal. They accused us of selling out to FIFA, with a post-colonial narrative that we, as white Europeans, were trading the social capital of the network for our own benefit.'

The relationship with some of the Dissenters had not always been easy. 'They had consistently taken a hard-line stance about how we should position the network,' says Jürgen, 'and were understandably very protective of our identity. In my opinion, it was rooted in a loathing of commerce and capitalism, yet at the same time they were prepared to accept funding from FIFA. Nonetheless, I had always regarded some of the Dissenters as good friends, and several times I had defended their behaviour internally when others had spoken against them. Early in my career, I had made a conscious decision to be trusting, not recklessly, but to give my trust easily to many. On the whole this has paid off, and I always accepted that there would be disappointments, but with the Dissenters the approach failed with very negative consequences.'

I looked around the room. There were many weary faces, but Gert, the founder of Altus Sport, now well into his 70s, stood up and made a rousing defence of streetfootballworld, the founders, and, it seemed, the integrity of sport in general. Pete and I remained silent. We were focused on enjoying the festival, and like the vast majority of network members, we accepted that a partnership with FIFA would involve some compromises alongside the huge benefits for our organisations and the young people we served. We didn't, and perhaps couldn't, relate to what some of the Dissenters were saying, but it was more than that, we also instinctively trusted Jürgen, Vladimir and the streetfootballworld team to do the right thing, to represent us appropriately and to act in our collective interests.

Vladimir adds, 'In my opinion, some of the Dissenters walked between two worlds; they were zealous anti-establishment figures fighting the system, but they also wanted a place at the table of decision-making in our movement. I believe that it created a dangerous ambivalence that was destined for conflict. At times they were attacking the partnerships that we were building, while also holding out their hand on behalf of their projects.'

Ana Arizabaleta, who was leading the Colombianitos delegation, recalls, 'I was quite new to the network environment, and I was struggling to understand what the issues were. There were lots of small unofficial meetings during the festival between the Latin American delegation leaders. Some of them were talking about leaving the festival and going home. I tried to keep out of it.'

After nearly two hours, Vladimir brought things to a close, 'Well, I think this started as a good meeting, but it has ended as a very bad meeting.'

The room emptied in silence as people returned to their rooms. It was the start of an episode that would take the streetfootballworld network to the brink of destruction.

Tuesday, 6 July

While the young people enjoyed a rest day, the first general assembly of the streetfootballworld network took place in the school hall, with representation from 60 of the 82 organisations now within the network. Vladimir says, 'Theoretically it was a good idea to hold the assembly during the festival, because we had so many people already present, but in practice it meant that the meeting was dominated by tensions surrounding the event.'

The Dissenters resumed their narrative, voicing their collective discontent and once again accusing streetfootballworld of selling out, and selling them. 'In my opinion, some of them were acting as demagogues,' says Jürgen, 'and using the circumstances of the festival to turn people against us. We tried to appease them, and rightly agreed to give the South American network members much greater control of the planned festival and the social legacy programme for the next World Cup which was taking place in Brazil in 2014.'

Another topic of contention that attracted negativity more broadly across the network, and which I believe temporarily damaged Jürgen's reputation, was United – a planned online global community of football fans. It was the early days of social media and Jürgen believed that United could become a source of funding and momentum for Football for Good, competing alongside the likes of Facebook. But the idea lacked support, both within the streetfootballworld team and across the network.

Vladimir says, 'In 2007 Jürgen was made an Ashoka Fellow, a recognition of leading social entrepreneurs – people who are finding innovative solutions to the world's problems. From that moment he changed, ultimately in a good way, but initially he started to speak a language that I didn't understand, and to put forward ideas that seemed crazy. I was asking myself, who is this guy? It was the start of a period where we disagreed on many things and it led to internal conflicts between Jürgen and the rest of the team. United was the first big example of him trying to take things in a direction that other people did not want to go.'

Jürgen reflects, 'After joining the Ashoka ecosystem, and soon after being awarded the Schwab Foundation's European Entrepreneur of the Year at the World Economic Forum in 2011, I was increasingly exposed to a mindset of maximising impact, sustainable financing and cross-sector collaboration. In simple terms, I was transitioning from a charitable to an entrepreneurial way of thinking, and it would result in loneliness as a leader, struggling to take the streetfootballworld environment with me on a journey and causing massive resistance at a moment when I was expecting support and trust. United would subsequently fail, admittedly because the idea was not mature enough, but without the support of others, it never stood a chance. Looking back, I am sure that I could have been more strategic with my internal communication and perhaps more empathetic, but having to fight for innovation on two fronts – internally, and for investment and positioning on the market – was energy-sapping. It was a scenario that would be repeated many times in the coming years, and with every innovation I'd bring to the table there was opposition to leave the comfort zone of a typical NGO rationale, and go beyond a linear, step-by-step approach to development.'

'Jürgen needs people alongside him to implement his ideas,' says Vladimir. 'With United, no one was willing to drive it forward. Later, when a different concept of a global football community emerged, the right person was there to help it break through and to realise Jürgen's vision.'

'Sometimes we need things to fail,' adds Jürgen, 'in order to learn and understand what we actually need to do, and how to achieve it. United failed, but the concept of uniting the global football community to achieve social change was far from dead.'

The defining moment of the assembly was the election of the new network board. Statutes and by-laws, enshrining the advisory role of the board within a legally binding framework, had been agreed and voted on by network members prior to the assembly. Jürgen says, 'This empowered the network, enabling elected representatives to provide guidance to the decision-making of the streetfootballworld entity in Germany, without having to take on fiscal responsibilities, which none of the local organisations were interested in nor prepared for. In my opinion, this became a major issue for the Dissenters, who wanted the board to have full control of the organisation without taking on any form of liability.'

Despite these challenges, the election was, according to Vladimir, 'a triumph for democracy', with the following organisations and representatives appointed to serve a two-year term:

- KICKFAIR (Germany): Steffi Biester (Steffi had left the confederation in Baden-Württemberg in 2007 to co-found KICKFAIR, which was already delivering a range of sophisticated social and educational interventions across Germany)
- Mundo Afro (Uruguay): Adán Parreño
- Street League (England): Charlie Gamble
- Mifalot (Israel): Gal Peleg
- Grassroot Soccer (various African countries): Kirk Friedrich

Jürgen and Vladimir remained on the board as two permanent representatives of the streetfootballworld organisation in Berlin, with staff member Christophe Mailliet appointed in an administrative capacity, with no voting rights.

The general assembly concluded and everyone climbed on to the stage for a group photo. There was a happy atmosphere, but there was also a sense of tension and, for me, a quiet feeling of confusion, which I later discovered was shared by many others.

We could relate to some of the issues, and appreciated the need to question and hold people to account, but we were struggling to understand why some of the Dissenters seemed compelled to undermine a community that was contributing so much to our mission, and for which we already held a deep affection.

Wednesday, 7 July
Spain defeated Germany 1-0 in the semi-final in Durban, with a towering header by central defender Carles Puyol securing the win.

Saturday, 10 July

There was a lively atmosphere on the final day of the festival, and the stadium was aflutter with the orange, black and white of the streetfootballworld logo. 'We printed hundreds of small flags which we gave to the delegations,' says Vladimir. 'It was a petulant act but we wanted to make a point about the lack of visibility.'

For the closing moments, everyone crowded on to the pitch. MYSA had once again taken the title, but the signature moment was the presentation of the Fair Play Trophy to the team from Spirit of Soccer. The conduct and manner of the young Cambodians had captured the hearts of everyone at the festival, and as Federico handed over the trophy, receiving a scarf in return, there was an outbreak of mass euphoria, as players and delegation leaders broke down in tears, screamed with joy and ran around the pitch embracing each other. I remained relatively reserved, standing with Pete and Madleen as we witnessed the astonishing outpouring of emotion. Despite what Jürgen and Vladimir were experiencing and feeling, for many of the young people it was the most uplifting moment of their lives.

Sunday, 11 July

The World Cup Final between Spain and the Netherlands took place at Soccer City in Johannesburg. It was a poor match featuring 13 yellow cards and one red, with Dutchman John Heitinga sent off in extra time. In the 116th minute, with penalties looming, Cesc Fàbregas played in Andrés Iniesta to score, giving Spain their first World Cup. Juan Mata says, 'Without a doubt it's one of the most important moments in my career, if not the most … when the referee whistled the end of the match … we all went crying to our families on the stands.'

Jürgen had tickets to the match, but he gave them away to some of the project team, much to the chagrin of Elida and the girls. Six years later he and Juan would meet, and together they would start to shape a new future for Football for Good, and for the football industry as a whole.

34

The Opening of the Lesotho Football for Hope Centre, September 2011

THE PITCH on the outskirts of Maseru was characteristically ravined, with a combination of stone and compacted earth that rendered studs a non-starter. We had been warming up for some time when we saw the bakkie approaching at speed on the road adjacent to the field. There were already several hundred children surrounding the pitch, who had made their way on foot from the local school to watch their teachers take on the Kick4Life All Stars. And now the teachers arrived in style, the full squad standing, crammed on to the back of the vehicle, which turned with a wheel spin on to the pitch, dust rising as they elegantly disembarked, dressed immaculately in bright-red kit, eliciting wild cheers from their students.

The All Stars was a concept that had been running almost from the start of our operations in Lesotho. It is based on the model of a regular overseas charity trip, but instead of undertaking a physical challenge, participants are fully immersed into Kick4Life and made to feel a part of the organisation. They learn about our work, interact with the team and, most significantly and always the highlight, they are trained to deliver interactive health education sessions to young people, fully supported by our expert life-skills coaches. As well as learning about Lesotho and concluding with an adventure trip to the mountains, there is, of course, the chance to play football, with matches against local teams, often in stunning locations. The tours raise money in themselves, but even more significantly, they have created an international community of supporters, and when people return home, they invariably continue assisting Kick4Life in various ongoing capacities.

We had organised an All Stars tour to coincide with the opening of the Lesotho Football for Hope Centre, and had squeezed in a match against the teachers at Thetsane High School the day before the big event. As I lined up at centre-back, I looked across the defensive line. Alongside me, in the centre was David 'Motts' Moteane, who had been reading the *Daily Echo* in Southampton back in 2006 when an article about a new charity seized his attention. Motts's father was from Lesotho but had moved to the UK for work in the 1960s and started a family. Growing up in England, Motts was an excellent footballer and was given an apprenticeship at Portsmouth in the late 1980s before a knee injury ended his hopes of a professional career. Motts had always dreamed of visiting his father's homeland but it had never quite happened. The article in the newspaper seemed too improbable to be true. He looked again – two local brothers were organising a ten-day football tour to Lesotho, a country that most people had never heard of, and they wanted people to join them. He had signed up, and by 2011 Motts was on his third of many trips.

At right-back was a younger guy, Chris Bullock, who had attended his first tour in 2009. A football fanatic, Chris had fallen in love with Lesotho, and the feeling seemed to be mutual, with the Basotho people taking to his natural humour and laid-back nature. Two years after this tour, Chris would move to Lesotho to work for Kick4Life and would go on to play a major and continuing role in the country's football ecosystem.

Completing the back line, and next to me at left-back, was a ringer – Mike Geddes, the now ex-BBC reporter, whose piece on Spirit of Soccer had changed the direction of George Springborg's life. Mike was also now a part of the streetfootballworld team, working in the communications department, and was in Lesotho to cover the centre opening. The tour concept would leave a lasting impression on Mike and he would subsequently create a social enterprise – The Third Half – with the aim of scaling the All Stars model, offering similar travel experiences to destinations around the world, hosted by local streetfootballworld network members.

There were similar stories throughout the team, as well as first-timers starting their journey with Kick4Life, such as Oya Mustafa. With no particular interest in football, Oya had signed up via a friend, and had become the heart and soul of this group, winning the coveted Spirit of the Tour Award for the first of several times.

Despite the superior appearance of our opponents, we started well, going 3-0 up early on, before they pulled one back in the second half. With a few minutes to go I attempted to roll back the years with a marauding run forward, only to be slammed by one of their midfielders, falling heavily on my side with a deep thud. I've never been one to complain with injury and I managed to get up and carry on for the last few minutes, but as a crate of Coca-Cola was pulled off the bakkie for a mutual celebration and photos, I realised that my arm was not moving and was swelling ominously. Pete, who had slipped away from the event preparations to play in the second half, now found himself driving me to a local clinic for X-rays. An hour later, I emerged with my arm in a sling; I'd broken my elbow and cracked three ribs, just in time for the biggest day in Kick4Life's young history. Meanwhile, at the airport, guests were starting to arrive.

* * *

As the small plane began its descent into Maseru, Vladimir looked down at the Orange River which marks Lesotho's western border with South Africa. This was his first trip to the Mountain Kingdom and another tick on the growing list of countries to which streetfootballworld had taken him. He had already attended seven centre openings, in seven different African countries, with the remaining 12, after Lesotho, scheduled to be inaugurated in the next three years.

'We were sometimes criticised for not having the 20 centres completed by the World Cup in 2010,' says Vladimir, 'but that was never the intention. It was a purposeful decision to ensure that we didn't just walk away at the end of the tournament, which is so often the case with large sporting events. Instead, we were committed to a more enduring social legacy. It was also unrealistic to responsibly complete the initiative in such a timeframe. This was not just a replicable build project, it involved creating and managing 20 different and complex multi-sector community partnerships, across 16 countries from Cape Verde and Rwanda to Cameroon and Mali, all with their own regulations related to construction and ownership. I think the link to FIFA, and to a mega tournament, where construction legacy often fails, led people to presume or desire failure, but in reality, 20 centres for 2010 is arguably the most successful legacy project in the history of major football events.'

In 2008, streetfootballworld had partnered with Architecture for Humanity (AFH), a US-based charity specialising in architectural and design projects in the development sector. AFH led on the design and construction of the 20 centres, each one created differently to fit the local physical and visual environment, and to meet the particular needs of the local community and the network member host. A qualified design professional was sent by AFH to live and work at each centre site during the development process, working with local construction firms, contractors and community groups.

'There are core features,' says Vladimir, 'including a five-a-side artificial pitch and a building with rooms and spaces for health, educational and other social programming, but each centre has its own distinctive identity and design. This includes various sustainable features such as solar panels and floodlights, and roofs designed for water capture. In Mozambique, instead of the regular fire bricks which are contributing to deforestation in the region, a new type of compressed earth block was used for the construction, resulting in the creation of a new local business manufacturing this more sustainable product.'

Having progressed through Maseru's miniature airport, Vladimir was met by a Kick4Life driver and taken to his hotel, where he joined Federico and several other members of the Football for Hope team. The star guest, Lucas Radebe, was arriving in the morning.

* * *

With the pain in my arm and ribs almost completely concealed by the mysterious pink and blue tablets from the clinic, I joined the All Stars for breakfast. Later, when the hotel and restaurant were built, tour groups would stay on-site at the centre, but for now we used the rudimentary but pleasant rooms at the Lesotho FA's HQ a mile up the road. Despite the early hour, there was already an electric atmosphere, not just fuelled by excitement for the day ahead and the fabulous weather but by the spirit of solidarity that seems to infuse every tour group. Bringing people together from different backgrounds in a new environment, with novel and positive experiences, the ingredient of sport and a shared purpose, perhaps unsurprisingly, brings out the best in people, and quickly creates a strong and unifying bond that endures well beyond the trip.

Pete arrived, and bidding the group a temporary farewell, we drove to the centre for a pre-event briefing with Radebe. Born in Soweto, the South African had attended anti-apartheid rallies in his youth before establishing himself as a gifted central defender at Kaizer Chiefs, one of the country's top sides. In 1991, with rumours circulating that he might be leaving the club, Radebe was shot in the back while driving with his brother. Whatever the true motive, and unlike Andrés Escobar three years later in Colombia, Radebe escaped serious injury, and in 1994 he moved to Leeds United in the English Premier League, becoming a cult hero and inspiring the name of the local indie rock band, the Kaizer Chiefs. A huge star in Lesotho, Radebe went on to captain South Africa at two World Cups, in 1998 and 2002, being described by Nelson Mandela as 'my hero', before retiring in 2005. He was now, among other things, working for FIFA as an ambassador, and was eager to know the circumstances of my injury, which I briefly described, before Daniela ran through the plan of action for the event.

What followed was our own festival 06 moment, condensed into a single day, with dancers, live music, football freestylers, a mini youth tournament and a showpiece match on the new pitch between former Lesotho internationals and a Kick4Life select team. Motts, with tears in his eyes, was invited to play for the Lesotho team, with Vladimir stripping off to represent Kick4Life, reunited on the pitch with Pete, and running, arms outstretched to the crowd, after finding the net. A lectern was then carried on to the pitch for a series of speeches, with Daniela, who had contributed so much to the success of Kick4Life as our first country director, recognising the contribution of our young team and thanking our corporate sponsors, who had now committed to funding the majority of the social enterprise block. It would be more than three years before the opening of the restaurant, hotel and conference centre, but the extended legacy in Lesotho of the first African World Cup was already guaranteed, and construction was starting soon.

With the afternoon sun beating down, Pete, Daniela and I lined up alongside Federico, Vladimir, Radebe and Lesotho's Sports Minister for the official ribbon cutting. The scissors clicked, and the blue ribbon floated towards the pitch in multiple parts, triggering celebrations that lasted late into the night. The beautiful voices of our local team, the lifeblood of the organisation – Puky, Refiloe, S'bu, Lash and many others – rang out in joyous harmony as we crowded together for a photo.

'There was a feeling of overwhelming emotion,' says Pete. 'Many of the team had been with us from the start in 2007. We had become a family, and now we had this glorious moment.'

Motts adds, 'It was surreal and emotional for me, and I struggled to get my head around how far the charity had come in such a short space of time, and also the impact that the centre was going to have on the kids in Lesotho.'

I looked around at everyone – our coaches and staff, the All Stars, the many local partner organisations, the kids from the neighbouring houses – and realised that, despite the incredible new centre that had just been opened, the most important asset that we had at Kick4Life was not the buildings, but the community that we had forged over the last six years. The centre now provided us with a home, and a dedicated, safe and inspirational place to deliver our programmes, and eventually to launch our social enterprises. This had been made possible through our commitment to the wider, global network of streetfootballworld. Being a part of that ensured that the Kick4Life community did not exist in isolation, but was connected to hundreds of projects, to thousands of coaches and practitioners, and to millions of young people around the world. We were stronger together than apart.

* * *

The story has never been confirmed, but it is rumoured that a small group of Kick4Life coaches returned to the pitch in the middle of the night, where, denied permission to incorporate the traditional practice within the formal proceedings, they conducted a blood sacrifice, slaughtering a chicken and asking the ancestors to bless the centre, and all who came there.

35

The Crisis

'PLEASE STAY,' implored Elida. 'If you go, something bad is going to happen.'

It was April 2012, and Jürgen was in Costa Rica for a Latin American network meeting.

'Eli had joined me for the trip and during the week it was my birthday,' says Jürgen. 'I decided to take the day off and go with her on a trip to the coast. She told me that I shouldn't leave the meetings; she sensed that something was going to happen while I was away.' From the start, Elida had advised Jürgen to be wary of the Dissenters. 'She has good instincts,' says Jürgen, 'and often sees things that I don't. But on this occasion, I felt it was an overreaction.'

* * *

When Jürgen left festival 2010, he had done so with confidence that the problems surrounding a minority of Latin American network members could be amicably resolved, with an outcome that was acceptable to all parties.

'Essentially, we were fighting for the same thing,' says Jürgen, 'to change the system in order to transform lives. We had different ideas about the best approach, but I believed that if we focused on the collective interest, we could find a way to move forward together.'

In seeking a positive outcome, Jürgen attempted to detach his personal feelings from the process, 'My commitment to the mission has always been superior to any clash of personalities. That doesn't mean I don't care about other people's feelings. In fact, the opposite. Nor that I can't feel upset myself. I was hurt by what some of the Dissenters had said, because it was everything I didn't want to be, but I wouldn't let it affect my focus, which remained fixed on striving for maximum impact.'

Despite Jürgen's determination to find common ground with the Dissenters, over the next two years it became increasingly difficult to align the different positions, 'It was a miserable feeling, but I believed it was right to protect what we had built, and to continue working with FIFA to maximise opportunities for social development. This sometimes meant standing alongside a system that I did not believe in, and I was open to redefining the relationship, but I could not see the benefit of completely walking away.'

After festival 2010, streetfootballworld and FIFA had an open conversation about the successes and challenges of the event. Jürgen says, 'It had been very well organised, and there had been many positives: the stadium was full, the local community was happy and the young people had enjoyed it immensely. But we remained unhappy about a lack of representation, especially given that delegations had paid for their own travel. Federico agreed that in future, at 2014 and beyond, this would change. With costs fully covered, and with the festivals integrated completely within the World Cup, we could accept that they would be branded exclusively as FIFA events.'

The subsequent festivals in Brazil in 2014 and Russia in 2018 again provided incredible opportunities for young people, but they would largely be hidden away. Jürgen says, 'In Brazil, due to concerns about protests, the event took place on the outskirts of Rio, while in Russia there was a reluctance among the local organising committee to talk about social problems; they did not want to admit that their system could have failings.'

In 2011, Jürgen and the team decided to withdraw the streetfootballworld name from the composite logo of the strategic alliance, 'Some people thought we were crazy to remove our visible presence, turning down so much exposure, but we felt it was important to distance ourselves, not from the partnership and the movement, to which we remained committed, but from the impression that we had compromised our independence. I believe that it caused surprise at FIFA.' Despite the change, the partnership remained strategic and strong, with continued and growing programmatic funding for network members as well as future forums and festivals in the pipeline.

But for some, changing the logo was not enough, and the Dissenters also remained unhappy about the governance structure of streetfootballworld. 'With the hybrid structure,' says Jürgen, 'it wasn't possible to hand over control of the streetfootballworld entity in Berlin to the network without also handing over the fiscal responsibilities that came with it. We remained resolved to work towards a governance model that would put more control into the hands of the network but it couldn't happen suddenly, and it had to be driven by the network board.'

Once again, a major point of contention was United, the online community that Jürgen wanted to build as a sustainable funding mechanism for Football for Good, but which the Dissenters viewed as another imposition designed to leverage the social capital of their organisations, without their consent and support. 'It raised the question about what they wanted from us, the team at streetfootballworld,' says Jürgen. 'Did they want a conceptually dormant and purely operational body that simply responded to the requests of network members, or did they want us to contribute strategic vision and leadership, as part of a collaboration?'

* * *

After a pleasant day on Costa Rica's Atlantic coast, exploring some of the places Jürgen remembered from his time in the country more than 20 years earlier, he and Elida arrived back at the hotel.

'I discovered that an additional meeting had been scheduled for the following morning,' says Jürgen. 'I didn't know what it was about, but again Elida predicted that something was going to happen. The next morning as I walked into the room, it felt like I had entered a trial. The chairs were shaped in a U, and I was sitting at the front. Video cameras were also set up to record the meeting.'

What followed was a series of personal attacks and accusations from some of the Dissenters, accusing Jürgen and streetfootballworld of exploiting the social capital of the network for personal gain, and selling out to corporates. 'Many people remained silent,' says Jürgen, 'and I had the impression that it was carefully orchestrated.'

Jürgen was tense, and despite Elida's warnings, he was caught off guard, 'I'm a transparent person and I try to share what I feel and to defend my position, accepting that people won't always agree. But in that meeting, I didn't have a voice. In my opinion, it had been scripted in advance by the Dissenters with only certain people permitted to speak, and designed to prevent me from responding.'

'I was still on the outside,' says Ana Arizabaleta, from Colombianitos, who was present at the meeting, 'and I was struggling to understand what they wanted to achieve. In my opinion, it was all highly political and there were power dynamics at play. I spoke privately to other network members who agreed that it had gone too far. The accusations did not represent how we felt.'

The meeting came to a close and Jürgen walked out of the room, alone and subdued. Soon after, he and Elida left Costa Rica.

'It was clear,' says Vladimir, 'this was now the biggest crisis that we had ever faced.'

36

Washington, D.C., August 2011– July 2013

AS THE crisis unfolded, Jürgen, Elida and the girls had moved again, leaving Berlin more than 11 years after they had arrived on that January night in 2000, when they had stood freezing on the street outside a locked apartment, inadequately clothed, while a furious domestic row proceeded inside. After that difficult start, and the following months of loneliness that Elida had experienced, the Griesbecks had found happiness in Berlin, but Jürgen now believed that in order to take streetfootballworld and his mission to the next level he needed to be in the United States. Washington, D.C. was the epicentre of the huge, global aid system, with a concentration of political foundations and an advanced approach to philanthropy, and Jürgen envisaged that he could embed Football for Good within this funding environment to achieve an international impact. The family packed up and left Germany, with the girls, now in their mid-teens, starting school in Washington.

'We found a good neighbourhood and easily made a lot of friends,' says Jürgen, 'though we did find that these relationships were often quite superficial. This also translated to the working environment – I liked the openness and how easy it was to engage with people, but it was harder to establish deeper and more meaningful connections. On reflection, I should have gone to New York or the San Francisco Bay Area which was already emerging as a hub of social innovation, and where there would have been a better alignment with our evolving approach.'

People in the team, including Vladimir, felt that it was a random move, and that it was an additional cost burden on the organisation as opposed to an opportunity for growth. 'To a certain degree, they were right,' says Jürgen. 'The immediate results were not what I had hoped for nor expected, and it might have been too early in our development to go to the States. The streetfootballworld brand was not understood, not only the use of "football" instead of "soccer", but also how it related to a global community. I found that the individualistic mentality of the US made it hard for some people to grasp our collective ambitions.'

Back in Berlin, Vladimir was heading the team, and with Jürgen distanced from the day-to-day realities of the organisation, it increasingly felt to Vladimir, and others, that he was in charge of the whole operation. Jürgen says, 'The physical separation created a wider, temporary distance in our relationship, and Vladimir and I discussed the possibility of him taking over, with me moving on to something new in the wider world of social entrepreneurship. There were some unnecessary frictions but we had an honest conversation. I felt that streetfootballworld was still the right place for me, and where I could have the biggest impact.'

Elida remembers, 'It was a very demanding and difficult time at work level for Jürgen; never until then did I see so much stress and pressure on him. Because his mission is much more than a job, there has always been a very strong symbiosis between Jürgen's professional and personal happiness. It put a strain on family relationships, but we got through it together.'

Two years into what was initially a four-year plan, the Griesbecks returned to Berlin. Vladimir says, 'It wasn't the success that Jürgen had anticipated, but I felt that for him it was personally and professionally beneficial. After so many years of intensive action, he needed a break and a chance to breathe, and despite the challenges that happened during that time in the network, he came back refreshed and refocused.'

For the family, there had also been many positives. 'We embraced the local culture, with all of its contradictions,' says Elida. 'We travelled a lot, we practised the language, we expanded our circle of friends for life, and we returned to Berlin together and united. Each one of us returned changed, and elaborated, with our futures shaped in different ways.'

The benefits of moving back to Germany were immediately felt, refortifying Jürgen's relationship with the co-founders, especially Vladimir, and strengthening his connection with the whole team. His time in the US had also consolidated Jürgen's belief in the need for collaborative and sustainable solutions in addressing the world's many urgent problems, shaping his emerging ideas for embedding social change within the football ecosystem, 'I saw the underlying divisions in society which were later manifested under [President Donald] Trump. It felt like a broken system, with everything organised around personal gain and economic growth, with very little invested back into service to people – health, education, public transport. It is hard to see how such a system is sustainable, for both people and planet.'

A decade on, Jürgen believes that his time in the United States is now finally paying dividend, 'I established a legal entity and developed a presence, a history and an understanding which has enabled us to re-enter the country in a significant way. This time we have done so with a brand and an approach which are much more appealing to the American market and mindset, and we are seeing the results.'

37

The Coup d'État, September 2012

ON SUNDAY, 9 September, Vladimir went to quickly check his emails before heading for a day out with the family, 'I saw messages coming through from network members and partners asking what was going on. I read some of the forwarded emails and saw what was happening. The day out was cancelled and the next eight hours, and the coming days, were spent dealing with the fall-out.'

The Dissenters had emailed all streetfootballworld network members telling them that Jürgen and the other co-founders were corrupt, and accusing them of using the network's social capital for personal gain. The message was clear – you are either with us, or we are enemies – and a deadline was given for network members to decide whether to stay with streetfootballworld or to join them in a new community of organisations. Ana Arizabaleta says, 'We received the message and I spoke to the board at Colombianitos. We were unanimous that we did not want to have any part in this. I sent a short reply to that effect.'

Messages had also been sent to streetfootballworld's partners and funders, saying that the founders had been misusing resources, had been dishonest and could not be trusted to represent the network. 'None of it was true,' says

Jürgen. 'In fact, it was the opposite of what we stood for. I could not believe it was happening; after everything we had done to build the network and to create a movement, after the shared successes and the collective progress that we had made. I felt undignified.' The Dissenters also asked the funders to abandon streetfootballworld and join them in their new venture.

'We explained our position to those who approached us for answers,' says Jürgen, 'but we decided not to respond directly to the Dissenters right away, nor to make any public statements denying the claims. I could not relate to what was being said in any way, and although some of the network board members sympathised with questions of identity, they advised us not to engage publicly. So we left it out there for people to make up their own minds. It was frustrating not actively defending ourselves, and disturbing to know that some people would be reading it, and wondering if it was true, but we could not see the benefit of fighting nor of interacting with the accusations.'

'It was a chaotic time,' says Vladimir. 'In my opinion, it was an attempt to destroy streetfootballworld and we did not know how people would react. Would they believe the things that were being said about us? Over the next few weeks, we spoke privately to concerned network colleagues and partners, and we waited, to see if any of the remaining network members in Latin America, or elsewhere, would join them.'

Gradually, it became clear that the 'coup' had failed. 'No one else left the network and no partners or funders abandoned us,' says Jürgen. 'I believe that our approach of non-contact led to stabilisation, and, more importantly, that years of building and investing in trusted relationships paid off. We sent a message to the Dissenters wishing them good luck in the future and applauding their brilliant work in the community. The collective had survived, but we had lost nearly ten per cent of the network, and it did not feel like a triumph.'

With the second general assembly of the network less than two months away, Jürgen, Vladimir and Johannes jointly decided that they should offer to step down, and hand over full control of governance to the network. 'Our roles and our integrity had been brought into question,' says Vladimir. 'The Dissenters had left, but we did not know how the rest of the network truly felt, and we were prepared to stand down and hand over control and responsibility. In order to continue, we needed to know that we had the backing and support of the remaining network members. The assembly would be an opportunity to give them a choice.'

38

On the Board

Lyon, December 2012

I WOKE up feeling groggy. The night before had been a spirited reunion of friends from around the world, as we gathered in Lyon for the second general assembly of the streetfootballworld network. The event was being hosted by the French network member Sport dans la Ville at their impressive facility on the banks of the Rhône River. As usual, it was predominantly the British delegates who had carried the festivities on into the early hours, led by the effervescent Marcus McGilvray of Whizzkids United, based in South Africa and Ghana. The Sport for Development sector is a close-knit group of people, and with our shared motivations and experiences, there is always a jubilant mood when we come together. But, on this occasion, I was now regretting those multiple craft beers; I had a presentation to deliver in 30 minutes and wanted to make a good impression ahead of the network board election that was taking place in the afternoon.

Pete and I had discussed whether we should put ourselves forward. Although we were still a young organisation, we had already benefitted tremendously from membership of the network, and we saw that a role on the board could be a valuable next step. I called Kirk Friedrich of Grassroot Soccer (GRS), who was coming to the end of his tenure on the board, and asked for his advice. Was the time commitment manageable? Did you enjoy the experience? Was it of benefit to GRS? Kirk was very clear, 'The board is not about strengthening your own organisational position, it is about putting back and contributing to all network members, and that means making impartial and sometimes difficult decisions that may even be against your own interests.'

We had understood that board membership was a responsibility on behalf of the whole network, and we had always believed in collaborating in order to maximise football's positive impact on society, but we had also been approaching it as an opportunity for Kick4Life. Kirk had put a different spin on the whole thing, and from that point on, we assessed our candidature based exclusively on our potential added value for the collective. Pete and I agreed that we had some useful skills and lots of energy to contribute, and decided to go for it.

With around 15 applicants and only five network member places available on the board, it was a competitive process, but I opted not to campaign too aggressively. Instead, in the weeks leading up to the vote, I messaged people that I knew within the network, explaining why I was standing, and asking them to consider voting in Kick4Life's favour. I focused on our emerging role around social enterprise and our commitment to sharing and collaborating, as evidenced by my book *Eleven*. I stayed clear of any politics. Kirk's tenure on the board had coincided with the Latin American crisis; he said it had been enormously challenging, but also that the worst was over. Pete and I had been aware that there were issues, and had witnessed events at festival 2010, but we had remained at arm's length, not fully understanding the issues nor the severity of the situation until the 'attempted coup'.

With the hangover slowly fading, I successfully completed my presentation, and even managed some last-minute lobbying over lunch. The atmosphere was surprisingly tense. A few of the candidates had printed out leaflets which were being left on tables and chairs, and some of the remaining South American delegations were in a huddle, clearly planning to vote as a collective, something that was completely within the rules, and an important opportunity to redefine the region's presence in the network. I looked around at the African network members spread across the dining hall – there appeared to be no plans for tactical voting. Despite being English, I was, of course, representing an African organisation, and with a high proportion of members from the continent, I wondered whether I should have stood on that ticket. It was too late now.

Just before we headed back into the conference room, Marcus approached me, and asked bluntly if we were in it for ourselves at Kick4Life. It was a fair question. We were friends, but we were also competitors, both with a strong focus on HIV prevention in Southern Africa, and often applying for the same limited funding. If he voted for me, would it be to the detriment of Whizzkids United? At Kick4Life we had been, and remained, extremely driven in pursuing funding to further our mission. Any charity that isn't will find it hard to survive and thrive. But we could also see beyond that. We had an instinctive belief that we could achieve more through collaboration, and that our work within Football for Good went beyond one organisation, or one community or one area of social need.

Even within the not-for-profit sector, I believe this spirit of union remains rare, but streetfootballworld had created an environment and provided the moral leadership for those values to be realised, and the words of Kirk had tipped us over the edge. I looked Marcus in the eye and answered, truthfully, that we would serve in the interests of all, and we walked together into the room.

Prior to the election, there were in-depth discussions about the crisis, with a planned vote between two options for future governance of streetfootballworld. Option one involved retaining the status quo with evolution towards further shared responsibility and decision-making, while option two would see the network take full control of the entity in Berlin, essentially accepting the resignations offered by the three co-founders. There was an intense and respectful debate with a small number favouring the more revolutionary approach, but it transpired that the vast majority of network members preferred option one, with some people expressing alarm at the possibility of making a rash decision that could severely damage the efficacy or existence of streetfootballworld. Subsequently, it was agreed that no vote on the day would take place, and instead the newly elected board would be responsible for guiding the future direction of governance. It was a de facto resolution in favour of the co-founders and a spontaneous round of applause broke out across the room.

'I was relieved, but it didn't feel like a victory,' says Jürgen. 'Looking back at the whole crisis, I'm sure there were some things I could have done or said differently, and I agreed with the Dissenters' assessment of historical wrongdoings and colonialism, and a lack of justice in the current global world order, but I didn't feel personally responsible for it, and I didn't want to be judged by it. I could also understand that some of the Dissenters did not feel represented or empowered within the governance structure, and were therefore uncomfortable with streetfootballworld leveraging their social capital to build partnerships. In my opinion, some of the things they accused us of were indefensible, but they had a right to voice their concerns and, ultimately, a right to walk away.'

With confidence in the founders and the existing structure reaffirmed, the formalities of the election began. It seemed to take an age, with a recess as the votes were counted, during which we gathered for a group photo in the cold afternoon on one of the outdoor pitches. As we headed back into the auditorium, I thought about Claire and the girls at home. Since 2005, when the girls were born and Kick4Life was established, it had been non-stop. If I was elected it would be an added responsibility and even more time away, but I knew that Claire would be waiting at home, anxious for a positive message.

We took our seats and moments later the appointed organisations and candidates were being declared:

Jill Robbins, Soccer in the Streets (USA).

Verónica Escobar, FUDELA (Ecuador).

There was loud and raucous cheering across the room, and I could feel beads of sweat running down my back.

Steve Fleming, Kick4Life (Lesotho).

And there it was! I remember being slightly dazed as Charlie Gamble, now of Tackle Africa, nudged me and indicated that I should join the others on stage. I giddily worked my way along the aisle and towards the front as the next names were announced:

Ana Arizabaleta, Colombianitos (Colombia).

Abhijeet Barse, Slum Soccer (India).

The cheering continued as the five of us stood arm-in-arm, looking back at the network which had just elected us to represent them.

* * *

An explosion erupted outside and I walked over to my balcony on the ninth floor of the Dayrell Hotel in Belo Horizonte. On the street below a large crowd and a line of police, carrying shields, were enveloped in smoke, or tear gas, or some other airborne substance which shrouded the protests in a translucent veil. I was in Brazil for the second Football for Hope Forum which was taking place during the Confederations Cup in June 2013, and after an epic journey involving four flights, I had crashed in my bed only to be woken a few hours later as the riots kicked off and persisted long into the night.

In the weeks leading up to the tournament, held as a trial run for the World Cup the following year, demonstrations had broken out across Brazil. Underpinned by growing inequality, the riots were triggered by an increase in public transport fares at a time when government corruption was endemic, and when expenditure on upcoming mega events – the 2014 World Cup and the 2016 Rio Olympics – was massively over budget. Along with anger at growing police brutality, there was widespread fury at FIFA for forcing through a temporary change in the law that would allow alcohol to be sold in stadiums during the World Cup, something that had been banned 11 years earlier to prevent violence at football matches. With Budweiser one of the main tournament sponsors, FIFA secretary general Jerome Valcke had enraged Brazilians, stating, 'Alcoholic drinks are part of the FIFA World Cup, so we're going to have them. Excuse me if I sound a bit arrogant, but that's something we won't negotiate.'

The Football for Hope Forum was originally planned to take place at the City Hall, but the building had been attacked in the days leading up to the event so the venue was switched to the hotel, with an opening panel to explore the underlying issues behind the riots. Despite the close proximity of the protests, the conference progressed smoothly, amid heavy security, and on the penultimate day we were taken to the Estádio Mineirão to watch the semi-final between Brazil and Uruguay. It was my first time watching a game in South America and I was blown away by the intensity of the emotion, with the home crowd continuing to sing the national anthem long after the band stopped playing. Brazil scraped through 2-1 with a late goal from Paulinho, and after the game we were held in the stadium for over four hours, as 125,000 protestors filled the streets of Belo Horizonte. The demonstrations were largely peaceful, but on returning to the hotel, a group of young, masked protestors chased and pelted the coach with projectiles, shouting and signalling abuse. It was a strange feeling; our organisations were dedicated to serving the most vulnerable people in society, and here we were being targeted in a fight for social justice. I guess that was a price we paid for the relationship with FIFA. That night a few of us put on our regular clothes and stepped out of the hotel and on to the streets, where we walked among the protestors. It felt much safer in the crowd.

While in Belo Horizonte, there was also an informal gathering of the network board. At our first official meeting in Germany, in early 2013, we had learned more about the crisis, and it was evident that Jürgen and Vladimir were hugely relieved that it was over. There were still, however, important decisions to be made, surrounding the partnership with FIFA ahead of the 2014 World Cup in Brazil, and related to the evolving governance model, alongside a restructuring that was happening in Berlin. I enjoyed making a genuine contribution to the network, as well as the chance to travel, with multiple trips to Berlin and Brazil and meetings in India and Ecuador.

During my two-year term, I also had the opportunity to work intimately alongside Jürgen, and to learn more about his character. From a distance, he had always appeared somewhat mysterious, often pensive and slightly removed from the present, but at the same time hugely inspirational and a person of action, who had created tangible opportunities that were benefitting millions of young people globally. I came to realise that he was a man of multiple contrasts, at once reflective and forward-looking, practical and intellectual, effusive and understated, considered and impulsive. I believe this mix of characteristics can result in some people misunderstanding him, becoming frustrated by his behaviour, and, without doubt, underestimating him. Other values and traits became evident as unimpeachable: his humanity, his ambition for impact, and his ability to imagine new versions of the future. Needless to say, he's not always right, and some of his ideas fail or need refinement, but he is unquestionably a visionary, and he presents concepts that others find exciting, but which can also make people uncomfortable, or which they simply believe are impossible. I've been there, and have found myself jumping to explain why the new plan is unrealistic or impractical. He sits there and listens, nodding. Vladimir says, 'In over 20 years of working together I've never seen him flustered or lose his cool.'

Jürgen adds, 'My greatest challenge is to articulate my ideas in order to convince people that we can do it, that we must do it.'

All of this was apparent during my tenure, as Jürgen emerged from the Latin American crisis, and his stateside intermission, and moved steadily towards his next great creation. It was an evolution that would go beyond Football for Good and the practical application of the game as a tool for social development, and even beyond partnership with official bodies of the sport. He believed that to truly unleash the power of football for social impact, the whole ecosystem had to be fundamentally changed. With so many urgent challenges facing both people and planet, and with the 2030 Sustainable Development Goals (SDGs) just 15 years away, football, with its unparalleled human community, that cuts across so many social divides, had to do more; it was no longer acceptable that the game of the people was structured to serve the few. But despite the gross disparities of wealth and poverty, for Jürgen, it was about more than money. Money was one factor in football's enormous potential for impact, but on its own, it was meaningless. For him, it was about intent, and the possibility, and the desire, to put something more than profit at the game's core. It was about purpose.

As it had done in Manrique, after the gangs had placed down their weapons, an idea started to form, and this time even more people would tell Jürgen that it was stupid, impossible, destined to fail. He would, of course, do it anyway, and there would be, as there had been in all of his successes, someone at his side in its execution. Elida had been a constant of loyalty and belief throughout, but new people had always appeared at the right moment to help carry the torch of his latest conception into the world of reality – Alejandro and Maria in Colombia, Uwe at the confederation, and Vladimir and Johannes at streetfootballworld. The next person was out there, seeking a new direction of his own, and he had just signed for Manchester United.

39

From Kick4Life to Kick4Life FC

THE ALL Stars bus was full and ready to go for a packed day of health education delivery and football. We were just waiting for one person – Chris 'Bully' Bullock – who had forgotten to hand his room key into reception. The front door of the Lesotho FA's HQ swung open and he appeared, carrying, and variously dropping, his items for the day: football boots, shin pads, a water bottle, a camera that he didn't know how to operate and various pieces of paper. At the time, it would have been ludicrous to consider that here stood the future of football administration in Lesotho.

Chris had quickly established himself as the joker of the tour, always up for a laugh and ready to embrace every aspect of the trip, from the community visits and education activities to the football matches and socialising. He came from Portsmouth, 17 miles down the road from Southampton, and this provided an immediate opportunity for banter, with the clubs from the two cities forming one of the most intense rivalries in English football. Chris, and his brother Andy, had grown up on the terraces, not only at Fratton Park, the home of Portsmouth FC, but at many of the local semi-professional grounds in the region, establishing an excellent knowledge of the game.

After his first tour in February 2009, Chris had returned to Lesotho several times, and alongside his job as an office worker for a large energy company, he had thrown himself into Kick4Life, fundraising prolifically, getting other people involved and even organising his own expedition up Mount Kilimanjaro. He was the type of volunteer that every charity dreams of, and with his love of football and positive attitude he was an embodiment of Kick4Life. By 2013, Chris was eager to get involved in Football for Good on a full-time basis, and had begun talking about starting his own project. Later, we came to regard this type of progression as a big positive, with people using their experience at Kick4Life as a platform to new opportunities and creations that were an extension of our social impact. But at the time, I was eager to keep Chris involved with Kick4Life, and I suggested to Pete that we should offer him a short-term role in Lesotho. 'The timing was good,' says Pete. 'Our men's football team were holding their own in the A Division South, but were in desperate need of structure and better organisation in order to progress.'

Since its establishment in 2009, the Kick4Life men's team had made steady progress, and although the squad still exclusively consisted of staff and volunteers, we were only one promotion away from the Premier League – the top flight.

Given all of the developmental challenges facing Lesotho, a lack of football infrastructure, investment and coaches, this is a far cry from the elite leagues in Europe, and even much of Africa; at the time, just one or two teams in Lesotho's Premier League employed players on a full-time basis, with the others a mix of semi-professional clubs and teams which represented institutions – Lesotho Defence Force (LDF), Lesotho Correctional Services (LCS) and Lesotho Mounted Police Service (LMPS).

That said, the opportunity to be a top-flight club offered intriguing possibilities.

Over the previous years we had continued to keep fairly quiet about the teams, remaining concerned that having elite sides could cause confusion about our social focus. But we had undoubtedly begun to see some real benefits for the organisation and our mission. Internally, the teams had created a strong sense of togetherness, not only between those playing, but throughout the organisation, with everyone coming to watch games and becoming part of a shared and fun experience each weekend. Outside of the organisation we also realised that the teams were helping to raise the profile of our core work around HIV prevention, as well as further motivating young people to get involved. If we made it to the Premier League these positives would only increase.

During my four years of working with Chris as a volunteer in the UK, he had undergone something of a transformation, becoming an excellent administrator who was capable of planning and managing multiple tasks. In that regard, he was unrecognisable from the figure who was late for the bus on that first tour, although he had retained his abiding spirit of geniality and good humour. On reflection, the organisational skills were probably always there, and it was his passion for the cause, and his enjoyment of the work, which drew them out. Either way, Pete and I agreed that with Chris involved, and having secured our first sponsorship for the team, we had a good chance of progressing to the top tier. He accepted the role, which eventually became director of football, and we gave him a clear objective – get us into the Premier League.

'Before I arrived,' says Chris, 'Curtis, the new country director, sent me a list of issues which the team had compiled themselves about why they had struggled the previous season: we drink too much, we don't support the coach, we don't train consistently. Promotion seemed a long way off.'

On arrival in Maseru, and with three months before the start of the new season, Chris immediately set about putting more structure in place, strengthening administrative processes such as player registration and developing clearer lines of communication and responsibility with the players and coaching staff. He also worked closely with the head coach, Motlalepula Majoro, to improve the squad, most notably, and improbably, securing the signature of Robert Mekomba, a central midfielder who had just captained Lioli to the Premier League title. Originally from Cameroon, where he had played in the African Champions League quarter-finals, Robert was inspired by the wider vision and work of Kick4Life, and dropped down a league to lead the team. 'Signing Robert was a big moment,' says Chris. 'We had a lot of young, talented players and Robert brought the experience and stability that we were lacking, along with a new level of quality to the team. It also showed our intent to become a more established and competitive club.'

After losing the first game of the new 2013/14 A Division South season, we went on a 16-game unbeaten run, putting ourselves in a great position to finish top and secure the one promotional place to the Premier League (one team also gets promoted from the A Division North). 'I learned a huge amount in that first season,' says Chris, 'from managing last-minute player registrations using the FA's ancient software, to negotiating player transfers with boots and balls included as part of the deal. At one away game we were minutes from forfeiting the match before kick-off because our socks were white, the same colour as the opposition. Our kit man, KB, ran into a local shop and bought some black spray paint. It ended up being a crucial 1-0 win.'

The season developed into a two-horse race between us and Liphakoe, but we edged ahead, and victory in the penultimate game of the season against Mountain Shades would be enough to secure the title. On the day of the game, I was in the Lake District, climbing England's highest peak, Scafell Pike, as part of a training day for the Three Peaks Challenge, an upcoming fundraising event. On the ascent, I'd been unable to get any signal to check for match updates on Twitter, but as we reached the summit, I pulled out my phone and held it up to the sky. The page refreshed and the result came through: Mountain Shades 1 Kick4Life 2. With two goals from our captain and longest-serving player, Moruti Thamahane, we had done it. We were Premier League.

'The atmosphere was amazing,' says Chris. 'All Kick4Life staff and volunteers had travelled to the game and it went crazy at the final whistle. The singing didn't stop on the bus journey back to Maseru.'

As the men's team had continued to progress and remained the primary focus of our attention, Puky had quietly been running the women's side, bringing through new players and competing well in the Maseru District League. 'I immediately saw her passion for the team, and for the cause,' says Chris. 'She wanted to fight for gender equality and she saw that the team and football was a way to break down a massive barrier about the role and perception of women in Lesotho. I started to build an operational team for the football club, and Puky became an important part of that department, not only running the women's team but supporting youth development, administration and marketing. We also started an outreach programme to strengthen links between the teams and the core work of the organisation, and Puky and some of the other women's players went into schools to deliver gender education.' This formed the basis of Girls United, a new curriculum which was subsequently created by the women's team with sessions on gender rights, tackling gender-based violence and sexual and reproductive health education.

Chris also became active in promoting the women's game at a national level, where it had been severely neglected for many years, 'There was no national league and not even a national women's team after it was stopped in 2011. It was symbolic of football's perception as a men's game, and there wasn't much interest in promoting or developing women's football.'

There were, however, a few people at the Lesotho FA who were trying to create a national women's league and Chris was invited to join the Women's Super League Committee, eventually becoming chair, 'The Lesotho FA could see that we were taking both women's football and administration seriously at Kick4Life, and I was asked to get involved. I started with the basics: keeping proper records of meetings, improving communication and building a presence on social media to generate interest.'

The first Women's Super League was launched in 2015, with Kick4Life one of eight founding teams. Puky says, 'It created massive excitement for our players, and it gave us recognition as footballers and as women.' In the same year, the women's national team was restarted, and it featured seven players from Kick4Life.

With these positive developments for both our men's and women's sides, Pete and I started to articulate an idea which had been forming for some time. It was no longer an option to keep quiet about the teams, certainly in Lesotho, where our men's team would now feature in the national newspapers. But why should we anyway? Having elite teams was adding so much to the organisation, giving us a powerful platform to promote our wider work, helping us to engage more young people and challenging gender stereotypes. It seemed crazy to hide all of that away.

But instead of simply embracing the teams as one part of our model, we believed that we could go a step further, and fundamentally change the nature of how we presented the organisation. We had three legal entities in Lesotho – firstly the Trust, which was our charitable body, secondly a new non-profit business entity through which we would run our new social enterprises, and thirdly a football club entity as a means of operating the teams.

The latter two were effectively owned by the Trust, ensuring that they existed to serve our charitable objectives. This legal structure would stay the same, but I proposed that we could rebrand from Kick4Life to Kick4Life FC, a small but very significant change that would shift our identity from a traditional charity to a social enterprise football club. The rationale was simple: we could achieve more social impact, more easily, by integrating the different parts of the organisation under the shared presentation of a football club, than we could by keeping them apart. It would be a bold statement, that a football club could exist and thrive and compete at the top level with an objective that was not financially driven. We would still pursue success on the pitch and financial sustainability off it, with the teams remaining responsible for funding themselves, through sponsorship and other forms of income generation. In fact, we hoped that in time, the teams, like our other social enterprises, would generate sufficient income to invest directly into our core charitable activities. But the ultimate bottom line of the club would never be sporting success or profit – they would be enabling factors for a higher goal: purpose.

I researched online and could find nothing similar. There were many small community football clubs run purely for local people to enjoy sport with no interest in profit, and there were numerous foundations linked to professional clubs. The latter were typically charities themselves, doing positive local community work, often on a large scale, aided by the financial leverage and fan bases of the clubs. The Saints Foundation, for example, linked to Southampton FC, delivers a wide range of programmes for the local community, from health and education to tackling homelessness, providing access to sport for people with disabilities and promoting social inclusion of older people. Through our links having grown up in the city, Pete and I had worked with the Saints Foundation at Kick4Life on several occasions, and had seen the excellence of their work. However, despite being independent charities, these foundations still operated on the periphery of a much larger business model. We were proposing something very different. It wasn't a case of taking the moral high ground and saying that our way was best. We recognised that a model of private ownership made it possible for clubs like Southampton to have a deep and far-reaching social impact, but we also wanted to show that there was another way of running a football club, where purpose was central to the whole model, and that, in time, it too could be successful.

Perhaps the closest example we found was Right to Dream, a Ghanaian football academy set up by Tom Vernon from the UK, which Jürgen had read about during his early research into Football for Good. While they didn't have a football club in Ghana, Right to Dream had been meaningfully combining social impact and elite football from the start, providing academic support, football coaching and personal development to help underprivileged young people with footballing talent to secure student-athlete scholarships at universities in the USA. These genuinely life-transforming opportunities could lead to professional careers, and by 2015 more than 100 Right to Dream graduates had established themselves as footballers in Europe, Africa and the United States. Many others had achieved successful careers in alternative industries, with professional football just one of many possible progression routes. Although we didn't know it at the time, Tom was on the verge of an astonishing development that would take him further into the world of elite football, with even greater potential for social impact.

Back in Lesotho, the concept of becoming a social enterprise football club had gained internal support at Kick4Life. That was a crucial first step, but although we believed strongly in pushing traditional boundaries of both charity and sport, I remained concerned that the move could harm our reputation with funders and other stakeholders, who might not understand the change, or who might be alienated by the link to elite football. We conducted a consultation exercise to understand how the transition would be perceived, and received positive feedback from our partners at the Laureus Sport for Good Foundation, Beyond Sport and streetfootballworld. They emphasised the importance of ensuring that the senior teams remained independently financed from outside of our charitable operations and that full transparency was maintained with an independent audit. This was something that we were already committed to, but it underpinned the critical importance of building understanding with our various stakeholders. It was apparent that the change would require constant communication, and ongoing reinforcement of how the model worked, with our teams existing solely to serve community objectives. It was a radical idea, but we were determined to make it work and in August 2014, with a new logo and a new website, Kick4Life became Kick4Life FC – the world's first football club exclusively dedicated to social change.

'I loved the transition,' says Chris. 'It was a new level of innovation, and it encouraged everyone at Kick4Life to further buy in to the different parts of the organisation. We could see how the different departments were connected with a shared goal, and it made me even more determined for us to succeed on the pitch.'

* * *

In the years that followed, the Kick4Life men's and women's teams became established sides in the Lesotho Premier League and Super League respectively. The men's team achieved their highest finishing position to date in 2016/17, coming fourth, with the women's team securing the club's first major trophy, winning the Women's Super League Cup in 2018. Multiple players from both squads have been selected to represent Lesotho at full international level, and Kick4Life became recognised for raising standards of football administration in the country, with other clubs following suit.

The move also led to the creation of an academy, in the same vein as Right to Dream, with Tom and his team helping us to create a holistic programme of football coaching, academic tutoring and character development. We have since supported six young people to fully funded student-athlete scholarships in the United States, among them the first woman in Lesotho's history to secure such an opportunity, Senate Letsie, who, aged 15, in 2009, had starred for Kick4Life at the opening of the Football for Hope Centre in Khayelitsha. In the coming years, we hope to play a central role in developing a new generation of Basotho footballers, with some of the academy graduates already playing professionally in the US. Others are working towards careers with potential to become leaders of social change in Lesotho, across academia, civil society, business, health and the environment.

After five years in Lesotho, Pete had moved to New York, establishing Kick4Life as a charitable entity in the USA, and further expanding our fundraising reach. With the launch of the academy, he was also well placed to start building links with US universities, securing scholarship opportunities and developing a support structure for students coming over from Lesotho. It all seemed such a long way from our epic dribble in Malawi, when we started out with no money, no contacts and very little knowledge about the world of international development. The journey had taken us in many unexpected directions, and now, together with the whole Kick4Life community, we were pioneering a new type of football club. It was far from perfect, and discrepancies remained between our women's and men's teams, most significantly related to investment. The idea of full equality would first be raised by a future country director, Hana Taiji, a former Canadian under-20 player and Harvard graduate who joined the organisation in 2016. It was a nice idea, but at first, we didn't take it too seriously; with all of the complications and financial implications that it would entail, it was much easier to maintain the status quo.

But with Hana's persistence, combined with the extraordinary circumstances of a global pandemic, seven years later, we would once again lead the football industry into new territory.

40

The Social Enterprises

WAYNE BLYTHING walked out through the court doors and on to the streets of Liverpool. He thought about what the magistrate had said – one more offence in the next 12 months and he was going to prison. 'It felt like a crossroads. Either I could carry on with the life I was leading,' says Wayne, 'a life of crime and drugs, or I could try a different way.' He turned left and walked towards the Job Centre. It was worth a look.

Wayne was born in 1984, and after six months his dad left, 'He was a heroin addict. I was too young to remember him, but afterwards my mum and I moved into a hostel and then into different council properties.' By age 11, Wayne was drinking and taking drugs, and increasingly involved in crime, 'I was stealing cars, robbing houses and selling drugs. It was the only life I knew.' Expelled from every school he went to, Wayne was regularly in court, and now aged 18, prison seemed an inevitable part of his future. He arrived at the Job Centre and looked at the board, 'There was very little that appealed, but there was one thing that caught my eye. I decided there and then to do it, and I made a promise to myself to go down a different path.'

A week later, Wayne started out as a trainee chef.

* * *

By the middle of 2013, construction of the social enterprise block in Lesotho was almost finished. Since the opening of the centre two years earlier, we had first developed the shell and then completed the ground floor which included office space for the growing Kick4Life team, and two large rooms intended for the conference centre and restaurant. With funding from Rotary International we installed a kitchen and opened a very basic café offering a simple lunch service, with a grizzled American ex-pat chef and a small team of inexperienced trainees. The upstairs floor, where we had plans for 12 bedrooms, had remained an empty shell for over a year, put to good use for open-air events with everything from yoga to movie screenings.

The funds were eventually secured from a number of sources, notably the Vodafone Foundation, who had supported Kick4Life intermittently since we started, back in 2007. Since then, we had worked hard to diversify our income, recognising the risks of being too reliant on a small number of often short-term funding streams. We had subsequently developed partnerships with more grant-based funders and foundations, as well as expanding our fundraising activities in the UK and later the USA. The enterprises, if successful, would be another part of a balanced mix of income, strengthening our financial sustainability and independence with a more predictable and long-term income stream, that would complement the accountability, credibility and expertise that came with more traditional grant funding.

With construction completed, there was a big question mark about how we then created a functioning and thriving hospitality business. The café had shown us that the restaurant space and location could work, but it was not the basis for a successful income-generating enterprise.

We had a vision of the three components – restaurant, hotel and conference centre – coming together to provide a high-quality range of hospitality offerings. Pete says, 'We realised that a big selling point for guests would be the knowledge that their custom was helping us to change lives, but we also knew that, first and foremost, we had to provide a top-class service. In fact, as a charity, we believed that we would have to work even harder than an ordinary restaurant to build a reputation for excellence.'

From the start, Pete and I had been conscious of 'White Saviour Syndrome', the post-colonial idea that Africa needed people like us to come and rescue the continent. In the early days, our understanding of development was unquestionably basic, and we had a lot to learn, but there was no Football for Good programme in Lesotho at the time, and we believed such a project had huge potential in the country, so we went out and created one ourselves. But we always had an aim of long-term local empowerment, whether that was developing life skills for maintaining good health, training young coaches to lead delivery, recruiting a local board of trustees or working towards locally led management. Even the All Stars tour model was designed to empower local coaches to educate the tour participants about the issues in their country, not the other way around. With the enterprises, we also had a vision of developing young people, providing them with the skills to gain full-time employment either with Kick4Life or externally.

The vision for the enterprises was clear, but we had very little relevant experience and even less capacity in the team to make it a reality. There was also an absence of experienced professionals within Lesotho, or in fact anywhere, who possessed the precise skillset that we needed: hospitality management, culinary skills, environmental health, and the ability, empathy and patience to take a group of vulnerable young people with almost no experience and turn them into a high-performing team.

Thankfully, I knew two people who would be perfect. We just had to persuade them to leave their jobs and home in London, and move to Maseru.

* * *

Tessa Moon was in the final year of her degree in Textile Design at the University of the West of England. She had taken a part-time job as a waitress on a barge which had been converted into a restaurant, and as a natural 'people person' she loved being part of a dynamic team, as well as interacting with customers, 'I enjoyed providing a service that helped people to relax and have a great time, and I liked paying attention to detail; customers often appreciated the small touches and it created an experience which encouraged them to return.' Tess was also intrigued by her boss, the head chef, a blond, long-haired Scouser who, intentionally or not, caused her to fall about laughing every time he opened his mouth.

Wayne had 'fallen in love' with cooking, and after completing his three-year traineeship had started working as a chef in various restaurants and hotels in Liverpool, 'I wanted to further expand my skills and horizons, and was accepted into the University of the West of England to study Environmental Health.'

To fund his living costs, Wayne worked most evenings on the barge, and the ebullient waitress from London had caught his eye. It wasn't long before Wayne and Tess were a couple, and after finishing university they moved to London where Wayne started work in environmental health while Tess took on various jobs, working in restaurants, managing a swim school and volunteering at a helpline for victims of domestic abuse. They were always on the lookout for an opportunity to travel, and in 2010 one of their friends recommended a trip to Africa. 'I liked football,' says Wayne, 'but it was the whole experience which appealed to both of us.' Later that year they joined an All Stars tour to Lesotho.

I'd kept in touch with them after the trip, and when the particular mix of skills and personalities that we needed for the social enterprises became apparent, I sent an email asking if they'd be interested in moving to Lesotho, initially for a six-month spell.

'I was working in sound control at the London Borough of Ealing, and was sitting in a bleak council office when the message came through,' says Wayne. 'That night Tess and I had tickets to a masquerade ball, and in the taxi on the way there we discussed the opportunity in Lesotho. We didn't have too many ties and it was a chance to live in another country, something that we'd dreamed of. Later that evening, I remember us looking at each other in Venetian masks and deciding that we'd do it. We'd follow our hearts to Lesotho.'

'A few months later we walked into the restaurant space,' says Tess. 'There was a tiled floor, painted walls and a basic kitchen. The bedrooms in the hotel were also empty spaces. It was a blank canvas.'

On the second day, Wayne and Tess were introduced to the trainees, all in their late teens. 'They had been picked out from Kick4Life's employability programme,' says Wayne, 'and they all came from vulnerable backgrounds, living in poverty and some victims of domestic violence. Curtis, the country director, told us that we would probably need to let some of them go for various reasons. One of the girls, Tsepang, was so timid that she couldn't even speak to us. Others had lots of attitude. I remembered back in Liverpool when I walked out of court and had the opportunity of a traineeship, and we decided to give them all the same chance.'

Tess says, 'It was a huge cultural learning curve for all of us. The relationship that the trainees had with food was about eating to survive. The concept of preparing food to taste and look nice was new to them, and they couldn't believe that we would serve things like salad which offered very little sustenance, or blue cheese which was completely different from anything that they had tasted before. They had also never eaten in a restaurant or a café and had no idea about basic customer service or even how to hold cutlery. We took them out to a few of the existing restaurants in Maseru so they could begin to understand the concept of a customer experience.'

Over the coming months, Wayne and Tess created an intensive training programme which introduced the trainees to all aspects of the emerging enterprise, from cooking and customer service, to stocktaking, hotel management, room servicing and even cultivating herbs and vegetables in a small garden at the centre. 'We invested in them completely,' says Tess. 'Building mutual trust was so important, and we did everything to empower them and give them responsibility. We saw a transformation. Some showed particular ability and interest in the kitchen, others front of house or in management, eventually specialising in these different areas. They all excelled.'

Alongside the training programme, Wayne and Tess prepared the businesses for opening. 'We had to do everything,' says Wayne, 'from creating the identity and installing the décor to managing suppliers, setting up a payment system, developing menu plans and getting all of the necessary certificates and licences in place. We had almost complete freedom and flexibility to create something that we believed in, and that's one of the reasons we felt so connected to the project.'

The restaurant, named No.7 – a nod to some of the iconic footballers who have worn that shirt number, such as David Beckham, Cristiano Ronaldo and George Best – had a rustic feel, with local artwork and traditional designs. The menu theme – international cuisine with a Basotho twist – combined classic dishes with subtle local flavours.

It had taken three years, a staged construction and a titanic effort by Wayne and Tess, but in August 2014, with a brilliant young team, the social enterprises were opened by King Letsie III of Lesotho and Queen 'Masenate Mohato Seeiso. Since Pete's unexpected summons to the palace on his first visit to the country in 2006, we had maintained a good connection with the royal family, building a strong relationship with Prince Seeiso, the King's brother, who had co-founded Sentebale with Prince Harry. The King's son, and heir to the throne, Prince Lerotholi Seeiso, also occasionally played at the Football for Hope Centre.

Wayne says, 'Tsepang, who had struggled to speak to us when we first met her less than a year before, was now part of a confident team that was serving the royal family. All the trainees were immaculately turned out and the food and service was impeccable. For the rest of my life, I'll never forget the pride that I felt that day.'

* * *

Four months later, in December 2014, I travelled to Porto Alegre in Brazil for the third general assembly of the streetfootballworld network. After two great years on the board, I had turned down the option to stand for re-election for a second term, deciding to focus fully on Kick4Life. We had two busy years ahead with the transition to Kick4Life FC and the recent launch of our hospitality social enterprises. After the assembly, as I waited in the hotel reception for a transfer to the airport, Jürgen asked me if we could host a handover meeting at the centre in Lesotho, and six weeks later members of the outgoing and incoming boards arrived into Maseru. It was a fitting conclusion to our tenure, and a chance to show the progress that had been made since the centre opening in 2011.

Jürgen says, 'It felt very special to meet, stay and dine at the centre, to speak with the young people and to see Football for Good activities happening on the pitch. It was a visible manifestation of a unique model of social entrepreneurship, and for Vladimir and I it was further justification for the centres project and the partnerships that we had constructed to make these opportunities possible for network members like Kick4Life.'

At the end of the board handover in Lesotho, Vladimir drove directly to Kimberley in South Africa where he met Federico for the opening of the 20th of the 20 centres, hosted by loveLife. 'It was the end of a remarkable eight-year project,' says Vladimir, 'and one that continues to have a profound impact on the host communities.'

Not long after they opened, both the restaurant and the hotel were ranked number one on TripAdvisor for the whole of Lesotho, and were contributing approximately 25 per cent of the charity's income, supporting the growth and sustainability of our Football for Good programmes. After an emotional graduation ceremony, the trainees progressed to full-time positions, with many remaining at Kick4Life for years and others moving on to hospitality careers elsewhere in Lesotho and overseas. It had been a steep learning curve, and as with the football teams, there would be an ongoing process of communicating the nature and purpose of our business model. We also started to explore how we could share our experience of social enterprise development with other organisations in Sport for Good, with so many facing the same challenges of financial sustainability.

Two and a half years after they first walked into the empty restaurant, Wayne and Tess returned to England in March 2016. 'It was a painful decision to leave,' says Wayne. 'We had an incredible bond with the team, which went beyond an employer-employee relationship. It was like leaving our own children behind. But Tess was pregnant and we felt it was the right time to move on to something new. We also recognised that the team would need to succeed without us in a more formal working environment. It was hard for them at first but the depth of training and support that we gave them stood the test of time.'

A year later, in recognition of his work alongside Tess in Lesotho, Wayne received an outstanding achievement award from the Chartered Institute of Environmental Health in the UK, 'I'd come a long way on a journey that started on the steps of the court in Liverpool. It's been hard work and I've made mistakes, but I've kept the promise that I made to myself, to go down a different path.'

In their absence, the enterprises continued to thrive, eventually coming under the local leadership of Rosc Mabathoana. With the future looking brighter than ever, in March 2020, as the coronavirus pandemic gripped the world, a national lockdown was announced in Lesotho and the businesses had to cease operations overnight. With no government furlough scheme in place, Wayne and Tess would play their part in the emergency response, with the creation of a new charity, the Catering, Hospitality and Education Foundation – CHEF.

41

FIFA Corruption Scandal, 2015

ON 27 May 2015, plain-clothed police officers descended on a luxury hotel in Zürich where delegates of the 65th FIFA Congress were staying. Seven arrests were made on behalf of the US Department of Justice, following a three-year investigation by the FBI into 'rampant, systemic and deep-rooted corruption'. A simultaneous raid took place in Miami, at the offices of CONCACAF (Confederation of North, Central America and Caribbean Association Football), while back in Zürich the Swiss authorities opened an investigation into bribery surrounding the selection of World Cup hosts Russia in 2018 and Qatar in 2022. In the following months, decades of corruption were exposed, with convictions for racketeering, wire fraud, and money laundering, and with top-level FIFA executives found guilty of accepting bribes for the awarding of television and sponsorship rights. The scandal would also lead to the resignations of president Sepp Blatter and vice-president Michel Platini, who would subsequently receive long-term bans from football-related activity.

As the story broke, Jürgen released a statement expressing his sadness about corruption in football and calling for accountable administration throughout the game. He said that the corrupt system of governance did not, for him, reflect the true soul of football, which was embodied by the game's billions of fans and, more than anything, in the work of streetfootballworld network members 'promoting equal rights for women and girls in Kenya, providing education and employment to youth in Haiti, creating a path back to society for homeless men and women in the USA'.

He continued, 'A movement is growing in the world of football to recognise, elevate and leverage the power of football to become a force for social change. We are heading toward a more globalised, connected and interdependent world. A world that will need more global, connected and interdependent solutions. I believe that, despite all the successes of the grassroots in changing lives, in many cases saving lives, the real power of the game is still to be unearthed. Like every football fan, I look forward to the day when the word "football" is synonymous with a powerful global force that carries the purpose of its business – adding value to society – at its core.'

In response, on social media, a former streetfootballworld colleague in Brazil wrote, 'Nice words Jürgen Griesbeck but I would have loved to read why, even knowing about the huge levels of corruption at FIFA, an organisation like streetfootballworld received all along these years important donations and consultancy contracts from FIFA. "Partnerships" like these are not always healthy even if you name them Football for Hope.'

Jürgen says, 'It had been a careful and conscious decision in regard to the scope of impact that we aspired to. It would have been easier and more comfortable to limit ourselves to working with a small number of like-minded individuals and organisations, but to achieve lasting system change we recognised that multiple stakeholders had a role to play, and we understood that this would necessitate working with organisations that were underpinned by different values and motivations. We were also able to look beyond the institution to the individual, and with FIFA, the alliance was founded on the strength of our trust-based and value-aligned relationship with Federico. Without that it would not have been possible.'

It was a question that we had also carefully considered at Kick4Life, and as board members of streetfootballworld. We could have walked away, but we never saw the benefit of doing so, not for our beneficiaries nor for our ability to affect change in the industry. When we considered everything that the partnership with FIFA had enabled in Lesotho, including a facility that was used every day to deliver health, gender and education programmes to vulnerable young people, it was difficult to see the morality of turning it down. Ultimately, every person, and every organisation, had to make their own judgement, but in order to benefit those on the margins of society, the vast majority of network members consistently decided to accept the compromise of partnership with an institution where they knew that corruption existed.

But while the benefits for our participants were clear, it was much less apparent how the partnership with FIFA was enabling us to affect change in the industry. Undoubtedly, Jürgen and the team at streetfootballworld had instigated change at FIFA, working alongside Federico to create a genuine approach to Corporate Social Responsibility and the creation of a Football for Good movement, but this was an institutional change, not a permanent systemic one that cut across the whole football ecosystem. Achieving the latter was a seemingly impossible endeavour, but it was a challenge that was already on the table at streetfootballworld.

A year earlier in Berlin, while still on the board, I had attended a Theory of Change workshop, a process to explore and understand how organisations can achieve their desired change or results. Jürgen says, 'The crisis was painful, but it was an opportunity for greater self-understanding, and we wanted to press the reset button and ask what streetfootballworld would look like if we started again, with a blank sheet of paper. What had we learned? What did network members want from us? How did we need to restructure to meet the challenges and opportunities of the future?'

The workshop was framed around the aim of maximising social change through football, and we identified three pillars of activity needed to achieve this. The first two related to work that was already under way: the further growth and development of the Football for Good sector with the network at its core, and the establishment of partnerships and funding sources to enable that sector to thrive. By 2014 these activities had grown significantly, with 105 network members across 67 countries benefitting 1.2 million participants. The scope of work and support had also expanded, with global and regional events and forums, and the development of shared resources such as a football3 curriculum based on Jürgen's initial model of Fútbol por la Paz. Direct investment to network members had also increased with ongoing support from the Football for Hope programmatic fund, and there were new initiatives through partnerships with government ministries such as the US Department of State, football institutions including CAF – the Confederation of African Football – and corporations such as Adidas and Sony.

There was also a new European Youth Employability project, supported by Hyundai, responding to the urgent challenges precipitated by the financial crisis of 2008 and

2009. It was a realisation of what Jürgen had envisioned more than a decade earlier, when he and Vladimir had stood by the railings of a park in Berlin watching their daughters play. 'He was thinking ahead back then,' says Vladimir, 'and saw the particular potential of football around youth employability. He kept the idea, and when the right time and partnership arrived, it came to life, and it has continued to be a key strand in the network.'

The third pillar that emerged through the Theory of Change process was the embedding of Football for Good and social development within the football industry. 'We knew how hard this would be,' says Jürgen, 'in an industry which is inaccessible and resistant to change, and we had no plan, but we knew that to fulfil our mission, it was something that we needed to do. There had been some informal conversations with FIFA in the past about introducing a top-down regulation that would systemise social development, but that seemed neither realistic nor desirable. We would need to find another way.'

The scandal at FIFA was a dark episode for football, but I was pleased that action was being taken. We had all known that corruption was endemic within the game's governance, and the criminal proceedings would mean that administrators could no longer act with such blatant impunity. Things would have to change, but although football fans across the globe were angry and disillusioned, Jürgen believes an opportunity was missed to drive more radical change, 'Loyalty of many fans to their teams is so entrenched it seems to override anything else, with governance and club ownership far removed from their experience.'

The attempted breakaway of a European Super League six years later would be met with a more militant reaction, with the character of the clubs and the league system more directly challenged. 'In a world with so many problems and with so much injustice,' says Jürgen, 'I believe we are gradually reaching a point where fans are prepared to walk away if systems and even clubs don't represent their values.'

Regardless, in terms of global governance, the FIFA corruption scandal felt like a new low, and the need to embed a deeper purpose in the game was more pertinent than ever.

42

The Boy from Oviedo

IN THE 88th minute of the 2012 UEFA Champions League Final at the Allianz Arena in Munich, Juan Mata of Chelsea ran to take a corner. Five minutes earlier a dominant Bayern Munich side had taken the lead through Thomas Müller, with Chelsea's star striker Didier Drogba almost in tears as his, and Chelsea's, dream of a first Champions League trophy seemed all but over.

At 23, Juan was coming to the end of a successful first season in London, and seeing Drogba's despair, the attacking midfielder approached his team-mate, 'Believe Didi, you have to believe.' With just two minutes of normal time remaining, Juan swung the corner in with his left foot and it was met by Drogba at the near post with a powerful header into the top corner, sending the game into extra time and sparking wild celebrations from the Chelsea fans behind the goal as the Ivorian striker ran towards Mata at the corner flag.

Chelsea's remarkably resilient defensive display continued throughout extra time, taking the game to penalties, with Drogba once again finding the net with the winning kick. As the celebrations broke out, Juan looked around at his team-mates, 'I saw something truly beautiful.

As well as our unique striker from the Côte d'Ivoire, we had a keeper from the Czech Republic, a defender from Serbia, and another from Brazil, midfielders from Ghana, Nigeria, Portugal and England. We came from all over the world, our backgrounds had little in common, and we spoke many different languages. Some had grown up in countries ravaged by war, or entrenched in poverty, others, like me in Spain, had known peace and relative comfort. This democracy of football is one of the things that I love most about the game; there are very few barriers to play, and if you are good enough, and determined enough, you can make it. From our different backgrounds, we had come together and collaborated as a team, united for a common purpose, and we had done it. We were champions of Europe.'

Juan's father had also been a professional footballer, playing as a forward for Burgos CF and Real Oviedo in northern Spain. 'I was born in Burgos,' says Juan, 'but when I was four, we moved to Oviedo and it was here that I made friends and grew up playing football. I was surrounded by a loving family; I was very close to my sister and to my grandparents, and I developed a strong connection to the Asturias region, which has lasted for a lifetime.'

Juan's passion for football started early, 'As soon as I could walk, my sister and I played in the house, kicking a ball and breaking ornaments.' From there, Juan played with friends in the street and at school, and aged ten was taken into the youth system at Real Oviedo. His talent attracted the attention of Real Madrid, and still only 15, he moved to the capital to join their youth academy, La Fábrica, eventually representing the club's reserve team, Real Madrid Castilla, in the second tier during the 2006/07 season. After an impressive campaign, Juan was signed by Valencia, and spent the next four years making his name in La Liga – Spain's top flight – before joining Chelsea in 2011 for a £23.5m fee, soon becoming a recognised star of the English Premier League.

Juan's success at club level had been mirrored internationally, and having progressed through Spain's youth system he made his debut for the senior side in March 2009 in a World Cup qualifier against Turkey. In doing so, he became part of Spain's greatest-ever squad, alongside Xavi, Andrés Iniesta and David Villa in one of the most successful international teams in history, adding the 2010 World Cup to the European Championship they had already won in 2008. Juan went on to represent Spain 41 times, coming on as a substitute in the final of the European Championship in 2012 and scoring the last goal in a 4-0 thrashing of Italy as Spain won their third consecutive trophy.

Throughout all of these successes, Juan endeavoured to remain balanced and to stay connected with the world outside of the football industry, 'No matter how many trophies I've won nor how successful my career has been, my family has always been there to support me and to keep me grounded and humble. Football has given me an incredible life, and through the challenges and the many highlights of my career, they have helped me stay true to my roots and to my values, and to continue thinking about others. The game has taken me to the World Cup Final, to Champions League glory, and to global renown, but I am still, in my heart, the boy from Oviedo who dreamed of being a star.'

After two and a half extremely successful seasons with Chelsea, twice voted the club's Player of the Year, and winning the FA Cup and UEFA Europa League alongside the Champions League, Juan was suddenly out of favour with new manager José Mourinho. Halfway through the

2013/14 season he was signed by Manchester United for £37m, quickly establishing himself as a key part of another exceptional team alongside the likes of Rio Ferdinand, Wayne Rooney and Robin van Persie.

Juan was now 27, an established professional who had already achieved glittering success at club and international level. He had always taken an interest in the relationship between football and society, and alongside his pursuit of further success on the pitch he began to think more deeply about how he could use his platform as a footballer to make a social contribution, 'I had worked previously with large organisations such as UNICEF and had done many things with club foundations throughout my career, but I was also interested in setting up my own initiative and had started to consider the pros and cons of launching my own foundation. Through my various experiences, with charitable projects, I had always been particularly interested in those which used football as a part of their model. Over the years, from personal experience I knew the value of the game in developing skills and values that were useful in others areas of life, and I had an intrinsic appreciation of the game's potential for positive change.'

In November 2015, Juan was interviewed on Spanish TV and asked about wealth within the football industry, 'I mentioned that I would be theoretically willing to take a pay cut, if it meant being able to help people who are less fortunate. I didn't think too much about it, but a few days later I received a call from Ben Miller, a football agent that I knew from my playing days in Spain. He asked if I'd be interested in talking to an organisation that ran a global network of social football projects.'

A few weeks later, one morning in December, Juan left his house and headed to a hotel in Hale, Greater

Manchester for a meeting that would change his life, and change football.

43

Manchester, 2015–2016

JÜRGEN LANDED at Manchester Airport and took a taxi through the rainy streets to a nearby hotel. A few weeks earlier he had seen an interview on Spanish TV featuring Juan Mata which had grabbed his attention. It was similar to the moment when, late one Saturday night in 2001, he had heard Jürgen Klinsmann talking on a German show about the wider potential of the 2006 World Cup. On that occasion, Jürgen had made contact with Klinsmann via email, and it had led to their co-founding of streetfootballworld and festival 06. Now, 14 years on, he had the same feeling, as Juan spoke about the role of football in society, and specifically about the concept of taking a pay cut, recognising the inordinate level of player salaries at the top of the game. It resonated with Jürgen, and aligned with the third pillar which had emerged through the Theory of Change process, of embedding social impact within the football industry.

To make contact with the Manchester United player, Jürgen called Ben Miller, who worked in Barcelona for a sports management and marketing agency representing several top footballers. Jürgen and Ben had met during the Football for Hope Festival in Brazil the year before, when Ben had accompanied Spanish defender and FIFA ambassador Gerard Piqué to the event. 'Ben was different from a lot of the agents that we met,' says Jürgen, 'and I sensed that he was disillusioned with how things were working in the football industry. He asked a lot of questions, and I believe the experience at the festival had a big impact on him.'

Ben didn't represent Juan, but he was able to make the connection, and, less than a month after seeing the interview, Jürgen was standing in a hotel lobby waiting for the player to arrive. Moments later, Juan walked through the entrance, apologising for his late arrival. Jürgen looked at his watch, 'It was only two minutes after the agreed time, and I was surprised that he felt the need to apologise. It's only a small thing, but it made an immediate impression.'

In the same way that a shared language had helped to create a bond with Federico back in 2005, Jürgen's ability to speak Spanish fluently made an instant connection, 'It was comfortable with Juan from the start. I knew that we hadn't, but it felt like we had met before.' The pair walked through to a meeting room which Juan had reserved. 'It was very informal,' says Jürgen, 'and the chairs and tables were stacked. We got them down and arranged the furniture ourselves.'

Over the next two hours, Jürgen and Juan spoke broadly around the social dimension of football. 'I was very interested to hear Jürgen's story,' says Juan, 'including what he had achieved in Colombia, and how he had used that experience as a platform to connect similar projects around the world.'

Jürgen adds, 'It was clear that Juan had a good grounding in philanthropy having been involved with several large charities, projects in Oviedo and through the Manchester United Foundation. I gave him an overview of streetfootballworld and the Football for Good sector, and he seemed very keen to learn more.'

Juan mentioned that he had considered starting his own foundation. 'I believe that he had doubts about it already,' says Jürgen, 'and I shared our experience of player charities, often, but not always, falling short in terms of impact, as other distractions and a lack of expertise prevented them from succeeding. Through the network, I was able to show him that there were already many Football for Good organisations out there, doing incredible work that needed support to sustain and grow their impact.'

Following their first meeting, Jürgen and Juan kept in close contact, and Jürgen planted the seed of an idea, 'I mentioned what Juan had said in the interview, about taking a pay cut. What if you actually did it? What if you took a self-imposed pay cut, and committed the money to Football for Good? Instead of setting up another charity, maybe others would follow and a movement could grow out of that.'

In April 2016, Juan was unveiled as streetfootballworld's first ambassador, with an event overlooking Old Trafford at Hotel Football, owned by former Manchester United players including the Neville brothers, Ryan Giggs and Paul Scholes. Jürgen says, 'Despite operating for 14 years, we had never previously had an ambassador. We wanted to develop our own identity first, to look and feel authentic, and to avoid exposure to the sometimes unpredictable and inconsistent nature of the industry. By 2016 we had matured as an organisation, recognised for what we were, and in Juan we had an ambassadorial commitment that was deeper than surface level. He had a long-term vision, and instead of going through an agent or a club, we had open and direct communication with him.'

Teenage Jürgen at the Berlin Wall.

Elida at the house in the Andes, with one of Jürgen's beloved dogs, rescued from the market, 1994.

Jürgen and Elida on their wedding day, with the 1954 Ford Crestline, Saturday, 23 July 1994.

Andrés and Elida during her time volunteering as a photographer at Atlético Nacional.

Street football in Medellín, with the green and white of 'El Nacional' on show. Taken by Jürgen on a return visit in 2015.

A Street Football for Tolerance session in a Soviet-era hangar, Brandenburg, 2001.

Coach Maturana, Federico and Jürgen during festival 06.

The Fútbol por la Paz delegation, with Coach Maturana, present the Copa Andrés Escobar to a packed crowd at the scaffold stadium in Kreuzberg, 2 July 2006.

The three founders of streetfootballworld in 2010: Johannes, Vladimir and Jürgen.

Roosevelt Mpinganjira of the Malawi FA makes the first symbolic kick as Pete and I begin our 250-mile dribble in 2005.

The centre opening in Lesotho, September 2011. I'm front right (arm in a sling), Lucas Radebe is centre (in white), with Pete, left (in sunglasses). Back right is Federico, next to Vladimir. Credit: FIFA.

Tess gives a final briefing to the No.7 trainees on opening night, August 2014.

The streetfootballworld network at the fourth General Assembly in Lyon in 2016. Such an amazing community of people and organisations. Credit: Dana Rösiger.

Juan and Jürgen during the trip to India, June 2017.

Ashok, with two children from OSCAR's Football for Good programmes.

Jürgen and Megan after their first meeting in Seattle, July 2017.

Kick4Life win the Lesotho Women's Super League in July 2021, becoming national champions for the first time.

The Griesbeck García family in Andalusia.

After the event in Manchester, Jürgen flew home, not to Berlin, but to the Spanish region of Andalusia, where he and Elida had recently moved. After 14 years in Germany and two in the United States, Elida was craving a life that was culturally, spiritually and climatically closer to what she had known in Colombia. The girls had also moved out, to study and travel, and with a shift in Jürgen's role away from the day-to-day management of streetfootballworld to a more entrepreneurial focus, the personal and professional ties that bound them to Berlin were no longer so strong. Spain was the obvious choice due to the language, culture and climate, and with good connections to the rest of Europe.

Jürgen says, 'We found a pleasant coastal village close to Malaga – La Cala del Moral – the Bay of Mulberries – with a place overlooking the sea. It's an old fishing village, very Spanish and largely untouched by the nearby tourist trade, but still only 20 minutes from the airport.'

Elida adds, 'The south of Spain was the ideal place, a bridge between Europe and South America, and I felt reborn, listening to my language again in the streets, meeting happy people, being in contact with nature, and seeing the sea from the window. I felt that my life mission in Germany had been overcome, and it was our moment to start anew; reworking our daily lives, getting to know each other again as a couple, meeting new people and building a home, where the girls come often to renew their energy.'

A month later, in May 2016, Juan picked up his first silverware with Manchester United, scoring in a 2-1 win over Crystal Palace at Wembley. Off the pitch, conversations with Jürgen about the social role of football continued, and while he recognised the very positive impact that player foundations could make, Juan had decided on a different approach, 'Through talking with Jürgen and Ben I became increasingly interested in identifying a mission that was more holistic, and in creating a team approach that could offer a solution across the football industry.'

44

The 1%

THOMAS PREISS was at a café in central London, chatting to the agent of a top player in the English Premier League. 'It was going well,' says Thomas, 'until I mentioned the purpose of the meeting. He knew it was related to a social cause, but when I said it would involve the player committing 1% of his annual salary, there was a visible, physical reaction. The meeting was effectively over.'

A few weeks earlier, Thomas had met a younger and more junior colleague of the agency, who had been very enthusiastic about the concept, 'It felt like a generational difference, and a reflection of a greater willingness to embrace purpose amongst the next generation. We had high hopes, but the more senior agent quashed them.'

It was another no.

Thomas had joined streetfootballworld three years earlier in 2014, with the task of operationalising the third pillar which had emerged at the Theory of Change workshop in Berlin – to mobilise the football industry for social change. 'There was a lot of freedom to think creatively,' says Thomas, 'and to explore and study industry-wide movements that existed in other sectors. streetfootballworld was still largely rooted in a charity mindset, and tended to operate and think in terms of products, with a portfolio of forums, festivals and toolkits. These were all valuable, but the third pillar was an opportunity to think differently, and to develop a mechanism that would create system change.'

Thomas had completed a Master's in International Economics at the University of Göttingen in central Germany in 2011, having spent a year of his course at the University of California, 'During my time on the West Coast I met a lot of social entrepreneurs, working across many industries, and I was interested in how I could apply my business and economics knowledge in a similar way.' After completing his Master's, Thomas co-founded an ecommerce company selling sustainable lifestyle products, 'It was a nice concept, but the model was overly complex, and when I arrived at streetfootballworld and started to explore how we could implement something across the whole football ecosystem, I saw that we needed to keep things simple, with a clear message.'

Jürgen and Thomas also considered how 'the industry solution' could support the other two pillars – further growth and development of the Football for Good sector with the network at its core, and the establishment of partnerships and funding sources to enable that sector to thrive. Their thought process reflected a consistent message that kept coming from network members – more than anything we need sustainable funding to help us deliver and grow. It was something that resonated with us at Kick4Life; the short-term and unpredictable nature of grant funding was one of the primary reasons that we set up our social enterprises. A lack of funding, and the energy-sapping effort necessary to generate income, was the biggest challenge that network members (and charities in general) faced, and Jürgen and Thomas saw that the new industry initiative must be a part of the solution.

'We developed several concepts through a venture creation process,' says Thomas, 'and one idea stood out – the 1%.'

There were a number of existing examples, including One Percent for the Planet, through which companies donate 1% of their sales to environmental causes, and Founders Pledge, which involves entrepreneurs pledging a portion of proceeds from the sale of their businesses to charity. 'They have both raised hundreds of millions of dollars,' says Thomas, 'and they proved to us that, if done properly, and with a powerful narrative, the model could work. We believed it could be successfully applied to the football industry, with players and organisations donating to a collective pot that was distributed to Football for Good projects. We liked the potential of this approach to systemise social commitment, going beyond project-based Corporate Social Responsibility, and encouraging companies and institutions to make purpose an inherent part of their organisational DNA.'

Together with Juan, the idea was mapped out, based on a simple 1% contribution of income across football. 'Players were the obvious starting point,' says Jürgen, 'being the most visible representation of the football industry, but we also saw them as a bridge to engage the rest of the ecosystem – clubs, federations, agents, brands and fans. We wanted to unite the world of football behind a shared mission, and the name of the movement grew from that ambition – Common Goal.'

Juan had been heavily involved in the co-creation process, and committed to donating 1% of his annual salary as the first player within the movement, 'I loved the idea. It was something new in football, and it was simple and easy to grasp, but at the same time it represented a deep and meaningful commitment. I also liked the potential of Common Goal to strengthen the connection between players and fans. Without one or the other there is no industry; we need them to exist in harmony, and a shared purpose could help us to achieve that.'

With the concept now established, Juan, Jürgen and Thomas started to speak to players and agents to gauge their interest and to get a feel for how the idea would be received. The plan was to launch with a starting XI team of players already committed, and Juan initiated conversations with some of his closest colleagues, 'I spoke to some players about joining the movement, but it was not easy to gain commitment given that Common Goal did not yet formally exist. Some were also already focused on their own community projects. In the last few years, it has become much more normal to talk about social development and charitable giving, thanks to people like my team-mate Marcus Rashford and his campaign for free school meals, but at the time these subjects were not often discussed.'

'We faced a lot of rejection, and even ridicule,' says Thomas. 'Some agents listened politely and said they would speak to the players, but we never heard from them again. Others, such as the agent at the café in London, were more direct with their dismissals.'

The situation matched our experiences at Kick4Life. The expectation was, in fact, usually the opposite of making a contribution, with players and agents requiring payment in return for representing the charity, whether it was an endorsement on social media or attending an event. In the early days we had been surprised when a request for a former player to attend one of our tournaments came with a price tag that we simply couldn't afford. Later we realised that this was 'peanuts' compared to what players received for attending charity events run by the likes of FIFA. We understood the market dynamics behind this, but it still mystified us that some ex-players could receive three months of our organisational turnover, covering a team of 50 people, for attending a one-day charity football event. No wonder Thomas was having trouble asking for money. It was a radical idea and it required a mindset shift.

Conversely, other people, mostly outside of the industry, criticised the idea because 1% was not enough, given the enormous wealth involved. Jürgen says, 'We felt instinctively that to pitch the request any higher, or to specify a particular amount, would be a mistake. 1% made it a realistic amount. Anyone could do it, and given the unparalleled scale of wealth and finance across the football ecosystem, if it became a standard across the industry, that 1% would represent billions of dollars leveraged for social development. Besides, 1% was always a minimum, and people could give more if they felt comfortable and able.'

In early 2017, Jürgen arranged to meet Tom Vernon, founder of the Right to Dream Academy in Ghana, which had helped to inspire our purpose-driven club model at Kick4Life. Since its founding in 1999, the academy had been incredibly successful, creating a pathway for players to Europe, but Tom had an even bigger vision, and in 2015, with the support of his board, the academy had purchased a professional football club in Denmark – FC Nordsjælland. Jürgen saw great potential to embed the Common Goal model throughout the club, 'We met in London at a café near Baker Street. I explained what we were trying to achieve and Tom looked at me aghast, seemingly appalled at the act of stupidity I was about to commit.'

Tom says, 'I told Jürgen that, in my experience, the football industry was too individualistic and did not work as a collective, and that the influence of agents would unfortunately prevent it from succeeding. It was before the time of Colin Kaepernick taking the knee, and others like LeBron James, Megan Rapinoe and Marcus Rashford using their platforms as leading sportspeople to speak directly to their fan bases, and to influence and drive real change, and I couldn't see Common Goal gaining any traction.'

There was also a lack of enthusiasm for the idea internally at streetfootballworld. 'There was resistance,' says Jürgen, 'to what was perceived as the latest innovation with a high chance of failure. We had been trying for several months to get a second player to join Juan, without success, and I remember having a call with Vladi and Johannes to ask for their support and trust. I asked them, are you with me? If not, I accept it, but let me know, and I will take the idea elsewhere.'

'I was sceptical,' says Vladimir. 'I saw great value in Juan's ambassadorial role, but I could not see the 1% idea taking off. But I trusted Jürgen. He had proved himself, time and again as a visionary, not always right and not always at the right time, but Johannes and I gave him our support. We would have his back.'

The involvement of Thomas also gave the other co-founders confidence. Vladimir adds, 'With United, Jürgen had no one beside him to take responsibility for driving his idea forward. Thomas brought this to the table. He understood and appreciated Jürgen's entrepreneurial approach as well as contributing strong and decisive operational and management skills.'

Thomas says, 'Jürgen is a visionary, a skill that needs to be recognised, but he also has perseverance and endurance to stay in the game, and I believe this ability to both conceptualise and to commit for the long term has been central to many of his successes. Juan is actually very similar and these shared personality traits have enabled them to work together very effectively.' Thomas also saw the need to cultivate a culture of focus, 'Jürgen is very energetic. He always questions things, and he trusts in innovation. This is very positive but it also creates an environment where there are lots of ideas. My role was to connect the entrepreneurial and the operational spheres, to set parameters and to ensure quality and focus in what we decided to pursue.'

Common Goal would once again see streetfootballworld venture into new territory. Jürgen says, 'We did not have extensive contacts, or a well-recognised brand, and apart from Juan we were not well-known individuals with significant personal influence. But we did have expertise in developing trust-based relationships and this was the foundation on which we aspired to build and grow Common Goal organically within the football ecosystem.'

But despite this vision, and despite Juan's position as a figurehead for the movement, after a year of trying they had failed to persuade a single player to join him in signing up for Common Goal. 'It was disappointing,' says Jürgen, 'and we had a conversation about whether we should kill it or have the guts to publicly launch with only Juan. He had the most to lose in terms of his reputation if it fell totally flat.'

'I always thought it was the right idea,' says Juan, 'and the difficulty that we faced in recruiting a starting XI never affected my determination to make it work, nor my belief that it would work. We decided to go for it.'

A date was set for the public launch of Common Goal – 4 August 2017 – and to further strengthen Juan's connection to the network prior to the announcement, a trip was arranged in June that would take him, and his girlfriend Evelina, to the frontline of Football for Good.

45

India, June 2017

ONE DAY in 1999, when Ashok Rathod was 11, he and a friend skipped school and ran to the fish market where his father worked in the Mumbai slum of Ambedkar Nagar. They wanted to earn some money for themselves, and spent the following hours collecting discarded fish in a bucket and selling them to passers-by. 'One lady gave me 100 Rupees,' says Ashok, 'and it felt like a fortune.' In the coming weeks, Ashok and a growing group of friends, attracted by stories of great wealth, continued to abandon school in favour of the market.

It was not long before Ashok's father became aware of his son's activities, 'He told me, either you go back to school and stop going to the market, or you leave my house and never come back. I returned to my studies, but several of my friends did not, and in the coming years I saw what happened. At first it was okay, they made even more money, but soon they were getting involved in drugs and working long, hard hours. Some of them got married very young, to girls who were just 14 or 15 and they soon had families of their own to support. Most of those boys that I went to the market with are now dead, and I realise that my father saved me.'

Having spent most of his life working at the fish market, Ashok's father had wanted something different for his children, 'Every morning he started work at 4am and finished at 7pm,' says Ashok. 'There was not much respect, and even though he was paid very little, there were gangs who would try to mug the workers on their way home, so sometimes he would sleep at the market and only come home the next day when it was safe.' Ashok's mother also worked long hours, and from the age of four, he and his siblings were left at home during the day. 'Life in the slum is not easy,' says Ashok, 'and it is hard to think about the future when the present is occupied with day-to-day survival and earning enough to eat.'

Eighteen years later, Juan, Evelina and Jürgen listened intently as Ashok led them through the busy fish market, pointing out boys collecting fish as he once did, and explaining how the experiences of his youth had inspired him to set up OSCAR, a network member of streetfootballworld, 'In my late teens I was still studying and working part-time as a mentor, and I remember seeing some kids, sitting around smoking. They had dropped out of school and there must have been people telling them they were making bad choices, but they weren't listening. I wanted to tell them how my life, and the lives of my friends, had been very different since I had returned to school, and they had stayed in the market. As a child I had loved to play, so I asked if they wanted to come to a football session. They said they preferred cricket, but I couldn't afford the equipment so it was football or nothing. Thankfully, they agreed and I started running a regular session for 18 children.'

At first, Ashok found that young people from different castes and religions would not interact, 'I started to mix the teams, so that they would have to work together, and they quickly forgot about the things that separated them and became friends.' He also discovered that in a sporting environment, the participants were much more willing to listen to his story about the importance of education. The sessions continued, and gradually more young people came, and by 2010 he was running regular activities for 300 children.

The project was having a positive impact, and Ashok was directed to various funding opportunities to grow and formalise the programme, 'It became evident that we needed a name. I remembered a group of friends that I had played cricket with years before. We called ourselves OSCAR, because one of the guys was a big movie fan, and he said that we should try to be the best of the best, and in the film industry that was winning an Oscar.' The aspirational nature of the name appealed to Ashok, and he decided to use it for his football project, but when he went to the charity commission office in Mumbai he was turned away. 'The officer said we could not use the name because we might get sued, so I went away and came up with a new name – Organisation for Social Change, Awareness and Responsibility, or, for short, OSCAR. The officer accepted it!'

The following year, Ashok was accepted on to a coaching course in Jordan for young entrepreneurs around the world, and it was there that he met Stuart Christie who worked for Albion in the Community, the foundation of English club Brighton & Hove Albion. Stuart, and several colleagues, took Ashok under their wing and encouraged him to apply for membership of streetfootballworld. Since then, OSCAR's growth and impact has accelerated, and today the organisation has a team of 45 staff, working with 3,000 children across Mumbai as well as supporting other NGOs throughout the region. 'We are still focused on education,' says Ashok, 'but we understand the holistic needs of young people, so we now also deliver activities around health, hygiene, gender and employability.'

By 2017, OSCAR was recognised as a leading Football for Good project, and with Ashok's inspirational story, Jürgen had suggested India for Juan's first visit to a network member. 'Before launching Common Goal, I felt it was important to connect to the network more deeply,' says Juan. 'I wanted to feel and breathe what was happening, and it was incredible to see what Ashok and his team had achieved, and to sense their passion and energy.'

As well as visiting the fish market, Ashok took Juan, Evelina and Jürgen to visit his parents at their home in the slum. 'They had very little,' says Juan, 'but they welcomed us generously and we shared chai. I was touched by their kindness, and throughout the trip I was moved by the ability of people to find joy and positivity, despite the desperate struggles they were facing.' After visiting the house, Ashok led the visitors to a pump where he had collected water as a child, and where his parents still accessed their supply.

Jürgen says, 'The trip was very low key as Juan wanted to connect authentically with the community and the participants. There were no security guards, no police escort and no media. Only on one occasion did word get out that a Manchester United player was in the slum, and hundreds of people turned up to see him. He was, as ever, generous with his time, relaxed and happy to meet people.'

During the trip, the group visited an OSCAR football session, and after joining in some activities a promotional video was filmed that would be a key part of the upcoming launch of Common Goal. Jürgen says, 'We filmed Juan playing a football match against 11 young people from the programme. Despite being a World Cup winner, he, of course, lost, being so vastly outnumbered. We wanted to emphasise that football is a team game, and that for Common Goal to succeed, we also needed a team of players to join Juan. He couldn't do it alone.'

As photography enthusiasts, Juan and Evelina took hundreds of pictures during the visit, and after returning to the UK an exhibition was held at the National Football Museum in Manchester. Juan says, 'Like football, photography is a way to express ourselves, and it was a special way to connect and share the experiences and memories of the trip with fans in England.'

More than 40,000 visitors attended the exhibition, among them a group of young people from OSCAR whom Juan had invited from Mumbai. 'We still talk about it today,' says Ashok, 'and wonder if it really happened.'

The trip to India consolidated the growing friendship between Jürgen and Juan, as well as strengthening their shared determination to make Common Goal a success. 'I left with mixed emotions,' says Juan. 'I was sad to see the stark inequalities and the terrible challenges that so many people were facing, but I was also uplifted by the amazing work being done by Ashok and his team. I was even more convinced that the football industry had to do more, and that to make a genuine difference, we had to act together.'

* * *

A month after returning from India, Jürgen flew to Oakland in California where he joined Mike Geddes, the former BBC reporter who was now leading streetfootballworld's operations in the United States. Mike was in the process of setting up The Third Half, a social enterprise offering travel experiences to Football for Good projects around the world, and was also in the early stages of conceptualising a new purpose-driven soccer club in Oakland. Mike had arranged a meeting with Megan Rapinoe, a star player of the United States women's national team and at the time playing for Seattle Reign FC. He and Jürgen travelled to Seattle and met Megan for lunch at a city-centre café.

'She was already recognised as one of the best footballers in the world,' says Jürgen, 'but not yet the global icon she became after winning the 2019 World Cup, refusing to visit the White House, making powerful statements about LGBTQ+ rights and suing the US Soccer Federation for equal pay. She was, however, already clearly motivated to work towards broader change in the football industry, and when we told her about the imminent launch of Common Goal, she committed to signing up after the announcement.'

It was the biggest indication yet that Common Goal might just take off.

46

The Launch of Common Goal, August–December 2017

Friday, 4 August

The room was packed with journalists waiting for the player to arrive. At 12.39pm a dance track temporarily blasted out from the speakers, and with cameras rolling and amid flashing lights, he entered, embracing a series of people en route to the stage. The music died and a voice announced, 'Welcome everyone, and welcome Neymar to Paris.'

By complete coincidence, the biggest transfer in football history was being unveiled on the same day that Common Goal was introduced to the world. The previous record, set the year before, had seen Paul Pogba move from Juventus to Manchester United for €105m. That figure had just been smashed, more than doubled, with Neymar transferred from Barcelona to Paris Saint-Germain for €222m. His weekly salary would be €600,000.

A few hours earlier, 376 miles away in Manchester, the Common Goal story had broken, with an online and media launch led by Ben Miller. It included the release of the Juan v XI video, which had been filmed in India, and an article by Juan in the *Players' Tribune*, inviting his fellow professional footballers to join the movement. Thomas says, 'Speculation around Neymar leaving Barcelona had been building up for several weeks, but we had no idea that it would happen on the day we announced Common Goal. We were worried that Neymar's transfer would eclipse and detract from our news, but it had the opposite effect, generating a counter-narrative which the press picked up on.'

'It gave the launch of Common Goal a boost and amplified our message,' says Jürgen. 'On the same day that the wealth of football reached a new zenith, Juan was announcing that he was giving away a portion of his salary, and asking other players to join him and use the game for social impact. The media and the public responded very well. They saw that it was not a PR stunt, and although some journalists referred to it as the launch of a charity, instead of a movement, the Neymar move, based on the strength of our message and campaign, gave the story legs.'

Juan says, 'There was uncertainty, but also excitement as we made the announcement. Now we had to wait, and hope, that others would join.'

Monday, 7 August

There had been no immediate sign-ups and nothing over the weekend, but on Monday morning Juan received an email from German international and World Cup-winner Mats Hummels of Bayern Munich. Mats's management team had already been in touch with the team in Berlin to express interest, but the message to Juan confirmed that he would become the second player to make the 1% pledge and join Common Goal. 'I didn't know Mats personally,' says Juan, 'so it was a wonderful surprise when he got in touch.'

Juan was no longer alone.

Thursday, 17 August

Mats Hummels was publicly announced as the second player to join the movement, stating, 'As soon as I heard of Common Goal, I knew this was a chance for football to improve our world, and I wanted to be part of it. I feel we could be doing more to connect the increasing revenues in football to some kind of deeper purpose. Through the 1% pledge we're building a bridge between football and its social impact around the world … I'm putting the call out to all my fellow footballers: join Juan and me and help to take the game to the next level.' The media once again picked up the story, with extensive international coverage, something that would be repeated time and again in the coming months.

On the same day, at the office in Berlin, Thomas opened an email in the info@common-goal.org inbox:

> *Hello. I'm Giorgio Chiellini, player of Juventus.*
> *I'm interested to support your program and I would like to give my congratulations to Juan Mata for finding the time and having the idea to support through football people less lucky than us.*
>
> *I'm not interested in advertising; I only want to support a brilliant project.*
>
> *Sorry for my English. I try to make the best as possible!*
>
> *I wait for your answer about complete the registration.*
>
> *Bye,*
> *Giorgio*

At first, Thomas thought it was a prank, 'For a player like Giorgio, an established figure with Italy and Juventus, to introduce himself in such a way, and to reach out personally, seemed improbable.' A reply was sent requesting a Skype call. 'We were delighted when Giorgio appeared smiling on the screen,' says Thomas, 'and we quickly found out what a humble and authentic guy he is. It gave us faith that Common Goal could work, and that there were more players out there who wanted to be a part of it, without expecting anything in return, and with a genuine desire to collaborate and make a difference.'

Thursday, 14 September
Megan Rapinoe delivered on her promise to join Common Goal once it was up and running, and her friend and team-mate in the United States national team, Alex Morgan, joined with her. They were announced as the third and fourth members. Megan said, 'We are really looking forward to growing the Common Goal movement from here – sky's the limit at this stage.'

Jürgen added, 'It was incredible to have two global stars of women's football sign up, and it provided an excellent platform for the movement to grow in parallel with the exciting growth of the women's game.'

Friday, 29 September
With a personal video message, Giorgio became the fifth player to be unveiled.

Thursday, 5 October
German international Serge Gnabry, on loan at TSG 1899 Hoffenheim from Bayern Munich, became Common Goal's sixth player, stating, '1%. It's not a big figure, but it can make a huge impact if we commit to it as a team. I want to make giving back part of football, and make football feel good about itself again. I want to change the game for good and that's why I'm with Common Goal.'

Over the coming days and months, more people kept coming forward, pledging 1% and joining the movement. Thomas says, 'With momentum in the media and online, we saw the contagious nature of Common Goal. Unlike before, when we had struggled to gain commitment, the concept was now a real thing and the information was visible. When players saw the likes of Megan and Serge joining, it gave them confidence and inspiration to also become a part of it.'

The diversity of those joining was also encouraging, with a range of nationalities, ages, genders, levels and backgrounds, reflecting the ubiquitous appeal of Common Goal. They included, with their clubs at the time listed, Charlie Daniels of AFC Bournemouth, Spanish international Verónica Boquete of Paris Saint-Germain, Colombian forward Nicole Regnier of América de Cali, Kasper Schmeichel of Leicester City and Denmark, German international Pauline Bremer of Manchester City, Juan's former team-mate at Valencia, Bruno Saltor, of Brighton & Hove Albion, Heather O'Reilly, a USA player and Women's World Cup winner, Japan's Shinji Kagawa of Borussia Dortmund, Hasan Ali Kaldırım of Fenerbahçe and Turkey, and Julian Nagelsmann of TSG 1899 Hoffenheim, who became the first head coach to join.

Behind the scenes, the team in Berlin were working hard to finalise and implement the financial infrastructure and processes that were needed to manage and distribute donations. Common Goal would exist as a project of streetfootballworld, but in order to facilitate cross-border donations from multiple nations the fund would be hosted by the King Baudouin Foundation in Belgium. The foundation was already part of the Transnational Giving Europe Alliance, meaning that charitable tax reliefs which exist in each country could be applied. In the UK, for example, the government's Gift Aid scheme would mean an additional 25 per cent on each donation. Meanwhile, a call for proposals was prepared, inviting network members to apply for funding, with more than €500,000 contributed by the end of the year.

Saturday, 25 November

I had been among those who loved the idea of Common Goal but struggled to see it taking off. When the campaign was launched and players started to commit, it was incredibly exciting and my lack of faith quickly turned into enthusiasm. News of the movement reached Kick4Life FC men's captain Bokang Mothoana, who also captained the national Lesotho team. He spoke to Chris, our director of football, about his interest in the scheme, and a few weeks later 'Lefty' was publicly announced as the second African player to join the movement.

Wednesday, 29 November

Jürgen and Juan arrived at the House of European Football, the headquarters of UEFA which overlooks Lake Geneva in the Swiss town of Nyon. A few weeks earlier Jürgen had received an email from Pascal Torres, general secretary of the recently established UEFA Foundation for Children, saying that the UEFA president, Aleksander Čeferin, was interested in Common Goal, and would like to meet during an upcoming visit to London. Juan had travelled down from Manchester and Jürgen from Berlin, and together they told Aleksander more about their ambition to embed Common Goal across the football ecosystem. By the end of the meeting, Čeferin said he would personally sign up, and in the coming weeks a live stream event announcing his commitment was planned to take place in Nyon.

As they waited for the event to start, Jürgen and Juan walked up and down a corridor that was filled with UEFA's various trophies: the European Under-19 Championship, the European Under-21 Championship, the European Championship, the Europa League and the Champions League. Juan walked up to Jürgen and said, 'It's funny, I've won all of these [men's] trophies, but I've never before stepped into the building of a federation or a governing body.'

In that moment, Jürgen felt the disconnectedness of football which had for so long separated fans and even players from the institutions and the club owners who controlled the game. He remembered when the DFB had told streetfootballworld, still in its infancy, to stop interfering with football, and he reflected on all of the problems at FIFA. Everything he and his colleagues had done since had sought to close that gap, and to bring the global football community closer together – the network, Football for Hope and now Common Goal. The divides had to continue being bridged, and that bridge had to be purpose.

During the live stream, Aleksander, Jürgen and Juan discussed the social dimension of the game, and took questions from around the world, before announcing that Čeferin was joining Common Goal. His commitment, as the first football administrator to join, and at such a high level, was a huge statement. 'I want to join the initiative Common Goal, and I want to pledge 1% of my salary,' said Aleksander. 'As Juan said, football players are very privileged to live from football and to be part of football. We are also privileged, football politicians, so I think we should join.'

Sunday, 31 December
By the end of 2017, 34 players, coaches and administrators from 18 countries had signed up. 'We had believed in the

idea,' says Jürgen, 'but it came to life in a way that exceeded our expectations. We knew there was still a long way to go, and that the media interest would not always be at the same level, but we now had a platform from which to build both a global community and a long-term source of sustainable funding for network members to continue their life-changing work.'

47

Right to Dream

TOM VERNON looked out over the pitch at Right to Dream Park, home ground of FC Nordsjælland (FCN), a Superliga club in Denmark. Flags of red and yellow, the colours of the home team, were being waved enthusiastically across the packed stands as the players lined up against the reigning champions, Midtjylland. As a child growing up just ten minutes from Wembley, Tom could not have guessed that his life would lead him first to Africa and then to Denmark, nor to the ownership of a club pushing for another season of European competition. But three decades on, in April 2021, as he watched Nordsjælland complete a 3-2 victory, it felt like the realisation of a dream; in the starting line-up were nine players from Right to Dream's youth development system, some like forward Kamaldeen Sulemana who had progressed via the academy that Tom had first established in Ghana in the late 1990s, while others such as midfielder Jacob Christensen had come through the coaching structure in Denmark. A link between a European club and an African project is not unusual, with the world's richest clubs seeking to unearth some of the game's undiscovered stars, but Right to Dream is different, unique – in 2015, the academy in Ghana had taken the extraordinary step of purchasing FC Nordsjælland. They had flipped the dynamic. And there was more to come.

A football fan from a young age, Tom was happiest away from the classroom, 'I was dyslexic, and there was very little recognition and support at the time, but I was able to express myself differently, and by the age of 12 I was already running two businesses, videoing school productions and selling copies to parents, and running a pay-to-play five-a-side league.' It was an early indication of the entrepreneurial spirit that would define Tom's future, but his natural abilities in business went largely unremarked, 'It is a continued failing of the education system that talents outside of traditional academia are not properly acknowledged or encouraged.'

Tom's own experiences would help to shape the support structures that he would later build at Right to Dream, 'Most young people have barriers to overcome, whether it was me in the UK trying to find my place in society, or a boy in Ghana walking ten miles home after training, or a girl in Denmark facing the pressures of social media.' When Tom started coaching, it was perhaps inevitable that his approach to youth development would be holistic, with support on and off the pitch going hand in hand.

After finishing school, Tom completed his coaching badges, but initially struggled to find a position in elite football in the UK, 'In the 1990s there was still a strong culture of former professional players dominating coaching opportunities, so when a friend invited me to coach in Ghana I quickly accepted.' Aged just 19, Tom was soon appointed head coach of Accra Great Olympics, one of the top clubs in the country, 'I had a huge amount of unlearning to do. I was a child of the 1980s and had grown up in the era of Bob Geldof and Band Aid, and I arrived with many unconscious biases about how I could benefit Ghana and what Ghanaians could learn from me. I was struck by the immediate warmth of people in the country and the very strong sense of community, but it took me over a decade to gain a proper understanding of the deep and rich culture that existed. As a white man, in a country that has been so negatively impacted by Britain's colonial influence, it also took a long time to build trust around my motives for being there.'

This was particularly important given Tom's involvement in football, 'Unscrupulous behaviour across the football industry is not exclusive to Africa, but in Ghana, and across the continent, vulnerable young people are persistently tricked into parting with money for opportunities that don't exist.'

Tom had a particular interest in youth development, and given the raw talent and technical ability of the young players that he saw in Ghana, he imagined what might be possible if they were given the same structured coaching opportunities as kids in high-income countries, 'We held a trial in Nima, one of the poorest communities in Accra and identified 16 lads whom we started coaching in the evenings.' Over the coming months, Tom and his girlfriend Helen (now his wife) developed a strong connection with the boys. 'We saw more intimately the challenges they were facing,' says Tom. 'Most had inadequate diets and some were victims of domestic violence, and we realised that it wasn't just an absence of qualified coaches or a lack of facilities that was holding them back; to achieve their potential on the field, they also needed an education, healthcare, safe housing and proper nutrition.'

In 1999, Tom and Helen took a bold step, converting their house to include dorms, a classroom and a dining hall, and inviting the 16 boys into their home. Tom says, 'We wanted to provide them with holistic support across all areas of their lives, and worked closely with their families to build trust. It was a huge learning curve, but we started to see real progress on the pitch, in the classroom and in their overall wellbeing.'

It wasn't long before Tom took a scouting job with Manchester United, enabling him to step away from club coaching and affording him much more time to focus on the newly named Right to Dream Academy, 'We were learning as we went along, but we believed completely that with the right structures in place it could become a sustainable model for developing young footballers. We realised that not every young person would make it to the professional game, but the holistic approach and education would ensure that there were multiple career pathways, and we quickly discovered that Ghana's underdeveloped potential extended far beyond the football pitch.'

Early on, Tom recognised the critical importance of character development, and the need to equip the boys with life skills to overcome challenges they might face in the future, such as rejection, injury and adapting to new environments. He also cultivated a culture of giving back, 'We later learned that this philosophy was already strongly embedded within local culture, with African players often generously supporting their families and communities, but from the outset we sought to promote an ethos that Right to Dream was about more than individual objectives. The players were there to achieve their dreams, and we were careful to avoid creating an expectation of servile gratitude, but we did want our boys to recognise the value of their opportunity, and to nurture a responsibility and a motivation to use their platform and success to create opportunities and impact for others. That was where the idea of wider purpose first developed in the project.'

From the initial intake of 16 boys, drawn from a trial of 100, three went on to represent Ghana at full international level, five played professionally in Europe, and six graduated from NCAA Division 1 universities in the United States with fully funded scholar-athlete degrees. That process took ten years, but the astonishing success rate showed Tom the enormous potential that existed, with many more players already coming through the academy, 'We registered as a foundation in Ghana, enabling us to formalise some of the relationships that we were building with clubs like Everton and Fulham.' Through his scouting role, Tom was also able to secure training opportunities with Manchester United each summer in the UK for two Right to Dream Academy players.

By the early 2000s, with its inherent social objectives, coupled with a focus on talent and performance, Right to Dream was operating in a unique space which cut across both the football industry and the Football for Good sector. Tom says, 'In terms of our mission, it was very closely aligned with traditional charities using football for social change, but we used elite football as a primary vehicle to achieve it.' As a result, Tom rarely accessed charitable funding, with donors put off by the elite component. Instead, the first decade of Right to Dream was funded by a sports travel company which Tom had founded, offering gap-year opportunities in Ghana for young coaches from the UK and the USA, but when the business collapsed in the financial crisis of 2008, it was the commercial approach of Right to Dream which enabled it to scale and grow. Tom says, 'More than 95 per cent of our income has since come from first-refusal agreements, sell-on fees and agents' commission, and this has been reinvested in opportunities for more young players to receive intensive and holistic support, which has genuinely and permanently transformed their lives.'

In the following years, the Right to Dream Academy has achieved enormous success, with the opening of a US$2.5m purpose-built facility in 2010, including a fully residential international school. Each year there is an intake of 20 boys selected for their academic, character and footballing potential, drawn from across West Africa, with the model extending to girls in 2013, supporting the development of a new generation of female footballers and leaders. With a growing team of coaches, tutors and operational staff, the academy has now seen more than 60 graduates progress to professional football, with over 40 representing their national teams and over 70 accessing student–athlete scholarships at international universities.

Yet despite all of these success stories, and the meticulous work that was undertaken at Right to Dream to prepare players for the psychological demands of moving to play in a new country and culture, Tom was dissatisfied with the club support structures which young players faced when they graduated from the academy, 'With the universities in the USA there was a strong alignment of values, and the institutions were eager to develop the young people holistically as a continuation of their journey, but the vast majority of the clubs in Europe were different. They primarily viewed our players as commercial assets; they weren't interested in providing wider support and they didn't see it as their responsibility. At the academy, our holistic approach prepared our players to perform optimally, while in Europe, there was a narrow focus on profit that paradoxically prevented them achieving their potential on the pitch.'

At the same time, and after 15 years in Africa, Tom increasingly reflected on his own journey, from a mindset of European superiority to recognising that Ghanaian society had culturally rich solutions that could be a guiding light for other nations, 'For so long, Africa has been viewed with a negative lens of corruption, poverty and violence, and as a young white guy moving to Ghana, I had arrived with an ingrained neo-colonial superiority that I knew best. It took years for this perception to be gradually unwound and to fully appreciate the strong values and culture which had survived colonial interference. I wanted to create an environment where local ideas and principles could thrive, and ultimately that meant stepping away from decision-making and empowering the team to lead.' Tom's value system was already reaping rewards in Ghana, but it couldn't be imposed on the clubs to which Right to Dream graduates were progressing in other parts of the world.

At a board meeting in 2013, Tom expressed his frustrations, 'I told them that all of the power was rested in Europe, and that the whole system felt like it was designed to stop us from progressing. It was rooted in a post-colonial relationship, with the European clubs taking the best talent without being truly invested in the wellbeing of the players, and without any genuine interest in the development of the communities from which they came.'

The board asked Tom how the situation could be addressed. 'We could buy our own football club in Europe,' he replied, in jest. 'I said it, I didn't mean it, but the board considered the idea and believed that we should do it.'

Tom was able to find additional investors and started an analysis process to identify a suitable club to purchase in terms of strategy and price point, 'We narrowed it down to a few countries including Portugal and Austria, and we also looked at Belgium, but felt that many failed attempts at Belgian player development in Africa would pre-define how the project would be received locally.' Instead, there was one country which stood out, 'Denmark would enable us to compete at the top level with a young team. Universal fluency in English would also be very helpful, both for our operational staff and for young players coming over from Ghana.'

FC Nordsjælland, an established Superliga club in Farum, a town in eastern Denmark, was pinpointed, and a cold approach was made to the owner. 'They rejected it,' says Tom, 'but a few months later their circumstances changed and they were open to selling. We also had the support of incoming head coach Kasper Hjulmand, who has since gone on to manage Denmark men's national team. He believed in our vision, and wanted to be a part of it.' In December 2015, a deal worth €10m was agreed, and Right to Dream took ownership of FC Nordsjælland, with Tom becoming one of the youngest club chairmen in European football history. FCN was purchased within a for-profit structure but declared a non-dividend policy on incorporation.

'The immediate challenge was to build understanding with fans and stakeholders in Denmark,' says Tom. 'There was understandably concern and uncertainty about our intentions, and about an experimental model that had never been tried before. We had to make the project locally relevant, and we made small adjustments to an already successful academy at FCN that would enable young people to be holistically supported as they were in Ghana. In the same way that my own understanding of Africa had been reversed, there was a process of trying to change perceptions in Denmark, to show that Ghana had values and approaches that could benefit western society. What if our model of holistic support, character development and purpose, rooted in African values, could be applied to young footballers in Denmark? Surely that would be a positive thing?'

Equally, Tom recognised that it must be a two-way process of learning, with the empowerment of local people to shape the project in Denmark, 'We never believed there was only one right way of doing things, but we did have an understanding that if we looked after the basics – an education, life-skills development, nutrition, good mental health – then we could let the local projects flourish independently, and share what they learned with each other. We organised exchanges for players from both academies to interact with each other, and this built a shared understanding that manifested in a common mission when players from both projects started to come through into the first team at FCN.'

Tom believes that as societies in Europe become more reflective of their past, and begin to look and think beyond the parameters of their own values framework, there is an increasing opportunity to create shared purpose, 'There is a long way to go, but with fractured societies like the UK and the USA, and with the negative consequences of individualism becoming more evident, people are starting to question what has been lost, and what can be learned from other parts of the world. Applying this to football, if principles of community, of giving back, of the successful few supporting the many can become a systemic part of how we develop all young players, then the likes of Juan Mata and Marcus Rashford won't be the outliers, they will be the norm.'

Since the takeover, the club has consolidated its position in the Superliga, consistently qualifying for the top six championship round, and placing third in 2017/18, which ensured qualification for the UEFA Europa League. These successes have been achieved with the youngest squad in Europe, averaging just 22, and with 80 per cent of the first team consisting of graduates from Ghana and Denmark.

A professional women's team and academy system has also been established, with the senior team progressing to the top flight, the Elitedivisionen, and winning the Danish National Cup in 2020.

Tom says, 'The achievements on the pitch, and the progression of academy players to bigger clubs such as Mohammed Kudus moving to Ajax and Mikkel Damsgaard to Sampdoria, both in 2020, have helped to build local confidence and pride in our approach, as well as generating funds to reinvest in future youth development.' In 2019/20, FCN was the 13th most profitable club in Europe with an operating profit of €2m, and in 2021 the transfer of Kamaldeen Sulemana to Rennes for €21m shattered the Scandinavian transfer record, 'Over the years many people have told us that a purpose-driven academy and club model cannot be sustainable or successful. We keep trying to prove them wrong.'

* * *

After his meeting with Jürgen in London in early 2017, when he had expressed his reservations about Common Goal, Tom had watched events unfold with interest, 'I was pleased to see that a good number of big names were signing up to the movement, and some of my colleagues in Denmark started to push for us to get involved.' Contact was re-established, and in early 2018 Jürgen and Thomas visited FCN's winter training camp in Murcia.

Jürgen says, 'I strongly believed that the Right to Dream and the Common Goal journeys must go hand-in-hand, and I proposed that FCN become the first club to join the movement. It helped that a number of Nordsjælland players, including Alex Rúnarsson, now of Arsenal, had independently taken the pledge to give 1%.'

'We saw it as an opportunity to further embed purpose at Right to Dream,' says Tom, 'and to join an ecosystem that extended beyond our own organisation.'

On 21 May 2018, before kick-off against FC Copenhagen in a Superliga play-off, FC Nordsjælland became the first club to join Common Goal, pledging 1% of their stadium revenues, including ticket sales, to the movement. The commitment was signed on the pitch by FCN chief executive Søren Kristensen and, on behalf of Common Goal, by Kasper Schmeichel, who had joined the movement in 2017. Søren said, 'We enter Common Goal without any hesitation or reservations. We are convinced that it is the right thing for us and for football.'

All ten members of FCN's management team at the time also made the commitment, with the 1% donation written into all new contracts for players and club staff, with the ability to opt out. 'It has helped to strengthen the presentation of our values,' says Tom, 'and has created a thread of purpose which connects everyone involved in the organisation including fans, players and staff.'

Jürgen adds, 'Many of the earliest football clubs started off existing to serve the community, and with FCN, Right to Dream has shown us that we can go back to these radical roots. The commercialisation of the game doesn't mean that purpose has to be left in the past. In fact, it enables us to do more, here and now.'

* * *

With the link between Ghana and Denmark successfully established, Tom and his management team started to consider the possibility of Right to Dream being scaled as a global concept, 'We looked at the City Football Group, which owns a portfolio of clubs around the world, and explored whether we could do something similar, but with purpose at the core.' Founded in 2013, and based on its flagship club, Manchester City, the City Football Group has gone on to variously buy and set up a global family of clubs in the United States, Australia, India, Japan, Spain, Uruguay, China, Belgium and France. The business model includes close collaboration between the clubs in terms of a common tactical philosophy, scouting and player sharing, enabling financial efficiencies and leveraged brand equity.

'We explored how we could build momentum for a similar concept based on the Right to Dream model, creating an ecosystem of clubs, academies and academic partners,' says Tom. 'It was a massive step to consider. We could keep the project small and fully within our existing influence, or we could give the idea wings and see the impact scaled, realising that we would lose an element of control in doing so. I saw that we should do the latter, but we would have to find high-net-worth investors who truly shared our ethos and ambition. We had a successful academy and club model, an exciting vision and a strong commitment, but at this level of investment, it proved extremely difficult to find genuine value alignment.'

There was, however, an existing supporter of Right to Dream – Loutfy Mansour, the CEO of Man Capital, the investment arm of the Mansour Group (valued at over US$7bn) – who was interested in the idea. Since 2013, when he supported the project philanthropically, Loutfy has been inspired by Right to Dream's work, and learning of Tom's plan for expansion, he initiated a conversation with his father Mr Mohamed Mansour, the founder and chairman of the family-owned conglomerate (for clarity, the Mansour Group is separate to Mansour bin Zayed Al Nahyan who is one of the principal owners of the City Football Group). Based in Cairo, the Mansour family are big football fans and have a rich family heritage in the game, with Mr Mansour's great uncle representing Egypt in goal at the 1934 World Cup in Italy. For some time, Mr Mansour and Loutfy had discussed the possibility of investing in football, and the idea of supporting the growth of Right to Dream would enable them to combine their love of the game with another of their great passions – purpose.

Tom says, 'We started a conversation about an investment based on our non-dividend model. It would enable us to continue pursuing income generation through commercial activities in the football industry, but would retain the reinvestment of profits into providing more opportunities for young people. On this basis the Mansour Group would not be taking funds out of the business and would only make money if they later sold the company for a profit, which they have been explicit in stating is not their intention. In effect, it would be an investment into growing the transformational impact of Right to Dream on young lives. We would also operate differently from many clubs where owners have to write a cheque every quarter to bring in new players and to keep things going. Instead, we would be building a self-sustaining model, and the fact that we had just made a profit at FCN, despite the impact of the coronavirus pandemic, showed the strength of our approach.'

Loutfy says, 'Right to Dream is a special organisation, and we love to be involved in special things and to help them grow. The model operates commercially, because that enables it to succeed and grow most effectively, but how we move forward will always be driven by a desire to invest the profits into more opportunities for young people.'

Mr Mansour adds, 'We were immensely impressed with what Tom had built. The values that he had instilled from the roots up at Right to Dream aligned with our values as a family, and the combination of football and education complemented our approach to empowering people across our portfolio of businesses. We were also excited by the opportunity to bring the project to Egypt, a country that loves football.'

The negotiations had started before the outbreak of the coronavirus pandemic, but the crisis only strengthened the desire of the Mansour family to buy Right to Dream. 'It showed us how broken and fragile the football industry is,' says Mr Mansour, 'and Right to Dream presented an opportunity to do things better and more sustainably.'

For Tom, the potential to keep ownership of the Right to Dream Group within Africa was very appealing, and the relationship that he quickly built with Mr Mansour also gave him confidence, 'My two previous inspirations, Alex Ferguson and George Weah, had great wisdom and charisma, and Mr Mansour is the same. We clicked, and his intention to work together for the long term, not just through the successes but also through the hardest and most challenging parts of our growth, matched my belief in how entrepreneurs can most effectively be nurtured and guided to the next level of success. In addition, we saw that it would be tremendously motivating for everyone at Right to Dream to know that the owners were not just in it to make a quick buck and move on, but because they believed in, and were a part of, our purposeful vision.'

Over several months a deal was negotiated, and on 20 January 2021 Right to Dream, including the academy and FCN, was sold to the Mansour Group in a deal valued at €120m, with Tom becoming a minority shareholder and chief executive of the Right to Dream Group, which remained a non-dividend company. The investment is intended to make the following possible: the creation of a new Right to Dream Academy in Egypt, additional funding for the existing academy in Ghana and FCN in

Denmark, the development and growth of a women's and girl's programme across the group, and the purchase of further clubs in new markets. 'In line with this,' says Tom, 'we want to strengthen our storytelling capacity, to show what is possible when you challenge the constructs that limit certain groups of people in society, and to inspire young people that they can achieve anything if they apply themselves and make changes that can transform the directions of their lives.'

With the new academy set to open in Egypt in early 2022, as he did in Denmark, Tom is keeping an open mind about building an approach and a curriculum that is locally relevant, 'It would be crazy to enter an ancient civilisation thinking that we have all the answers. The core pillars of character, academic and footballing excellence will remain, but we want an environment that will allow the best of Egyptian culture and talent to flourish. There will likely be strands that emerge in each location that we can take and share across the group, but we don't believe they should all be the same.'

At the time of writing, Right to Dream is in the process of purchasing a second club, in a new market. Tom says, 'We want to bring in other clubs where young people in the community are denied access to opportunities, and which can also be stepping stones for players coming through our academies in other parts of the world to progress their careers.'

A new management team is also being forged to conceptualise and drive forward a strategy for women's football. Tom says, 'I believe that women's football is being taken in the wrong direction and that there is an opportunity to change its evolution and build something better, with closer alignment to the original values and interpretation of the game. Inevitably, the game will be successfully commercialised, but it doesn't have to be created in the image of men's football, and perhaps it doesn't even have to be governed by FIFA.'

The expansion of Right to Dream is being guided by purpose, with social outcomes embedded within the fabric of the organisation more strategically and fundamentally than ever before. Tom says, 'In February 2021, Pippa Grange joined as head of purpose, bringing a wealth of experience in organisational culture, and leading a process of unlearning, purpose discovery and the creation of an identity, and a meaning, that goes beyond winning.'

As Right to Dream grows, Common Goal grows with it, with the 1% pledge extending across the group, and with Mr Mansour directing that a further US$2m should be invested in Common Goal, after a meeting with Jürgen and Juan. 'Jürgen and I are brothers in arms,' says Tom. 'We don't agree on everything, but we have a shared mission to transform football, and to put purpose at the heart of the game. We have a common goal, and everyone has a right to dream.'

48

The Common Goal Community

JÜRGEN PICKED up his pen and started to write. It had been a long time since he had composed anything by hand, other than a shopping list, but he felt that in contacting Jürgen Klopp, a handwritten letter would carry with it an authenticity that the Liverpool manager would appreciate. The five-page document was sent via Mats Hummels's agent, who also represented Klopp, and a few weeks later, in September 2019, Jürgen was on the rooftop of a hotel in Milan, discussing his compatriot's involvement in Common Goal. That night, the Best FIFA Football Awards were taking place at La Scala theatre, and Klopp was nominated for the Best Men's Coach Award. Jürgen says, 'We discussed that with moments of triumph come an extra portion of responsibility and, if he won, perhaps he could use the platform to send out a powerful message.'

A few hours later, Jürgen and Thomas took their seats in La Scala as the theatre filled with the stars and leaders of the game. Later that night, Lionel Messi and Megan Rapinoe would respectively pick up their sixth and first Ballon d'Or trophies, given to the best players in the world over the last 12 months. But for Jürgen, the big moment of the night was the men's coach award, and having won the Champions League with Liverpool, Klopp was named the winner, ahead of Pep Guardiola of Manchester City and Tottenham Hotspur's Mauricio Pochettino. In his unscripted acceptance speech, Klopp acknowledged his fellow nominees, and thanked his family, his team and his club, before concluding, 'I want to use that stage to say one thing … We are all here on the really good side of life … There are people out there who do not have the same situation. I'm really proud and happy that I can announce that from today on I am a member of the Common Goal family … If you don't know it, Google it. It's a great thing.'

That night, the Common Goal website temporarily crashed, as millions of people around the world followed the Liverpool manager's instruction.

* * *

Since the launch of Common Goal, new players have continued to join. Some are established professionals and well-known figures, while others are younger and just starting out in their careers. Every pledge is an endorsement of the movement, and while the initial rate of growth has slowed, the names keep coming: Pernille Harder, Christiane Endler, Timo Werner, Quinn, Paulo Dybala, Magdalena Eriksson, Michael Essien, Jessica Silva, William Troost-Ekong, Irene Paredes, Tim Parker, Vivianne Miedema and many others. Alongside Klopp, other coaches have signed up including Marco Rose, Oliver Glasner, Casey Stoney and Bo Svensson, as well as esports professionals including Michael Bittner and football freestylers such as Lisa Zimouche. In 2018, Eric Cantona joined as a mentor, working closely with Jürgen and Juan to grow the movement, and, as envisaged, Common Goal has grown to include people from the wider football ecosystem: media figures such as Melissa Ortiz and Alice McKeegan, and football executives such as former England player Eniola Aluko, who is now sporting director at Angel City FC in Los Angeles.

With approximately one new pledge per week, the total number of players is more than 200, with overall members standing at over 450. Jürgen says, 'On one hand it has been an incredible achievement. Many people said it could not be done, but we have brought together an amazing team of people to collectively drive purpose within the football industry. On the other hand, 200 out of 65,000 professional footballers worldwide is nowhere near fast enough.'

Jürgen and the team are working hard to expand the movement, and to encourage more peer to peer growth, something that has been particularly effective within women's football. 'Things have improved in the men's game,' says Jürgen, 'with players becoming more comfortable talking about social issues, but in women's football it is already a very natural topic and organic growth among players has generated many new sign-ups.'

To attract new members, and to motivate continued support and engagement of existing players, the Common Goal team are also striving to build links between members and the causes closest to their hearts. Juan says, 'Following my experience with Ashok and OSCAR in India, and a subsequent trip with Jürgen to Colombia to see the work of Tiempo de Juego, I always encourage my peers to visit the projects, and to see how their donations are making a difference.' Further trips have been organised, with Serge Gnabry visiting Tackle Africa in the Ivory Coast, his father's birth country, and Danish international Sofie Junge Pedersen travelling to Ghana where she spent time with Whizzkids United, learning about their work and delivering training sessions for young people in the programme. Remote links have also been established, with

Everton and England player Izzy Christiansen connecting online with Pauline, a young leader and coach at Society Empowerment Project, a network member in Kenya, and a player herself for the Kenya women's national team.

To date, more than €4m has been donated and distributed to Football for Good organisations via Common Goal. This includes Kick4Life, and in 2018 we applied to develop a project based on sharing our experience of setting up and running the social enterprises in Lesotho. Working alongside Football United in Australia and Tiempo de Juego in Colombia, among others, we jointly created and launched Social Enterprise Assist, with a range of tools and resources to support other network members in improving their financial sustainability. We subsequently supported organisations in Ghana, Kenya, Costa Rica and Myanmar, but it wasn't until the coronavirus pandemic, when many network members faced funding emergencies, that Social Enterprise Assist really came into its own.

Reflecting on nearly five years of Common Goal, Jürgen says, 'The biggest challenge that we face is capacity. We have an incredible staff team, but our long-term commitment to ensure that 90 per cent of donated funds go directly to the frontline, with only ten per cent used for running and growing the movement, means that we are always overstretched. The strength of Common Goal is the trusted relationships that we have built, and this becomes harder to sustain as the movement grows.' As a result, Jürgen sees the future of Common Goal as being increasingly decentralised, with organisations such as clubs, federations, companies and Football for Good organisations taking responsibility for growing and implementing the 1%.

Thomas says, 'We want to ensure that growth is not held back by the limited capacity of a central body, and at the same time we want to avoid building a large administrative team. Instead, we see Common Goal growing more independently and organically. There will still be a common validation process and a core team which coordinates the movement, but the money flows could be different, and the potential for growth can become much greater as more people and institutions take ownership of bringing new stakeholders on board. For example, an organisation like Kick4Life could organise some of its fundraising around 1% pledges that go directly to its work in Lesotho, sports brands could institutionalise the 1% across their product lines and operations to sustain their community interventions, or a club could encourage 1% contributions from its players, staff and fans to support its local community programmes. A similar model has evolved at One Percent for the Planet, enabling it to grow exponentially. We are also exploring how we can utilise new and disruptive technologies such as blockchain to ensure even greater efficiency and transparency in facilitating growth of the movement.'

In line with this evolution of the model, Jürgen envisages an expansion of impact beyond the existing streetfootballworld network, with more organisations and causes being supported through the movement. 'We have always had ambitions that are greater than our means, and with Common Goal we want to remove any barriers that could limit growth, whether that is our own capacity or because the network does not cover a particular country or social issue. To truly unleash the movement, we need to make it a home for everyone who is interested in using football for social change.'

In 2021, a proposal was put forward to reposition the streetfootballworld network as part of a much larger Common Goal Community. Network members were consulted, and with broad support for the change, a transition is planned in the near future. At Kick4Life, we had developed a fond attachment to the streetfootballworld brand, but we never felt it accurately reflected us or the majority of organisations in the network. Jürgen says, 'We have matured as a movement, and our growing stakeholder community needs a stronger and clearer identity, which Common Goal provides. The original streetfootballworld organisation will remain, but it will be renamed Common Goal, in line with our outward facing presence.'

Over the coming years, the Common Goal Community is expected to grow significantly, with many more organisations, clubs and player foundations coming on board, going well beyond the 150 organisations currently in the network. As part of this, a new quality seal is planned, providing accreditation, pathways for learning and growth, and a framework for implementing the 1% concept across the whole Football for Good sector. A new governance model will also be in place, with the creation of a congress which will meet regularly to debate and vote on key decisions. Jürgen says, 'It is an evolution of governance, with a new model of representation that will put more control over decision-making into the hands of the whole community.' Collective impact plans are also being agreed, ensuring that investment decisions are guided by the community, with the social capital of the movement leveraged according to that direction.

In addition to individual commitments, a range of companies and organisations have also joined the movement, including player agencies such as projekt b, BK Consulting, ROOF and Prosper EPA, and events including the World Football Summit and the Donosti Cup. FCN is also no longer the only professional club, with Oakland Roots in the USA making the 1% pledge, where Mike Geddes is now 'the first chief purpose officer in American sports and (I hope) not the last'.

In July 2021, during the delayed European Championship, Common Goal announced that Adidas was coming on board with an initial three-year commitment to pledge 1% of global net sales from footballs to Common Goal, with the aim of positively impacting 90,000 lives. With annual ball sales averaging €100m, it represents a big step for the movement, which Jürgen hopes will become permanent, with potential for expansion across product lines, 'There is an opportunity for brands like Adidas to show early leadership by collaborating in purpose-led partnerships. It is all about understanding who you are, not what you do when you have something left over or as an afterthought; who you are as a corporation, as an individual, as a government, as a country.' The online sports streaming service DAZN also joined the movement in 2021, making a multi-million-dollar pledge alongside a 1% global employee time and resource commitment.

Tom at Right to Dream recognises the progress of Common Goal in securing a wide range of support, and in generating valuable funds for social development, but says, 'It remains to be seen whether the movement can be successfully scaled and systemised across the football industry. With a club model founded on purpose at FCN we are fully bought in, but we need to see other clubs and businesses making the commitment because it makes commercial sense. Most companies are still rooted in pursuing charitable partnerships and initiatives that have a short-term commercial benefit, but with younger generations being more discretionary in their purchasing and brand loyalty on the grounds of social responsibility and revenue distribution, we will hopefully see this translate to longer-term, more embedded and more genuine commitments to initiatives such as Common Goal.'

With the ongoing growth of the movement, Juan remains heavily involved, finding time to contribute significantly alongside his career at Manchester United. Thomas says, 'Juan is extremely focused on his career as a professional footballer, but despite common misconceptions, players do have time to pursue other interests, and Juan is often involved, from reviewing new website designs to surprising candidates for new staff roles by attending interviews. He also supports strategic decision-making and attends key meetings, as well as welcoming new players taking the pledge.'

Juan says, 'Common Goal has brought greater meaning to my football career and has helped me to grow as an individual. It makes me feel good, and I'm curious and eager to keep learning through the process. I believe that other people in football are looking for something similar, and I hope that many others will join us.'

As Common Goal continues, so too does Jürgen's entrepreneurial endeavour, with the unceasing conception of new ideas and innovations. In a bid to mobilise billions of football fans around the world to take social action, he is now working towards the launch of a new initiative – Game of our Lives. Jürgen says, 'In 2019, when Megan Rapinoe spoke on the steps of City Hall in New York after the World Cup victory parade, she inspired millions of people. She said that we have to be better, we have to love more, hate less, and we have to know it is our collective responsibility to make the world a better place. People were ready to act, but they were not guided to any concrete actions or next steps, and had no framework to respond. This was not an isolated case, and now that we have a critical mass of influencers in Common Goal, we need a place where they can invite their audiences to team up with them for social change.'

Game of our Lives is intended to be that place, where a global community of football fans can take collective action, from signing petitions, promoting causes and sharing information, to making donations, volunteering at local projects and accessing resources to learn and empower themselves.

Vladimir says, 'Jürgen will not, cannot, stop innovating. He is a creative mind and he will keep generating new ideas and visions for the future. People will say he is crazy, sometimes he will be annoying and sometimes he will fail, but like he does on the pitch, he will pick himself up and go again, pushing forwards down the right wing until eventually there is a goal.'

For Juan, the personal connection with Jürgen has been central to the success of Common Goal, 'When you spend a lot of time together it is important that you have shared values and motivations. Through working alongside him, I have begun to see that Common Goal can be part of something bigger, that goes beyond Football for Good, and which integrates purpose across the industry. There are not many things certain in life, and I don't yet know what I will do after my playing career, but I do know that I will always, for as long as I can, be involved in trying to change the world through the game I love, football.'

49

The Pandemic

IN FRONT of me was a gathering of people, most of whom had already been a part of the Kick4Life adventure. And that's undoubtedly what it had been, an adventure. That's how it began, and despite the inevitable challenges and difficult times along the way, that's what it remained. What made it special was the shared nature of the adventure, and what started out with just Pete and I had grown, first to include close family and friends, and then to the many people we met along the way. The hopes and dreams that I had as a kid had always been underpinned by a desire to do something both adventurous and meaningful, and Kick4Life had been the vehicle for realising those ambitions. But without other people to share it with, it would have felt empty.

It was 20 February 2020, and the long-awaited fundraising launch for the Stadium of Life. Since repositioning as a purpose-driven football club, we had discussed the idea of having a small stadium, either on our existing centre plot or at another nearby site in Maseru. Over the years we had tentatively reached out to numerous funders, but it wasn't until one of our most enduring supporters, Preeti Shetty, then at the Football Foundation, put us in touch with the owner of SIS Pitches, George Mullan, that it started to become a real possibility. SIS is one of the world's leading pitch providers, and a year earlier, at a meeting in London, George had incredibly pledged to supply and fit an artificial pitch for Kick4Life in Lesotho as a part of their social commitment.

With the pitch locked in, we started to build a vision and a campaign for the Stadium of Life – 'the world's first football stadium purpose-built for social change'. In consultation with the staff team and the local community in Lesotho, we created a concept which included in-built health clinics for HIV testing and counselling, converted containers that could be used as classrooms and meeting rooms, and an outdoor stage for cultural performances. The most unique element would be the integration of nature within the stadium, with the possibility of a Biodiversity Stand, completely reserved for local flora, as part of our growing work on climate change education. With the pitch used for Football for Good activities, as well as providing a home ground for our teams, the Stadium of Life would serve our mission in multiple ways, enabling scaled programming for vulnerable youth and an extension of our social enterprise model. To bring the idea to life, we contacted our former country director, Daniela Gusman, who had since established rise – Relationships Inspiring Social Enterprise – an organisation which empowers young designers and architects in Lesotho and across sub-Saharan Africa. It was a great fit, and plans were drawn up. Now we just needed to raise the money.

As I looked out from the stage across the sixth-floor venue at Google HQ in London, hosted by one of our trustees, I saw many familiar faces: board members Dave Light and Alex Oswald, and some of our most loyal fundraisers such as Rosemarie Robinson and Shaun Jones. Motts was there too, and Chris had come over from Lesotho, shortly to be presented with an Outstanding Achievement Award in front of his parents. Wayne and Tess were sitting together near the front, and dotted around were representatives of many organisations that we had partnered with over the years: Beyond Sport, the Saints Foundation, the Laureus Sport for Good Foundation, Comic Relief, and the PFA among them. There were also some new faces, including several from the world of investment banking with potential to make significant contributions.

The event at Google was our big moment to build momentum for the campaign, with videos sent from our colleagues and participants in Lesotho, and a special message from Juan expressing his support and enthusiasm for the stadium. On the day we raised about ten per cent of the target, and having generated strong interest with some of the corporate attendees, we hoped that the remaining funding would follow in the coming weeks. But global events were about to take an unprecedented turn. We had followed the news about Covid-19 but we still expected the impact of the coronavirus in China to remain largely regional, like bird flu and SARS several years before. As it turned out, 20 February 2020, the day of our event, was the beginning of a market slide which reflected growing fears about the global spread of the virus, and within days it became clear that the situation was extremely serious. On 9 March – Black Monday – one of the largest stock market crashes in modern history occurred, and with it, all of the momentum for the Stadium of Life was lost.

England entered its first national lockdown on 23 March. Schools were already closed, and my daughters, now 14, would not return to classes until September. For the next few months it would just be the four of us at home. A week later, on 30 March, with cases surging in South Africa, Lesotho entered a national lockdown of its own. At Kick4Life, it meant an immediate cessation of our on-field programmes and football activities, with the Women's Super League and the men's Premier League both indefinitely suspended. We also had to close our restaurant and hotel, with an overnight loss of 25 per cent of our overall income, and no government furlough scheme to support staff salaries. The impact on funding would extend further, and still continues, with fundraising events such as the All Stars tours, which has been such a mainstay of our income model, shelved for the immediate future. All of this was happening at a time when the needs of our participants were greater than ever, and beyond the obvious and urgent demand for health education on hygiene and sanitation, there was an increase in mental health problems related to lockdown, a rise in protection issues and reduced access to medications for HIV positive youth, more vulnerable than ever to the impacts of poor immunity.

We went into survival mode, and started by looking at where we could reduce costs, with the exception of making any immediate staffing cuts at a time when livelihoods were most fragile. Some expenditure came down automatically as a result of reduced activity, notably energy bills and programmatic costs such as printing and transport, but we were also able to negotiate revised contracts with regular suppliers such as our internet provider and the hotel booking platforms to which we subscribed.

At the same time, we started to explore how we could adapt our Football for Good programmes to ensure that we could continue reaching our beneficiaries, as well as fulfilling our existing funding agreements, and in doing so covering salaries and other ongoing costs necessary to keep the organisation afloat. We knew that many young people in Lesotho had access to social media, and with a strong online presence already in place, thanks to the football club, we devised a plan to create animated versions of our health, life skills and gender education sessions. Our funders, including the Swedish Postcode Foundation, SOL Foundation, FIFA Foundation, Laureus Sport for Good Foundation, UEFA Foundation for Children and GIZ, supported the adapted approach, and by September the new animated content was being rolled out, featuring two virtual Kick4Life coaches, Kabelo and Lerato.

We also looked at how we could fundraise differently in the circumstances, moving our annual gala in New York to a virtual event, and researching new funding opportunities that were emerging through the crisis. We were able to access several unrestricted emergency funding pots from the likes of Comic Relief, enabling us to keep the whole staff team employed until the end of the year. Wayne and Tess, who had done so much to build the social enterprises, also chipped in through their new charity CHEF, raising funds that helped to cover the salaries of the former trainers, some who still worked with us, others who had already progressed to new opportunities.

The final area that we focused on was preserving the social enterprises, which became particularly challenging as society started to reopen, at least temporarily, in mid-2020. Business travel and tourism was, and continues to be, severely diminished, and we have faced numerous difficult choices, including whether to risk a full reopening with potential heavy losses, or to close completely until the situation improved, with a loss of staff and the subsequent task of rebuilding the business from scratch. Instead, we tried to balance the risks, with a series of scaled reopenings and closures as further lockdowns and restrictions were imposed and then relaxed. With the restaurant and hotel significantly hit, we worked on increasing and improving our domestic conferencing offering, while keeping a lookout for other new business and trading opportunities that might be emerging as a result of the pandemic.

As we reflected on our response, we realised that we had been instinctively working through a process – Reduce, Adapt, Fundraise and Trade – which conveniently created the acronym RAFT, and we started to consider how we could share the model with other charities around the world.

The impact of the pandemic on Kick4Life and our participants was being replicated on Football for Good organisations and their beneficiaries the world over. Some had fared better, others had fared much worse, and some were facing an existential crisis. Maybe we could play a part in a wider response.

We spoke to the team at Common Goal and suggested adjusting our current plans for Social Enterprise Assist, which had been focused on in-person workshops and on site consulting that could no longer happen. Instead, we proposed delivering remote emergency support across all areas of sustainability, and together with Anne and Esteban at Football United and Tiempo de Juego respectively, we created and started to deliver a new RAFT programme. With organisations facing urgent funding situations, we saw some quick and significant successes: Bauleni United Sports Academy in Zambia launching a soccer school enterprise that was generating US$500 in the space of a month, Open Field in Cameroon developing and opening a new equipment rental business, Grupo Desportivo de Manica accessing grant funding to continue their health and gender sessions in Mozambique. RAFT also gained additional funding from a Sport for Good Response Fund led by Laureus and Beyond Sport, and we were able to extend support to organisations using other sports: rugby in Eswatini and trail running in Afghanistan.

Meanwhile, in Berlin, the Common Goal team launched an emergency fundraising campaign, with donations distributed to the organisations most in need, and despite a significant financial impact on streetfootballworld itself, Jürgen says, 'We took a decision early on to interpret the crisis as an opportunity, and decided to scale despite the present situation of scarcity, accelerating towards our vision for 2030, and restructuring in order to focus on maximising football's contribution to people and planet. I think it was the first time that the football industry felt vulnerable; but instead of truly innovating and trying to create something more wholesome and sustainable, it feels like the goal is to return to the same relentless wealth generation, with the aborted European Super League taking things to a whole new, ugly level.'

Despite these developments, Jürgen believes that the initial global response to the pandemic, notably the collaborative development of vaccines, has shown us that humanity is capable of acting as one team, 'All of us have suffered one way or another, but what we have seen is an unprecedented global "team" effort to find a solution to a problem that was affecting everyone, everywhere. We have started to collectively understand just how interconnected we are, and we will see if global humanity will learn and act from the experience, or, once again, let political and economic interests prevail over the common good. If we can create a unifying global vision for the game, I truly believe that football, with its unrivalled fan base, and with its ability to transcend politics, has the potential to recapture that team spirit, and to contribute meaningfully to addressing other challenges that are even more pressing than Covid-19.'

* * *

During seven very successful years as director of football at Kick4Life, in which he had overseen promotion of our men's team to the Premier League and supported the establishment of the Women's Super League, Chris Bullock had become a well-known and respected figure in Lesotho football. For some time, a move to the Lesotho FA had been on the cards, and as the pandemic unfolded, a new opportunity emerged, with Chris accepting the position of deputy secretary general at the country's governing body. It was a brilliant progression, and an amazing story, and we were thrilled to see Chris transition to a new role where he would have great potential to drive positive change as a leading football administrator. Since taking on the post, he has helped to lead the Lesotho FA through one of the most challenging periods in its history, while significantly promoting women's football and creating a new social impact programme.

As Chris moved on, we also made a huge decision that would become the defining moment for Kick4Life in 2020. For several years we had discussed the possibility of moving to equal gender budgets for our men's and women's teams, and in doing so becoming the first top-flight club in the world to make the commitment. We knew that Lewes FC, a pioneering semi-professional club in England, had already made the move a few years earlier, but we could find no examples where both, or either teams, played in the top tiers of their country's football pyramids. It was an opportunity to make a powerful statement, nationally and internationally, at a time when lockdowns were triggering a dramatic increase in gender-based violence in Lesotho, and in many other parts of the world.

The main factor holding us back previously had been the financial difficulty of making the transition; without an increased level of funding for the women's team, we would have to significantly reduce our men's budget and in doing so risk relegation, undermining the positive message, and potentially demotivating other clubs from making a similar move. The strongest voice in pushing for the change had been our country director, Hana Taiji, who had travelled to her home country of Canada in early March 2020 for the funeral of a close family relative. Fully intending to return to Lesotho within two weeks, international travel was shut down as the pandemic took hold, and at the time of writing she has still been unable to get back, separated from her long-term partner for over 18 months. Nonetheless, Hana remained involved in supporting the management team remotely, and enthusiastically advocated for making the move to equal budgets which, relegation or otherwise, she felt was essential in order to truly match up to our organisational values.

We decided to go for it and invested in a PR campaign on the basis that it might help us to attract a headline sponsor for the club, enabling us to bring the women's budget up to the level of the men's, or even take both of them to a new height. Puky's story, of overcoming appalling gender-based violence and of subsequently forming our women's team, was a core part of the campaign messaging, and on 24 June 2020 the news broke, generating coverage far beyond what we had imagined possible. For most of the day the story was on the CNN home page, and was the main feature on the CNN Sport page alongside an article about Liverpool winning the Premier League for the first time in three decades. There was also prominent exposure on the BBC Sport website, articles in national newspapers such as *The Guardian* and numerous TV and radio interviews. Among our own professional networks, and in the wider Football for Good community, there was also a very positive and supportive reaction.

We had delivered a powerful message to the world, and in Lesotho we almost immediately started to see a shift in attitudes, both within the organisation and externally in the wider football community. Chris says, 'We had slowly started to see some changes since 2015 when we launched the Super League, with increased interest in women's football, amongst men and women. I'd pushed hard to generate more interest through social media, and developments at Kick4Life, such as Senate securing a scholarship in the USA, were changing the way people looked at the women's game. The equal budgets has moved things on again, massively, and has made it easier to drive forward change in my new role at the FA. We've also subsequently seen some of the bigger men's clubs, like Bantu, launch a women's team and invest in a women's development programme.'

We did, however, fail to attract a new club sponsorship deal, for which we had held out high hopes, with a unique opportunity for a company to align with such an important message at such a relevant time. We pressed on regardless, adjusting our budgets, and bringing through a few youth team men's players to replace some of the more established names who could no longer be kept on the payroll. With Chris moving on, we also had a new director of football, Lepe Seetane, who moved across from the academy staff, and for the first time, we had a fully Basotho senior management team. In Hana's absence, our deputy country director, Motlatsi Nkhahle, had stepped up, a move which became permanent in January 2021, with Hana moving to a capacity-building role. We always intended to make the transition to Basotho leadership, but perhaps for too long we had continued recruiting international staff for roles that could have been filled locally. We had spoken about the need to 'decolonise' our approach, but good intentions are not always enough, and sometimes it takes extraordinary circumstances to force decisions that you should have taken before. Hana had long been insistent that her successor should be Basotho. It just happened in a way that none of us could have foreseen. The pandemic has been the most difficult period that we have faced at Kick4Life since it was founded in 2005, and the challenges are far from over, but whatever lies ahead, we walk towards it locally led.

The 2020/21 seasons had been severely interrupted, but the men's Premier League resumed first, and despite our fears of relegation, our young team have held their own, maintaining a mid-table position. The start of the women's season was more significantly delayed, and we used the time to restructure and move towards the transition. On 18 March 2021, contracts were issued to the women's team for the first time, and Motlatsi informed us that many of the players were in tears as they arrived at the centre to sign, overcome by the significance of being recognised with a formal agreement for the first time. Puky says, 'I looked back to where we started and how far we had come. I believe in living my life to leave a positive mark, and this was a huge milestone, but it just motivated me to work even harder.'

When the Super League did resume, it was in a different format in order for the season to be completed in a reduced timeframe. Since the start of the league in 2015/16, Kick4Life Women had finished second on four occasions, and once third, with the dominant Lesotho Defence Force (LDF) winning the title every year. But with Senate Letsie temporarily back from her studies in North America, our team had an extra boost, and as the campaign progressed, there was a growing sense of belief that this might just be our year. On 11 July 2021, in a title decider against LDF, we prevailed 2-1, with two goals from Senate securing our first national title.

Back at my desk in England, I watched a video of the team in a huddle, singing and celebrating at the end of the game, and I reflected on the world of football that I had known as a boy in Southampton, when the women's game barely existed, and when those who did play were dismissed with derision. Thirty years later at Kick4Life, we had taken a small but significant step to move women's football forwards, and like Fútbol por la Paz in Medellín, emerging where and when it was needed the most, perhaps it was inevitable that it happened in a country like Lesotho, where gender inequality pervades every part of society. The person who had given the most in making it possible was Puky. She had overcome terrible personal challenges to become first a peer educator and a coach, before establishing the Kick4Life women's team, leading our gender programming, and promoting systemic change in women's football at a national level. In doing so, she has had the courage to keep telling her story. Every time she tells it, she suffers, but she tells it anyway, and every time she does, we move a little closer to a world where any girl, anywhere, can live, and play football, without fear.

* * *

In early 2021, I received a phone call from a number that I didn't recognise. I almost let it ring out, but decided to pick up, fully expecting to hear an automated voice. It turned out to be the owner of an English football club asking me about the Stadium of Life. A year earlier, I had sent their family foundation a fairly cold application, via someone Chris knew, and I hadn't thought too much about it since. In fact, after the pandemic kicked in I had almost given up on the dream of the stadium. For a few minutes, I was asked questions about the project, and as soon as the call ended, I thought of at least five things I probably should have said. A week later I received another call, and this time I answered without hesitation, with notes carefully prepared. Then it went quiet for a month or two before confirmation finally came through that we would receive a game-changing donation. We have come a long way since the long-distance dribble in Malawi, and although the construction has faced a number of pandemic-related delays, the Stadium of Life will be built, and our vision to empower every young person in Lesotho through football remains in focus. We kick on.

50

Reflections

WHEN THEY first moved to La Cala del Moral in 2017, Jürgen and Elida had spent most of their weekends working on the house, which had been neglected for many years. Now, with the most pressing decorations completed, the garden occupies more of their free time. Alongside two olive trees and two ageing palms, and among the many plantains, they have planted numerous fruit trees: papaya, mango, lemon, nectarine, orange, mandarin and banana, cultivating 'a true oasis, a treasured refuge where we can relax, disconnect and ground ourselves'. Part of the house has been converted into a rental apartment, with some of the décor handcrafted by Elida as part of a small upcycling business through which she converts discarded furniture and pieces of driftwood that wash up on the beach, giving them new life in the colours and iconography of Colombia. In the evenings, they sometimes meet with friends and neighbours, or dine out in one of the seafood restaurants dotted along the shore.

Remembering the moment in 1992 when Jürgen caught her eye in the lecture theatre in Medellín, Elida says, 'From that meeting of cultures, from the meeting of our love, I never imagined passing through so many places, meeting so many people and witnessing the acts of love and change of which people are capable in pursuit of a more just and liveable world. I believe in a destiny that presents us with paths; what we choose is our responsibility. Jürgen and I were born and raised in very different environments and cultures, and my life journey with him has not always been easy; it has meant leaving my country and my family, changing the direction of my career and reinventing myself. The biggest action in my life, and the one that gave me the most happiness, was having and raising my two daughters. I dedicated myself body and soul to being a mother, and now, looking back, I know I did well, I couldn't regret the path I chose.'

Before the pandemic, Jürgen travelled regularly, rarely at home for more than two weeks at a time. Now, for the first time in many years he has stayed in one place for an extended period, and, alongside Elida, has fallen into a daily routine that begins with walking their dog, Baloo, a Rhodesian Ridgeback, along the seafront just a three-minute walk from their home. The majority of Jürgen's day is spent in front of his computer, pausing for a late lunch in keeping with Andalusian time, before walking Baloo again before sunset, sometimes to the far end of the beach which is reserved for dogs, where once in a while they swim – Jürgen, Elida and Baloo.

During their walks together, Jürgen and Elida talk about their distant families and discuss the girls and the lives they are now leading in other parts of Europe. On some days Jürgen walks alone, with just Baloo for company, and in these moments he reflects on his life and career, and the people he has met along the way, 'I remember those early days in Colombia walking through the streets in search of direction, and the excitement of starting something new in companionship with Alejandro. I remember the difficult times in Berlin at the start, followed by that same feeling of shared adventure as we launched streetfootballworld, this time with Vladimir, Johannes and a growing network of friends from around the world. There have been difficult times, but they have always been on the road to something better. I do look back with emotion, but I tend not to dwell on past achievements for the sake of self-congratulation. I try to anticipate that things will happen, and if and when they do, I'm already moving on to the next thing, and the moment gets lost. But I am proud of never giving up, of being able to inspire some people along the way, and of never, to my knowledge, doing anybody harm.'

A nurtured aptitude for languages can perhaps be pinpointed as the personal skill which has contributed the most to Jürgen's journey, from his mastering of Spanish on the streets of Medellín, which subsequently enabled him to build so many important relationships, founded on shared sentiment and cultural understanding, to a fluency in English, which he describes as 'a necessary tool'. Reflecting on his personal attributes, he says, 'I struggle to tell myself what I'm really good at. After all these years, I still don't feel like I am an expert of anything. I have attended courses at Harvard Business School in Boston and THNK School of Creative Leadership in Amsterdam to improve certain skills that did not come so naturally, like communication, public speaking and some aspects of management, but when it comes to most things, I still tend to act on instinct.'

For Jürgen, the most important factor in all of his shared successes has been an investment of time, energy and honesty in building trust-based relationships, 'These haven't been constructed specifically with payback in mind, rather it is how I, and my closest colleagues, have instinctively operated, to appreciate, respect and value others. As a result, we can be disconnected from people for many years, without losing the strength of understanding and trust, with the link often bearing fruit for both parties much later.'

In line with this, Jürgen believes that relationships often have their moment, or moments, when the focus and interests of people and organisations align, 'Not every partnership is forever. Circumstances can sometimes bring us very close to other people, and then things change and our respective priorities take us in different directions, sometimes forever, sometimes to later reconverge. Understanding this is part of honest relationship-building.'

At the heart of this approach is Jürgen's conscious decision to 'give my trust easily to many, understanding that alongside the many positives, there will sometimes be disappointments. The episode with the Dissenters was the most difficult moment of my career, and something that I would not like to repeat, although we did come out of it stronger and with renewed direction, and that was thanks to the trusted relationships that we had built in the network and externally over many years. I continue to be trusting, although perhaps now I am more sensitive to some of the alert systems, such as Eli, who can help me to avoid potentially toxic situations.'

Jürgen also believes that accepting failure has been integral to much of the progress that he and others have made in promoting Football for Good, 'We have always aimed high, because if you don't aim for the impossible, you won't reach the possible, and if you don't fail then you haven't tried hard enough. Failure for me is part of the thought and building process, but in the development sector there is often an unacceptance of failure because you are directly impacting people or using resources that could have been applied elsewhere. But this culture prevents innovation and growth, whereas in the for-profit space, it is widely accepted that a significant proportion of new start-ups or products will fail, recognising that some will succeed and drive forward progress.'

This has been central to many of the greatest challenges that Jürgen has faced, to carve out space for innovation and to gain acceptance for failure as a vehicle for moving towards solutions that would otherwise remain hidden, 'We need more financial resources in our sector that are dedicated to properly testing solutions, and to finding new and better ways of doing things without the risk of reputational damage if the first attempt fails.'

While he has always tried to develop a culture of listening and contribution, Jürgen admits that he can be hard-nosed and immovable in the pursuit of vision, 'When you are convinced about the right direction, you sometimes need to resist strong headwinds, as we did with the launch of Common Goal. It doesn't mean that you stop listening, but people often have innate resistance to change, particularly when ideas are not yet fully formed, which is when I necessarily first bring them to the table. Because of this, ideas can be killed before they have the chance to mature. This is where the biggest internal frictions have occurred and sometimes it has been a lonely fight. I have tried to improve my communication and presentation of ideas, to bring people on board at an early stage.'

The intersection of Jürgen's personal and professional life has always been overlapping, with his career in Football for Good an extension of himself, 'I never wanted a job that ends at five o'clock and is forgotten until the next morning. It does come with challenges, but I've been very grateful for the opportunity to craft my own work-life balance over the years. It has helped us to be a happy family, and I like to think that I have been extremely present in our family life, but I am sure there are moments where I could have taken different decisions, or prioritised in a different way. I'm incredibly proud of my daughters, Sara and Hanna, and eternally thankful for the sacrifices that Eli has made along the way. None of it would have happened without her love and support.'

Many of Jürgen's professional relationships have also grown into personal friendships, 'I treat people the same in both spheres, and it would be unnatural for me to try to separate people into different categories, especially as those I work with often share the same interests and ambitions. It does sometimes make things more challenging, when difficult decisions have to be made that can negatively impact people that you care about, but through it all I try to stay true to my values, to interact with love, trust, empathy, and with a view on the common good.'

There have been many memorable dates and moments in the story so far: 17 May 1997 and the first session of Fútbol por la Paz, leaving Colombia for Germany on 25 January 2000, the first day in the new streetfootballworld office on 1 April 2002, the emotional final day of festival 06 on 8 July 2006 and the launch of Common Goal on 4 August 2017. But of all the dates, the one that remains most firmly etched in Jürgen's memory is 2 July 1994, the fateful day when Andrés Escobar – the Gentleman of Football – was gunned down in Medellín, 'Over the years, as I have met many inspirational people and seen many incredible acts of courage and kindness, new drivers have been added, but the moment that still motivates me the most, still pushes me on, and keeps me focused on maximum impact and purpose, is the senseless killing of that wonderful man.'

Jürgen's footsteps into the past are always, predictably, with an eye to the present and the future. What can be learned? What can be salvaged and recycled? What new way forward can be forged in pursuit of impact? How do we reach beyond the next horizon and create a new version of the future yet to be imagined? On some days, hot desert winds blow across the Mediterranean from Africa, and the people of La Cala del Moral take shelter in their homes. On other, cloudless mornings, when the sea lies flat like a millpond, Jürgen can make out the coastline of Morocco; he contemplates the grandfather that he never met, and the unknown cousins that might be there. For years, he and his father have spoken of taking a trip together, to connect with the land and a culture that represents a dormant part of their heritage. But for today, at least, he returns home, and continues with his mission, to change the world through football. He makes a coffee and sits at his desk. The doors to the garden are open, and the olive trees sway gently in the breeze, casting shadows in the room where he works, and the only sound is birdsong.

The Third Half

51

Radical Football

IN THE first half of the 20th century, English football manager Jack Reynolds introduced a new system that would go on to revolutionise football tactics. Born in Whitefield in Greater Manchester, Reynolds played as a winger for various clubs in the first decade of the new century, including Manchester City, Sheffield Wednesday and Watford, but he is remembered most as a manager, with three spells at Ajax totalling 25 years. During his time in the Netherlands he developed an approach to teamplay, whereby every outfield player could play in every position, creating a fluid and flexible system that was dependent on the adaptability and technical ability of every player. It became known later as Total Football.

Over the coming decades, similar tactical approaches were used to good effect in various parts of the world. At club level this included River Plate in Argentina in the 1940s, Burnley's English champions in 1959/60, and Pelé's Santos who dominated Brazilian football throughout the 1960s. On the international stage, the Austrian 'Wunderteam' of the 1930s and Hungary's 'Magical Magyars', inspired by Ferenc Puskás in the 1950s, both came close to winning the World Cup with an attractive style of play that was founded on the same principles as the teamplay pioneered by Reynolds at Ajax.

It wasn't, however, until the 1970s that Total Football became widely recognised, not only as a tactic but as a philosophy, containing fundamental values about how the game should be played. With the seeds sown by Reynolds, it is unsurprising that this happened in the Netherlands, championed by a generation of exceptional players, none more so than Johan Cruyff. With a pure brand of Total Football, Ajax won three consecutive European Cups in the early 1970s, with the national team finishing runners-up in both the 1974 and 1978 World Cups. The Dutch approach was based on extreme fluidity, maximising use of movement and space, and a high press that didn't rely on players falling back into a single fixed position when the opposition had possession. The system, like Cruyff as an individual player, was an expression of artistry, with a style of play that became synonymous with intelligence and beauty.

Following his playing career, Cruyff went into management and, after a spell at Ajax, moved to Barcelona, where he once again revolutionised football tactics. It was an evolution of Total Football, retaining many of its facets – the importance of technique throughout the team, the high press, and a focus on movement and space, but with an additional emphasis on movement of the ball in order to keep possession. Under Cruyff, Barcelona won four consecutive La Liga titles and secured their first European Cup in 1992, but his greatest legacy at the club was his philosophy, which later saw Barcelona (and the Spanish national team, featuring Juan Mata) achieve huge success in the years after his departure. Led by Pep Guardiola, one of Cruyff's former players, Barcelona developed tiki-taka, a further evolution of Total Football, with short passing, rapid movement and extreme possession which mesmerised opponents. Football was played in a way that was previously unimaginable.

* * *

In The First Half, I told the story of Jürgen as one of the pioneers of Football for Good, with the creation of Fútbol por la Paz in Medellín in the mid-1990s. He soon discovered that he was not alone, and that there were other people around the world using football as a vehicle for social development, in a great diversity of contexts. These early Football for Good projects materialised independently, but Jürgen envisioned what might be possible if they were connected, and this was realised through streetfootballworld and the creation of a movement, exponentially accelerating the growth and impact of the sector. The story of this emerging movement was told in The Second Half, with my own journey at Kick4Life, an example of how collaboration and collective action enabled far more impact than would have been possible if we had ventured alone. It also documented how Football for Good has, in the last ten years, begun to influence, and leverage, the football industry in pursuit of a new level of sustainable social impact.

Total Football changed the game on the pitch through a groundbreaking system, an innovative tactical approach and ultimate teamplay. Can a similar transformation occur off the pitch, in the management, administration and ownership of football, so that it is defined, no longer by money, but by purpose? It seems an impossible idea, but in the same way that Total Football emerged in isolated pockets before many of its components became mainstream tactics and features of the game, Jürgen believes that the beginnings of a new movement – Radical Football – are already under way, 'In the last ten years we have seen a growth of purpose-driven approaches and initiatives within the football industry. These go beyond Football for Good and the practical application of football as a tool for social development, which often exists on the fringes of the football ecosystem. And they go beyond Corporate Social Responsibility in terms of football businesses, clubs and federations having a social commitment alongside their main activities. Instead, these organisations are being driven by and are systemising purpose, and they are embedding social impact within their structural DNA.'

Common Goal is a leading industry-wide example of Radical Football, seeking to mainstream giving across the football ecosystem, with Right to Dream and Kick4Life FC pioneering new club-level endeavours with potential for replication in terms of their purpose-driven objectives and commitment to systemic change. These examples, among others, emerged from the Football for Good community, with the charitable and social enterprise sectors moving into and changing the football industry. But Radical Football is by no means confined to this sphere, and there are a growing number of purpose-led approaches appearing from within the more traditional and established structures of the game. These are happening in different parts of the world, and in different parts of the football ecosystem; individuals like Juan and Megan, clubs such as Oakland Roots in the USA, integrating purpose across their operations, and Forest Green Rovers in the UK who are pioneering a range of eco-innovations including a fully vegan model. Changes are also happening at federation level, with the Norwegian FA becoming, in 2017, the first of a growing number of associations to commit to equal gender pay for their national teams. And there are companies such as Adidas who, as part of Common Goal, have committed, as a starting line, 1% of their global ball sales towards driving social impact.

The attempted breakaway of a European Super League in 2021 has created an environment where fans are questioning, more than ever, the essence of football. The breakaway failed, but with all the changes of the last 30 years the industry has never felt more remote from the concept of a people's game. Jürgen says, 'In a world facing so many challenges, this magnificent game, which binds people together like nothing else, must realise its potential and play a bigger role in protecting and improving our collective future. Then it can truly be called the people's game once again, not just because it is popular, nor purely because we have a sentimental attachment to it, but because it is organised and exists to benefit society – people and planet. Football has been entrusted to the football institutions for exactly that reason, and not to reduce this unique game to yet another branch of an entertainment industry and the fan to a simple paying customer.'

In 2030, two major global events occur. Firstly, it is the deadline for the United Nations Sustainable Development Goals (SDGs), a collection of 17 interlinked Global Goals for achieving a better and more sustainable future, including health and wellbeing, education, gender equality, clean water and sanitation, reducing inequality, sustainable cities and communities, responsible consumption and production, climate action and peace, justice and strong institutions. The goals were created in 2015 by a wide range of societal stakeholders with ambitious and critical 15-year targets and indicators towards 2030, with the vision that we collectively take responsibility for achieving them – governments, businesses, development agencies, communities and individuals. Secondly, it is the centenary year of the men's World Cup, 100 years since the first global tournament in Uruguay in 1930, with billions of football fans set to unite once again around a shared passion. 'These two events present an unprecedented opportunity to drastically increase football's contribution to society,' says Jürgen. 'But we must start now. As a global community we are already a long way behind the SDGs, and while football is not a panacea for all of the problems in the world, we cannot afford to accept that its enormous potential contribution remains untapped.'

The response to the coronavirus pandemic, and notably the rapid creation of vaccines, has shown us what can be achieved when we, as humanity, take collective and urgent action. What if we apply the same teamplay and energy to transforming football, to replicating and pioneering radical approaches to ownership and administration, to taking meaningful and drastic environmental action within the industry, to sustaining and growing Football for Good interventions, to promoting a purpose-driven culture that inspires innovations yet to be thought of?

'We can do all of these things,' says Jürgen. 'We must. But we cannot do it alone. We need to find new and radical ways of collaborating that enable us to go beyond the accepted possible, and to find big and collective solutions. This is not a request for football to give something away, it is a rallying cry that we can make it better.' With 85 per cent of Generation Z believing that companies and industries should stand for more than profit, Jürgen argues that the need for Radical Football is, in fact, essential to the sustained extreme popularity of the industry, 'These are the fans of today and tomorrow, they want change, and we need them to demand it. The drivers can't be the appetite for power and money any more, purpose must be the driver.'

In the coming 11 chapters we ask the Radical XI – a team of leading thinkers and innovators from the worlds of football, media, business and development – how we do it, how we change the industry, how we can dramatically increase football's contribution to the SDGs, how we create a story with a narrative powerful enough to mobilise a global community of football fans in pursuit of radical social change, and how, by 2030, we create a movement that radically and permanently transforms the character and nature of football.

52

Love Football – by Katja Kraus

*Katja won multiple trophies as a goalkeeper
with FSV Frankfurt and the German national
team, including three national titles, four DFB
Cups and the European Championships. After
her playing career, she worked in marketing and
communications including a role as press speaker
at Eintracht Frankfurt before becoming the first
woman on the board of a Bundesliga club, at
Hamburger SV in 2003.*

WHEN I was a little kid – maybe eight or nine years old
– even before I played soccer in a club myself, I spent every
weekend at the sports ground of my home club Kickers
Obertshausen. From Saturday at noon, when the little ones
started to play, until Sunday afternoon, when the whistle
blew for the match of the men's first team. Not only did
I watch all the games, but I also took notes, which I later
catalogued at home: team line-up, evaluation of each
player, remarks about the game. At the time, my parents,
in particular, thought that was strange.

When I was able to calculate in larger numbers, I worked
out my remaining lifetime in European Championship

and World Cup tournaments. As a child, this resulted in a thoroughly reassuring number; today, as I approach the single-digit range, each individual tournament takes on a growing significance.

At school, among girls, I was always 'the soccer player', the only one! And the one who didn't go on class trips so as not to miss any training sessions. When I joined a soccer team, with men, and finally felt that I was joining a community to which I belonged, devaluation and sexism were open and commonplace. Prejudice against women playing soccer, the ritualised calls for a jersey swap after every game, no one found it encroaching or even hurtful.

When I became press officer at Eintracht Frankfurt after my soccer career, I was already denied suitability before I could make the first mistake. Without my own career as a long-time Bundesliga and national player, I wouldn't have had a chance – and yet it always remained just women's soccer. Later, when I spoke to the club members for the first time as a board member of Hamburger SV and actually had quite respectable figures and content to present, a substantial number of those present shouted 'Undress!' as I walked to the lectern. Among my male colleagues, no one did that.

Examples of minor everyday discrimination and structural inequality have been countless over the years. I did not problematise this at the time; instead I just worked harder. Today I problematise it because so little has changed, even if people no longer shout jersey swapping or undressing. But the decider in sports continues to be a homogeneous group of middle-aged men.

That's why it's so important for me to share my little personal story. Because I have always been different. And because there is still far too little room in the soccer business for people who are different. Because there might be a slow growing awareness of diversity, but there's still a long way to go before there's an understanding of what inclusion means.

That it means recognising the benefits of difference and giving people who are different the feeling that they belong. This requires the willingness to change one's own behaviour.

Homogeneity is comfortable. Divergence is exhausting. But only in different perspectives and approaches lies the chance for change, and for the best solutions to be found, in a time with increasingly complex challenges.

Homogeneous groups develop inappropriate feelings of superiority. A closed system allows only those solutions that the system legitimises. The 'can do solution' from hedging, instead of the most promising or daring one.

Soccer is in a crisis of confidence because it lacks sensitivity to social developments. Because it does not represent the people who love soccer in their tremendous diversity.

It is not in keeping with the times that there are no women in the leadership of a Bundesliga club, or a female president of a national association. That impulses from the outside are far too few, and that young people are excluded from decision-making. I myself did the most radical, courageous things at the beginning of my professional life. And even if experience is an inviolable value, it is strengthened further in combination with the impartiality of youth.

There are tons of studies that prove the value of diversity for businesses. That highlight the economic and cultural benefits. The expanded opportunities in a competitive job market are self-explanatory. And the social stimulus role of sport should be an obligation for everyone who bears responsibility in soccer.

It has long since ceased to be a matter of courtesy to allow women to participate. It is an economic necessity. In the future, diversity will be a competitive advantage and good governance will be a differentiator.

The facts are known to all. And yet they are met with the same arguments. Arguments against a diversity quota on grounds of competence. A cheap argument when at least 50 per cent of the population has not yet been able to make a decision. Or I often hear that there are not enough women available to take on leadership roles. Because, of course, they have not yet been able to penetrate a hermetic system. Because there are almost no role models. And the soccer business has long been turned into a secret science that is only explained to former professional soccer players.

There are, of course, women who can run soccer clubs – who can lead in business, in politics and in sport. What is lacking is the will to let them. To change this, you have to issue invitations, create conditions and set the framework wider than, for example, the regional associations of the DFB have just done again with their criteria for filling the DFB presidency.

Because this is still the case, and because there are too few men in decision-making positions who are willing to drive change and take action, we founded the initiative Fußball kann mehr (Football can do more). This is an alliance of nine women who love soccer and who have all had prominent careers in the game. The referee, the national goalkeeper and mother, the TV commentator, the chair of the supervisory board, the fan representative, and so on. They have all always been 'the one and only'. And they have all had the same experiences, which now bring us together to work towards becoming many. So that real change happens.

Soccer can then once again unfold its inherent power. So that people can identify with it again, so that spectacular games continue to create incomparable community results. That children continue to play soccer because it is one of the few places where values are conveyed.

But only through change will soccer be fit for the future. Because society is changing. And because people have a legitimate expectation for it to be impactful, spectacular, inclusive and diverse. Good governance will be the differentiator in the future, with good decision-making that is driven by facts, but also by love.

There is a lot of talk about love in soccer. Especially by those who believe they love it, and understand it, in a special way. More than others. And they derive a right of ownership because soccer belongs to them.

But love is divisible. And so is soccer. That's what makes it so special. And that's why we need people in charge who love soccer so much that they want to share it with everyone.

53

Another Way – by Dale Vince

Dale is founder and owner of green energy company Ecotricity and chairman of Forest Green Rovers (FGR), a professional Football League club in England. Recognised by the United Nations as the world's first carbon-neutral club, FGR is fully vegan and has been described by FIFA as the greenest football club on the planet. Dale is a UN Climate Champion for Sport.

FOOTBALL NEEDS to green itself up, not more or less than any other sector of society – or any other sport. We all need to take responsibility for the impacts we have on the environment. And we need to do so with greater urgency.

How to go about this is a good question, especially for any organisation relatively new to the issue.

This is my advice. Start at the core. Don't imagine you can bolt the environment on to your existing operation or just add environment polices to your current playbook – you can't deal with this through a CSR programme (Corporate Social Responsibility) – those are fig leaves, after the event mitigations, designed more for public consumption than actual impact.

They are BS.

You need to change the fundamentals of your organisation. Make the environment of equal importance to whatever your main purpose is. Put the environment into all of your thinking and decision-making. Start at the core. Change your DNA.

I did this with Forest Green Rovers (FGR), ten years ago. If you've not heard of us – we're reckoned to be the world's greenest football club – by FIFA and the UN. It's a great accolade on the one hand – but an indictment of our entire sport on the other. I mean, how can a club as small as FGR have done so much more than clubs with orders of magnitude more at their disposal? It's because we care. And we dare.

It's about willpower, starting at the core (to get it right) and being bold. Less bold than it was ten years ago, when we started – but still, to many, the things that need doing will seem bold, even radical. It's not as radical as it looks and the reception your fans will give is better than you think – that's our experience.

We use a simple template in all of our work, with a focus on energy, transport and food. These three areas of life are responsible for 80 per cent of all of our carbon footprints, personally – and the same holds true for organisations of all shapes and sizes. Including football clubs. It's about how we power ourselves, how we travel and what we eat.

At FGR, we installed solar panels on our roof and we power ourselves 100 per cent with green energy. We installed electric car charging points so that our fans could come to a game in the electric cars they didn't yet have – and get home again; quite vital. Most radically of all we changed the menu. All the food and drink we serve, to everyone (players, staff and fans), is plant-based; call it vegan by all means – though we've found that label to be unhelpful.

We've done other stuff, of course: banned single-use plastics and sugary drinks, achieved zero to landfill and UN certified zero carbon status. We have an organic pitch and we collect the water from underneath it – to use again. We have wildlife borders, slow worms and wild orchids. We've done all sorts of stuff around the edges of the three big things.

And we take the time to explain what we've done and why. We don't preach or lecture, don't tell people what to do. We do the things we believe in, show how it works, how it could work for them – and hope that people take some of that away with them, and start to change how they live. And we've seen that work. Players and fans have embraced 'another way' to live.

That's the name of the road we're on by the way – we changed it to Another Way; it's a simple, small but bold signpost to our club philosophy.

And we've seen it work far beyond the immediate boundaries of our club. Last year our global media footprint was five billion impressions! We have over 100 fan groups in 20 countries of the world. Some of these are fans of football, some of the environment – increasingly fans of both. We can see that we've not just created a new kind of football club, but a new kind of football fan too.

We're founding signatories of the United Nations Sport for Climate Action program – which seeks to engage the entire world of sports bodies and fans in the fight against climate change. It's an improbable place for us to be, from a simple rescue of our local football club ten years ago.

The combination of football and the environment is improbable, counter-intuitive – even now, ten years later, the fact that we are vegan is the big media talking point, and for other sport organisations – who want to know how this can be done without having a fan riot. This goes back to my earlier point – it's not as radical as it appears and fans will respond better than you think. It's time to be bold.

Sport has no greater or lesser responsibility to green itself up than any other sector of society. But it has a unique ability to reach people. Sport is an incredibly powerful, influential platform. That gives us a unique responsibility – to use it for good.

Start at the core, change your DNA, be bold and brave – it is easier than it looks – and join us.

54

Everybody Football
– by Khalida Popal

*Khalida founded Afghanistan's national
women's team in 2007. She was team captain
and the first woman to be employed by
the Afghanistan Football Federation, before
death threats from the Taliban forced her to seek
asylum in Denmark in 2011. She subsequently
founded Girl Power, an NGO which promotes
empowerment of women through football,
and since 2018 she has also been commercial
coordinator in the women's football department
at FC Nordsjælland. Since the return to
power of the Taliban in 2021, Khalida has
worked tirelessly to secure protection and support
for Afghanistan's female footballers.*

I'LL TELL you how you know the power of football. You
know its power when it's gone. You know when football is
taken away from you.

Twice in my life, football has been taken away: once
from me, and once from the people I cared about. I'm going
to tell you about both.

To understand these times in my life, you need to understand a separation between different worlds of football. I call these worlds: *everybody football* and *material football*. I realise that narratives of 'them' and 'us' are often not helpful. But when we are talking about a division that's real, unnecessary, and most of all consequential, I think we need to call it by its name.

When I say *everybody football*, what I mean is the essence of football: as an expression of love, of peace, of determination, co-operation, and of self-realisation. Football as: *I am here*. Football as: *you matter and I matter*. This is a game of fulfilling human potential, football as a solution. Football for *everybody*.

It's different from *material football*. That's the game we watch on screens. Big salaries, big clubs, big sponsors. Hospitality, private jets, and first-class service in heated seats in plush stadiums. Fans paying more than they can afford, just to see the team they love. In this football, you must have everything to be counted. All the material things. It's a game that says you lose significance when a game is lost, and you gain it when it's won. Suits and lots of men (sorry men, it's kind of true!). The technology around the game changes sometimes, and the uniforms get more fancy, but *material football* fights to stay as much the same as it can.

You see, I was born in Kabul, Afghanistan. I have fought for *everybody football* over many years. First, I fought for the right to play football for women in my country. Then, when I was forced to leave, I fought from afar against the sexual abuse of my team-mates. Then, most recently, when the 'freedoms' that we so briefly enjoyed were lost to the return of the Taliban, I fought to help my female athletes escape with their lives. In other words: I know what it is like to fight for the game I love, the *everybody* version.

My game? Our game! It's for *everybody*. It's a game of claiming your rights as a player, a woman, a person of colour, a minority, a disabled person. It's a game of being. It's a game happiest when it's free, and without too many lines, rules and uniforms. That's the game I love. That's the game I played with the girls as we fought to build the first ever Afghan national team for women. That's the game you probably play. If you're reading this, you can grab a friend and walk out your door and play it right now. And that is a power.

If you doubt that it's a power, think about this simple fact: if you're a girl in Afghanistan today, you cannot. You can no longer just play.

The sad thing about the separation between the two versions of football is that it has consequences. As *material football* tries to stay the same, *everybody football* is fighting for the value of being different. We fight to express our right to live, play and participate, while the other side of the game fights to protect commercial revenues, viewing figures, and the right to spend more on a player than it costs to buy most clubs. As *material football* tries to stay the same, voices that say 'things are not all fine' can be difficult to accommodate.

Think about it in wider society for a second. It's the same thing. Social movements, oppressed peoples and marginalised narratives struggle for representation. They fight for change. The institutions – strong, but hard of hearing – they fight for the status quo. There, too, the separation that exists between two versions of progress means change is only ever incremental, and only over very long periods. Revelations about the truth of what might be happening at the margins can be treated as difficult.

I didn't know about the separation between the two worlds of football the first time football was taken away.

When I started playing, I thought we were all playing the same game. But then I learned that people like me are outside the *material* game.

As it turned out, playing the game in Afghanistan, if you're a girl, is a very dangerous hobby. First, someone tried to kidnap me 12 years ago. Then, I was accused on national television of being a terrorist. When a bomb went off at the federation's HQ in Kabul, and I was first blamed, and then told my life was in danger, I knew that Afghanistan was telling me to go. It was telling me: you cannot play football any more. You play, you die.

Think about it: the energy in the game was so strong, so disruptive, that the old forces of supremacy in my country believed that if I continued to play it – just play – that they would have to change. They would need to kill me, or make me run, to free themselves from that. That's power. I couldn't understand it at the time, but when I look back now, I feel that power. That's how I know now: they had to take it away from us. They had to force me and my family to flee.

Then I felt the power of football through its absence. It had been taken, and I was heartbroken. I had lost my home, my activism had created the conditions for my family to lose theirs, my mentor (my grandfather) and my passion – that ball – were now lost to me also. I wept for months, as I fled across the border to Pakistan, then India, and later to Europe. My mother and father endured even harder times, first in refugee camps in the Middle East, before we were reunited in Denmark, eight years later (yes, when the game was taken away from me, so too for a very long time were my parents).

But when they told me I couldn't play football, they changed me. I had always been a fighter, but I became stronger than them in that moment. After grief, first came anger, and then determination for the women of Afghanistan. From abroad, I began to speak. I used my voice. At some stage they must have realised it was easier to have me working with them than against them (wink). When the Football Federation reapproached me and asked me to lead the national women's team from my new home in Europe, I said: I can do it, *I must do it,* and I can do it better than anyone. I wanted to give something to the women of my country, who could perhaps feel the football I used to love. I wanted to turn my pain into something positive.

My rediscovered optimism was short-lived. This was the second time I was reminded of the power of football. This time, it was taken not from me, but from others. It was when I discovered that those same old forces of tradition that had made me flee, now felt so threatened that some among them decided to sexually abuse my team-mates. And when those women found the courage to speak out, football was taken away from them also, as they scrambled to escape with their lives, leaving behind their country, their families and their futures.

In the weeks building up to the revelations, I got lots of reminders of the good of football; lots of opportunities to think about the freedom of football. There were matches against international opposition in amazing places on beautiful green-grass pitches. There were meet-ups, dinners, and wonderful evenings spent talking about everything and anything. Jokes, laughter. There was one training camp in Mexico, I will never forget it: the happiness, the moments. A reminder that in other places in the world, the experience of football was shared. There were people with very few material things, just like in my home country. Yet still they created wonderful moments through the game. Small communities where football was really something, and when it was played, the whole community feels like they have everything. Moments: sandals as goalposts, skirts pulled up, bare feet, avoiding rocks. That's football truly played. That was our football. And as we felt it there, it was like home.

But what I thought was a safe little bubble, away from the pressures of family and tradition in Afghanistan, had in fact been infected by a secret culture of abuse on the part of officials working with the team. Those old architects of male supremacy felt so intimidated by the power of women playing football that they had to dominate them, oppress them, and take away their right to their own bodies. Their dreams of realising their freedom on those beautiful green-grass pitches turned into nightmares in a locked dark room.

I felt terrible. Those poor girls whom I had recruited, in the naïve hope that they would feel only the best of the game. I thought about their parents who I had gone door-to-door to canvass back when I lived in Afghanistan, who put their faith and their daughters in my hands; 'after god, we trust you' they'd said. When I thought of that, I knew I could never return that feeling of innocence to them. But I could try to find a kind of justice for them. Now that I knew about what had been happening, I had to try.

So, I went to battle again. And I used the power I have. My power is my voice. It's a real power. If I don't use it as a force for good, I feel irresponsible. And so, I used it.

A long fight ensued, one well documented in international media. It took many months. The fight in fact was a fight against a broken system in football. We learned that there had been reports, earlier in 2017, given to the federation and to FIFA, but these had become stuck because no official channel for such complaints existed. The system did not have a strong enough fail-safe to protect against abuse.

This fight led, eventually in 2019, to the ban of Afghan football officials, and the issue of an international arrest warrant for the former president of the Afghan Football Federation, Keramuudin Karim (who went into hiding, where he remains).

But it took years for this small redress. Too long. Meanwhile, women suffered.

Every time I think about it, I ask myself: how can the organisations, the governing bodies, the institutions see all this and not do more? Why did it take so long? How do they forget these injustices and turn back to *material football*, as if everything everywhere else is all okay?

I cannot turn away. Perhaps the separation between our worlds of football is a separation of experience. When you are a young girl and you are being exploited, you know injustice. You'll never forget it. You know injustice when you are forced to flee for playing the game you love. You'll know injustice when you are forced to hide your sexuality from your team-mates. You'll know injustice when you are booed and verbally abused because of the colour of your skin or your religion. Maybe that's why the institutions are slow to force changes, and why they are so slow to change themselves: they are populated, in the most part, by those who don't truly know injustice. They can't feel it because they haven't experienced it, perhaps.

Furthermore, I'm not sure if the institutions from *material football* know the beauty of my football, and its richness. I wish and hope that they get to know it. Because *everybody football*, though it is vibrant and real, is also under threat from exploitation and marginalisation. Though it is full of the power of that ball, it is also vulnerable. Reinforcing *everybody football* requires that the leaders of *material football* add diverse voices from the more inclusive side of their game to their ranks. And not as tokenism: the prestige side of the game must truly listen to those voices and act on what they say.

Can the two footballs stand together? I hope so. But right now, we are not. To fix this, we are all responsible. Not just the people like me, my brave team-mates, and our voices.

Don't wait for football to be taken away before you discover its true power. And once you feel it, use that power for something good.

Something for everybody.

55

Natural Football
– by Pippa Grange

*Pippa is a doctor of sports psychology and
a culture coach working across elite sports
and business internationally. As head of
people and team development at the Football
Association, her strategies for 'fearing less' were
widely credited with transforming the mindset
of the England football team at the 2018 World
Cup. Pippa is currently group chief culture
officer with the Right to Dream Group.*

DIVERSITY, INCLUSION and equality have been live
topics in football for some time. They are critical subjects,
essential for the wellbeing of the game, the people within
it and the people who love it. I'm glad that the conversation
is alive and that work is being done. But something
consistently troubles me about our narratives on diversity,
inclusion and equality.

Underneath these narratives is the little idea that the
group to whom the game belongs need to 'make room' for
others, to share what is essentially and historically 'theirs'

and to do so is the just and fair thing. It is a position based on small nudges to the status quo. It isn't radical, it's a concession. To me, this is an *unnatural* position and a handbrake on the game evolving to its best version.

I have a vision for a game that is shaped more naturally and less industrially. A game where those who get to play are not chosen on the basis of category or their birth lottery, but on the basis of desire and talent. A game that is accessible in diverse ways and not restricted to commoditised, productised and exclusive watch-play-compete models, and a game that understands that being optimal is actually about complexity and harmony, not about sameness and false stability.

Nature already gets all of this.

In nature, harmony isn't just about equal parts, in fact it's not even about permanent balance. It's about true diversity that enables the whole system to flourish and evolve. We often hear people talk about football as a metaphor for life. Maybe we should think about that as a metaphor for *all life*, not just human life, and pick up some new ideas.

The principles of ecology, as taught to me by Dr Lori Pye at the Viridis Graduate Institute in the USA, would be an interesting place for us to start looking at how football could be shaped more naturally.

For example, the principle that *everything runs on energy*. In nature, this is about the constant exchange of energy required to sustain life on the planet, and there are different systems and types of energy. It's the same in the game; there is a psychological energy that underpins the way the game operates.

Today, I would argue that this psychological energy is a starkly competitive, self-interested and gain-oriented energy that inevitably leads to scarcity mentalities. In nature and in human nature, hypercompetitive systems where everyone and everything is competing for the same resources pretty much always lead to exploitation and extraction. The idea that the more others have, the less you will have reigns supreme, and so people seek to own resources like talent and exploit resources like money and power. If this is the primary energy of the game, the kind of abundance mindset that is necessary for real equality and real inclusion will never truly happen.

I suggest that the energy that the game needs is the one that is actually primary in nature (despite what we see on documentaries designed to highlight charismatic predators); and that is the energy of co-operation. This means those with resources understand that they need to share some of those resources for the whole system to thrive. It means not taking more than is needed and hoarding it, and it means operating in a way that maintains equilibrium and avoids extreme imbalance. We might call this radical co-operation, and it requires that we get beyond our egos and scarcity narratives and change the psychological energy of the game completely.

Another principle in ecology is that *change is inevitable*. Absolutely nothing stays static in nature, even if the change is happening across geological time that we cannot detect, like the redirection of a river or the breaking down of rocks to make sand, it is happening. As much as we relish the traditions, heritage and format of football, if we expect to thrive rather than just survive, we will need to embrace evolutionary change. Perhaps in leadership terms, this evolution should be about creating impact in the game and in the world beyond it rather than maintaining the efficiency of non-stop winning performances. Nature isn't all about efficiency. It is about successful regenerative strategies that will sustain the next generations and recreate life. We might call that radical leadership.

A third ecological principle is that *everything is interrelated*. The natural world doesn't have silos. The tree you can see out of your window doesn't really stand in isolation, it is part of an unseen system, and if one part of that system becomes unhealthy, undernourished, restricted or toxic, eventually the tree will suffer in size or in its ability to reproduce. What we allow to exist in one area of the game will not remain ring-fenced in its reach and impact. Racism in the stands, elitist breakaway leagues or financial corruption in the corridors of power can never be disregarded as somebody else's problem if we want to flourish. Perhaps it is time to accept that the game is really a system of relationships, not a system of divisions. We might call this radical connection.

Fourth is the ecological principle of *no waste*. There is no waste in nature, but plenty in human nature. Psychological waste can come in the form of ego, envy, misogyny, racism, elitism, homophobia, entitlement, better-than-you ideas, and fear of failure. This 'waste' leads to deep human loneliness and away from the joy and genius that playing or loving football can inspire. There is psychological waste in every story that gets told of needing to smash the opponent, every myth of who you have to be to win, and every fear-filled hyper-masculine environment that gets created where a person feels they cannot show their true identity. There is waste in our biases and in our old, dead ideas about who is a real footballer or a real coach; who belongs in the game. As in nature, we can 'compost' this kind of thinking and use what we have learned to create fertile conditions for a better, more robust future for the game – maybe we call this radical health.

The final principle in ecology is that *diversity is necessary to flourish*. As climate change is showing, sometimes we only notice how important diversity in nature is once we start to lose it. It's the same in the game. A lack of diversity relentlessly and sometimes silently erodes the full potential of football and its people. Diversity isn't just a numbers game, or an effort at representation. It is a raging resistance to sameness and staleness, a desperately needed avoidance of the monocultures that always lead to impoverishment. It is inviting chaos and conflict and difference as well as freshness of perspective and method, because it is those things that create opportunity and regeneration. Harmony in nature isn't always pretty and it definitely isn't stable. It is a constant rebalancing and recalibrating towards optimal conditions, and that requires difference – different bodies, different voices, different agendas. This would be radical harmony.

Perhaps 3.8 billion years of nature's intelligence has something to teach us about reshaping football, naturally.

56

Giving Back to Youth – by Pamela Coke-Hamilton

Pamela has served as executive director of the International Trade Centre since 1 October 2020. The International Trade Centre (ITC), the joint development agency of the World Trade Organization and the United Nations, is dedicated to supporting the growth of micro, small and medium-sized enterprises (MSMEs) in all developing countries and transition economies, and in doing so aims to develop and connect local economies to international markets, raising incomes and creating job opportunities, especially for women, young people and poor communities.

FROM CRICKET to football – with the national team called the 'Reggae Boyz' revealed to the world during the 1998 World Cup (and the 'Reggae Girlz'!) – to the development of athletics, sport really belongs to both the culture and the history of my country: Jamaica. Jamaica enjoys more victory per inhabitant in athletics than any other country in the world! Jamaican children start doing sports as an everyday activity at school at a very young age. Talented youngsters would often be offered scholarships for their education, a real chance to go to university and to escape poverty or criminal activities. And many of them will want to compete at 'The Champs', the Inter-Secondary Schools Boys and Girls Championships. This is where the story started for many of our champions from Merlene Ottey to Usain Bolt and, more recently, our female athletes, who dominated the sprints at the Tokyo Olympic Games in 2021.

I am proud that ITC started its Sport for Development initiative in 2019: Kick for Trade. This approach uses football to build youth entrepreneurial capacities and capabilities by offering educational opportunities and developing life skills transferrable to workplace and in community life. It fosters increased employability and entrepreneurship, particularly for youth, people with disabilities and other vulnerable groups, to enter and succeed in the labour market.

The world today hosts 1.8 billion young people. One in five is neither in employment, education nor training. Youths aged 15 to 24 are facing the challenge of joblessness with around a 15 per cent youth unemployment rate in the world. On average, youth unemployment is triple the rate of total unemployment (Source: ILOSTAT Database, 15 June 2021). Lack of skills and missing access to networks contribute to this tragedy. Kick for Trade aims to address some of the most pressing social challenges related to youth unemployment and limited new business opportunities. These interlinked factors inhibit sustainable economic development and engender vulnerabilities in communities, which can in turn create negative consequences, such as poor provision of health, education and social care services.

Mobilising capital for Sport for Development implies creating and building partnerships between different actors from the public and private sector and local communities, which requires mutual trust and understanding, as well as shared goals and leveraging the expertise of stakeholders. I believe that all professional football clubs should be part of this ecosystem through their foundations.

Football motivates and enthuses young people in a way that no other sport does. The investments made by the football industry on the economic and social development of young people (e.g. education, skills development and youth employment) have great potential for collaboration and action in advancing the Sustainable Development Goals (SDGs). However, Football for Good organisations, for instance, lack financial sustainability to implement their programmes. As argued by Ben Sanders (sportanddev.org), now is the time to ensure sport better serves society.

We know that MSMEs contribute both directly and indirectly to the Sustainable Development Goals, so it makes sense to strengthen their ability to become game changers in the respective sectors and countries in which they operate. The UN secretary general's annual report on SDG progress was clear that globally we are in a precarious place. The call was made to 'use the recovery to adopt low-carbon, resilient and inclusive development pathways that will reduce carbon emissions, conserve natural resources, create better jobs, advance gender equality and tackle growing inequities'. What is the football industry doing in that regard?

Today, developing nations are drained of their best players by the international trade and very little is done to support the further development of football and, beyond football, of the economy in those countries. It is striking to see that 18 per cent of French Ligue 1 players come from

Africa, representing half of the foreign players. The English Premier League, the richest league in Europe, has nine per cent of its players coming from Africa. Similarly, African players represent almost one-third (32 per cent) of players in the Belgian league. How can the economic success of those European leagues, increasingly built on markets in Africa and Asia, be redistributed to develop local economies and MSMEs in those parts of the world?

I would build on the current amazing Common Goal platform and would go a step further by changing some governance aspects and suggesting policies:

1. Make redistribution of 1% earnings from professional football clubs from the European leagues to developing countries mandatory in their status. The overall size of the European football market in revenue terms reached €25.2bn for 2019/20 (Source: Deloitte annual review of football finance, 2021).
2. Tax all player transfers by 1% to pledge to the Common Goal fund. Looking at the past ten years, football clubs spent a total of US$48.5bn on transfer fees (Source: FIFA report on ten years of international transfers, 2021).
3. Tax all agents' commissions by 1% to pledge to the Common Goal fund. Again, based on the FIFA report, US$3.5bn was spent on agents' fees over the past ten years.

With this change in the status and regulation of professional football, we could redistribute US$300m every year to emerging countries. This does not even count the generous efforts of players, managers or fans already members of the Common Goal platform. I would also suggest structuring the allocation of funds to nurture inclusive economic growth and provide job opportunities for youth and women in these territories, delivering on SDG8: Decent Work and Economic Growth. The structure added to the football clubs' status and policies in transfers would include the following:

1. Grassroots: Football clubs' foundations to support inclusive and safe access to sport facilities. Allocation of funds by territory could be done based on the nationalities represented in the teams. This would allow the clubs to build relationships with their local communities while enabling countries where players are coming from to develop football academies and simply football for all, with a mandatory focus on women to advance gender equality in football.

2. Sport for development programmes: in order to tackle the skills gap faced by youth including life skills for employability and entrepreneurship, equip them with the skills they need to succeed in today's labour market.

   At ITC, we focus on both soft and technical skills training and build linkages with the private sector to ensure positive labour market outcomes for youth participants. We believe in helping them find and create decent jobs for themselves, their families and their societies. By using Sport for Development, we achieve economic and social inclusiveness for youth – in their workplace and the community life. I believe the whole ecosystem (players, clubs, industry, sponsors, policymakers, etc.) needs to work together to support youth from all sides, to provide institutional strengthening and cohesion.

3. Access to capital for MSMEs in developing countries: at ITC, we will continue supporting enterprises to get

ready for the new green normal and the digital transition. However, youth in developing countries often lack access to capital to allow them to build inclusive and environmentally responsible business models and supply chains or even to capitalise on new technologies. We can offer tailored access to finance solutions to youth-owned MSMEs at different growth stages by partnering with the football industry to help raise capital for young people from poor communities, thereby contributing to inclusive economic growth.

57

Maximising the Social Benefit of Football – by Moya Dodd

Moya is a lawyer and a football administrator, who has been a board member at Football Federation Australia, the Asian Football Confederation and the FIFA Council, the highest governing body in football. She is currently a special advisor to the Centre for Sport and Human Rights and chair of Common Goal. During the 1980s and 1990s, Moya represented Australia at senior international level.

IF YOU'D met me as a kid, you'd have thought I was the least likely person ever to enter the halls of FIFA.

My mum was an Australian-born Chinese Seventh Day Adventist, and a great proponent of healthy eating and vegetarianism long before lentils were fashionable. My dad was a fireman, having worked as a professional acrobat in gangster-owned pubs before deciding on a less risky career in firefighting. We lived in a fire station – and no, we did not have a pole.

I grew up in Adelaide, Australia – a city where sport was men's sport, meaning cricket in summer and Australian rules football in winter. I played both, in backyards and schoolyards – but there was no place for me in a proper team.

So, there was I – a half-Chinese kid, living in an Adelaide fire station and taking Nutmeat sandwiches to school, where I kicked an egg-shaped ball with boys whose team I could never join. We didn't have a TV, so I'd never even seen a football game. The FIFA boardroom was as far away as it could possibly be.

Somehow, football found me. When colour TV came, my parents finally bought one. Immediately, the only football show became the best hour of my week. I watched, learned, imagined and practised. I found a team, played and represented. I won, lost, and had triumphs, injuries and adventures on grass rectangles from Port Adelaide to China, where, in 1988, I was subbed into the very first game of women's football that FIFA ever organised. Australia beat Brazil 1-0 to begin the journey that is the World Cup dream of today's Matildas.

After priceless years in the national team, a busted anterior cruciate ligament (ACL) took me from international football to recreational leagues with my mates, and another life completing an MBA and working in law, media and consulting.

Years later, football found me again. Would I be interested in joining the board of Football Australia? And how about Asia? They've just created quota positions for women. And now FIFA, too. Interested?

Somehow, I found myself taking a seat at a large square table in a vast underground room in Zürich. I'd arrived on the FIFA board, at the pinnacle of world football governance, as one of the first three women after 108 years of all male rule.

What I found in that boardroom was power and privilege, born of the universal popularity of football and its unique convening force.

The first piece of advice I was given – by a senior member of FIFA's board – was not to speak in meetings. Clearly, my political survival prospects were maximised by simply doing nothing. Yet the entire point of a quota position is to represent the under-represented group. My job was at the very least to advocate for women's football and gender equality. That could not be done by silence.

So, I decided to speak in every meeting. I was acutely conscious that women are perceived to speak more than they actually do (yes, there are studies on this), so I chose my topics frugally. I also avoided speaking in meetings if I could achieve the same objective another way, for example by speaking privately.

Because I was 'co-opted', I didn't have a vote. What I did have was access and proximity to power. I could observe, learn and understand. I could ask questions, tug on sleeves and make suggestions.

As for the people I met – they ranged from outright infidels (some of whom pleaded guilty to corruption charges and served jail terms) to loyal foot soldiers to real visionaries; from the deeply compromised to the truly outstanding.

But good people in a bad system are always at risk. And even when bad people are removed, a bad system replaces them with someone very similar.

As a case in point, I was present both times during 2015 when the famous Baur au Lac hotel in Zürich was raided by law enforcement agents who arrested various FIFA colleagues under indictments from the US Department of Justice.

The second time, the people who were arrested were the replacements of those who were arrested the first time.

It's clear: until we fix the system, it will continue to replicate itself.

How do we go about fixing a system as troubled as football? Many measures have been taken in recent years; some have been effective or retain the promise of being so. Gender equality provisions, human rights recognition and improved transparency have all featured. Their impact to date has been meaningful, but insufficient. There is much further to go.

What else is needed? For starters: wider diversity of stakeholders in decision-making bodies; greater transparency of decisions; term limits at all levels of governance; and meaningful enforcement and remedies when standards are breached.

But most fundamentally, football needs a profound rethink as to what it is and who it is for.

Right now, the game is a pyramid which draws the elite to the top. Can you score goals? Can you starve the other team of the ball? Can you make us win the league? Come on in! Since the first game of schoolyard pickup, we learned that we are valued for what we are worth to the game. The best players were given attention and opportunities; the rest just got by or dropped out.

Imagine – if you can – a game where our first question is not how good you are at football, but how good football can be for you. What would happen if we allocated resources and opportunities according to who would most benefit from them, instead of who is best able to help you win?

Sound revolutionary? Perhaps not as radical as it first sounds – because this is how markets work.

Economists talk a lot about efficient markets. One crucial concept is allocative efficiency, where resources and production are allocated to what society needs and values the most.

Imagine if the schoolyard pickup game chose players on the basis of how much they would benefit from playing that game of football. Among the first chosen might be the kid whose home life is difficult, the kid who has always been told she's no good at sport, the kid without friends, the kid who has never ever played before.

It is not the least bit revolutionary to allocate resources (the opportunity to play a game) to those who will derive the most value from it. Examples abound: public healthcare and social security systems are designed to provide access or support to those who need it most. Auctions are won by whoever bids the highest price, which is a proxy for how much the bidder values it. Why should sport, which belongs to everyone, not do the same in maximising the social benefit it can generate?

Imagine the aggregate value of that schoolyard kick-about, to each of its participants. Imagine the spin-off of social good if all of football leant into social purpose.

That's why I joined Common Goal, as chair of the steering board. I love that football's participants are taking responsibility themselves for ensuring that the game delivers a social dividend to the world.

Of course, football will always nurture the best players to put on a great show. But – as it turns out – winning isn't everything. I know this, because I see people who actually have won everything joining Common Goal because they want to achieve more. I see Juan Mata (World Cup, European Championship and Champions League winner), Alex Morgan (World Cup, Olympic gold medal, Champions League winner) and Jürgen Klopp (Champions League, Premier League, Bundesliga and Club World Cup winner) as team-mates in Common Goal, seeking to save the world through the UN Sustainable Development Goals.

That's football for good. And that's a team we all can join.

58

Team Game, Individual Roles, Collective Impact – by Serge Gnabry

*Serge is a professional footballer who plays for
Bayern Munich and the German national
team. He has won the Bundesliga with
Bayern Munich on three occasions as well as the
UEFA Champions League and the FIFA Club
World Cup. Serge became the sixth player to join
Common Goal in 2017.*

FOOTBALL IS a team game, and we can only succeed by working together. That's the foundation of our success at Bayern Munich. But teams are also made up of individual players, each with their own roles and responsibilities to perform, and if we don't play our part, the team does not achieve its potential. I believe the same applies off the pitch, in working towards a better world, and when I joined Common Goal in 2017, becoming part of an incredible team of players dedicated to making a difference through our collective efforts, I recognised that I had a role to fulfil.

When he was a young man, my father travelled from Ivory Coast to Germany. He didn't intend to stay forever, but he met my mother and together my parents provided me with a loving home and a privileged upbringing that enabled me to pursue my dreams. As my life and career have progressed, my parents and my close friends have kept me grounded and focused, and being socially aware has always been a part of this. I've also been fortunate to be represented by an agency that understands and shares my commitment to social contribution.

The link to Ivory Coast has always been strong, and when I joined Common Goal, alongside supporting projects in Germany, I wanted to further connect with my heritage in West Africa. In 2019, I went to Ivory Coast to visit Tackle Africa, a Common Goal organisation that delivers HIV and sexual and reproductive health and rights information and services to young people. It was a life-changing trip for me, and the first time that I had seen football used in such a structured and powerful way to engage, educate and inspire. I have stayed connected, and together with the team at Common Goal, we are now planning to develop a safe space facility in the country, combining a football pitch with an education and innovation centre, and providing health, education and employability programming for young people. The concept is inspired by a successful model pioneered by Amandla, an organisation in South Africa, and working together, we are hoping to extend the model globally, to provide more disadvantaged young people with a safe and inspirational place to develop and achieve their potential.

I am excited by what we can achieve in Ivory Coast, and further afield, and in parallel with my ambitions on the pitch – to win trophies and to hit certain targets for goals and assists – there are more things that I want to achieve in terms of social impact. Some of these are individual efforts, but within Common Goal they are always pursued within the context of a team, and when I hear about what other players are doing, such as Pernille Harder championing LGBTQ+ rights and William Troost-Ekong fighting neglected tropical diseases in Nigeria, I am inspired to fulfil my role and to strengthen my contribution. The more individuals who join us and play their part, the stronger the team and the more powerful the collective impact.

And that team goes beyond professional players. Football is a global community that unites people like nothing else, with so much potential for change. Imagine what could happen if every person and every organisation within that community decided to act collectively, and to embed purpose more systemically in the game. What if the 1% principle of Common Goal became standard across the global transfer system, so that every player sale reinvested something back into the football ecosystem? Ideas such as this are bold and innovative, but they are also achievable, and in the long term they are in the interests of the global game. So why not do it? Football is always changing and we need football leaders who are brave enough to pursue change that is purpose-driven.

That's what Radical Football is for me. A beautiful new way of playing the game off the pitch where everyone plays their part. Whether it's professional players speaking up for and supporting the causes that are close to their hearts, fans acting collectively to stop racism and injustice, or football administrators having the courage to be genuinely led by the interests of people and planet. In 2030, I'll be 35, and I hope that I can look back at even more individual and team success for club and country in the years between now and then. I also hope to reflect back on the contribution that I have made away from the pitch, in working as a team towards the Sustainable Development Goals. Whether it's through Common Goal or another way or playing your part, I hope you'll become a team-mate of mine in the coming years, on the biggest team on Earth, playing the most important game in history – the game of our lives.

59

Reconnecting with the Soul of Football – by Tom Vernon

Tom is founder and chief executive of Right to Dream, a group of academies and clubs in Ghana, Denmark and Egypt, with plans to expand to other parts of the world. Tom's story is told in detail in Chapter 47.

AT RIGHT to Dream, we are striving to show that football can be done a different way, that commercial and competitive success can go hand in hand with being purpose-driven. We hope that other clubs and academies will follow, not just because it is the right thing to do, but because it works.

We also believe that foundational changes in the game are essential, and where better to start than with the biggest stage of all – the World Cup.

Some things are too big to see. We can't retreat far enough to hold them fully in view, and therefore they seem like they are the whole world, everything, the only reality. So it is with structural racism within football; not bananas being thrown on pitches or banners flown over the Etihad – abhorrent and cowardly as these actions are, at least we can see them and see the perpetrators for what they are. Structural racism is the racism we don't see. The racism that means five World Cup spots for 54 African teams is accepted as normal. The racism that means Europe's money and ability to generate money cements its place at the top of the footballing pyramid.

To see these structures more clearly, we can take a few steps back in time.

England did not win the World Cup in 1966.

Sixteen teams participated in a football tournament in England in the summer of 1966; five were from Latin America (Brazil, Mexico, Argentina, Chile and Uruguay), ten were from Europe (England, Bulgaria, France, West Germany, Portugal, Spain, Switzerland, the Soviet Union, Italy and Hungary) and North Korea represented the rest of the world. Asia/Africa/Oceania had one spot.

Kwame Nkrumah, Ghana's first prime minister and president, instigated the idea for African teams to boycott this charade, partly because of the ludicrous unfairness of the qualification system and partly because of FIFA's inability to decide whether or not to suspend apartheid South Africa's membership (they didn't, then they did, then they didn't for a bit longer until finally they did), which says a lot about the organisation's moral courage at the time. This meant that Africa's population of approximately 328 million people had zero representatives (zero players representing African countries – the tournament's top scorer and best player, Eusébio, was born in Maputo, Mozambique). Three continents, one spot. No African nations represented. England did not compete against the world in 1966 because most of the world was not given the chance to compete. England did not win the World Cup in 1966 because a tournament that excludes the majority of the world is not a World Cup.

We would like to think that things have changed radically in the intervening 54 years, that football has become fairer and more just, and that the World Cup has become a truly representative celebration of our game. We would be wrong. Like Eusébio, many of Africa's greatest sons still play for foreign nations and the structurally racist exclusionary model is in full force.

The qualifying structures that have been put in place are still based on the colonial outlook of the 1960s. They keep European nations firmly at the top of the footballing pyramid. In Europe, 55 teams are competing for 13 places at the next World Cup. In Africa, 54 teams are competing for just five. 'European teams are better' come the indignant cries. Why are they better? Money. Europe is the pre-eminent footballing power because of money. Money for balls, money for stadiums, money for coaching courses, money so that there's enough food to eat, money so that everyone can go to school, money so that everyone can go to the hospital.

Money gleaned well into the second half of the 20th century from direct exploitation of Africa – when Pelé was playing in his first World Cup Final, over 90 per cent of sub-Saharan Africa was owned, was possessed, by European nations.

European nations have used wealth gained through the enslavement and exploitation of Africa to improve every part of their cultural and sporting lives, yet they still give themselves almost three times more places at the World Cup than they give to Africa: in 2018, the men's World Cup finals had 14 of Europe's 44 countries competing (31 per cent) and, in Africa, five from 54 (nine per cent).

This is what structural, systematic racism looks like.

Every time we allow this inequity, we hammer further into place all the injustices of the past. Injustices that have caused Denmark to have a better national side than Malawi, and Belgium to have played at 13 World Cups while the Democratic Republic of the Congo has played at one.

We are told that we are all part of the football family. In a loving and trusting family, the kind of families we all aspire to be part of, no one is undervalued or exploited or taken advantage of. But a family that sees some members as second class is not a family at all. If football were a true family, resources and opportunities would be shared equally. Africa would be properly represented at the World Cup and FIFA would play its part in redressing injustices visited by European nations upon Africa, and pay reparations to their football associations. But we are not a family, the idea of the 'football family' is merely an utterly cynical, morally bankrupt marketing tool.

African football must take a stand to achieve equal participation, to take reparative action for the injustice of the past 100 years in football and to remove the obstacles to future opportunity. A boycott of the World Cup by African teams and players would be a first step towards putting in place radical changes that are needed to right the wrongs of the past.

This could include the creation of an independent black managed reparatory fund, financed, but not administered, by FIFA to put in place the structures in African and Caribbean football that allow development of the game to world-class standards. Or a two per cent tax on turnover placed on every European and North American professional club as well as a 20 per cent reparation tax on national associations, to exclusively fund the creation of opportunity in football for people of colour, and to level the playing field in the long term.

And what about a World Cup qualifying campaign where we have 20 groups of ten? Each group has an equally divided number of countries per continent (so a group might be Argentina, Jamaica, Ireland, Portugal, Egypt, Kenya, Cameroon, Iran, India and Fiji, home and away). The top two qualify for the World Cup finals. The World Cup could then become truly global. Nigeria v England in Lagos! Spain v Mexico. It would take the best in the world, around the world. Sierra Leone v Brazil. Players and fans alike would be exposed to the global game and context, understanding its universal passion, but also the power it has to develop and bring change.

Football could also learn from the US sporting structures about how to give the teams at the bottom of the pile a route to the top. There is no better example of this in the NFL draft where the best player goes to the weakest team. Why not apply the methodology financially to the World Cup? The teams that finish last in the groups get the largest slice of the entire World Cup revenues. Would the impact of this structural and financial model achieve a levelling of the playing field over 50 years, and give everyone a chance?

Football is a reflection of humanity's soul. Its current construct reflects the structurally racist planet we live in. Radical change is needed, and what better place to start than football.

* * *

There are other areas of the game where foundational change must also be pursued. Women's football, for example, is entering a period of tremendous growth and opportunity, and in order to harness this energy into a major wealth generator for all of its stakeholders, does women's football need an unfettered unique constitution, focus and expertise? FIFA is a male construct, perhaps irreversibly entrenched in beliefs that might be a fundamental contradiction to the values and energy the women's game needs to develop a successful future. While the men's game must improve, does the women's game need the freedom to define its own future? Until recently, the positioning of the women's game as a 'department' (while there is no men's department) at FIFA reflects an institutional mentality that will not allow for this freedom. Instead, could the women's game be governed by a new global foundation?

Another example, could we abolish the transfer system? Having worked in player development for 20 years, the worst part of the job is putting a 'price' on your players and pushing for the club's financial upside which is potentially at conflict with your player getting the best possible contract at his next club. Again, looking to the USA, they have designed their top sports without transfer fees. The universities take care of the formation phase of an athlete's journey, and the franchises run the pro entertainment business. Meanwhile, in football, US$7.3bn was spent on transfers in 2019, and an estimated US$4bn–US$6bn was spent on youth development. What if this US$12bn was a tax on revenues of every professional club in the world, and redistributed to a global player development budget? We could have an academy with a budget of US$3m for every two million people in the world. In India and Africa combined, for example, there are not more than four academies with budgets this size – this model would create 1,000.

This could provide a long overdue fix to the unethical and relentless deselection of players in academies. The current problem is that staff are 'forced by the system' to view students as financial assets and make decisions accordingly. I believe 99.9 per cent of the people working in youth football don't want to think this way. They want to coach football and develop young people. Fixed budgets and players graduating as free agents, and moving as in the NBA, could fix this.

Some of these ideas might seem unrealistic, some might sound crazy, but we don't have to keep doing the same old things in the same old way, nor do we have to be guided by the same limited diversity of people and thinking. We must open up the conversation. No one owns football, and no group of people or institution has the right to tell us how to think about the game. The future of football can be great, but we must allow the whole global football community to contribute to shaping the vision. Only then can the true values of football, and humanity, shine through.

60

Shining a Light
– by Eniola Aluko

Eniola is sporting director at Los Angeles–based Angel City FC in the National Women's Soccer League. As a professional footballer, she won the Women's Super League with Chelsea on three occasions and Serie A with Juventus. Eniola was born in Nigeria and grew up in the UK, playing 102 games for England and representing Great Britain twice at the Olympics.

FOOTBALL IS a great socio-economic leveller. If you are good enough, and determined enough, you can make it. As a result, modern professional football is one of the most diverse and inclusive industries in the world, and it has enormous potential to leverage meaningful social change, and to positively change society.

My earliest memory was playing football. No one taught me how to do it, and the boys I played with instinctively included me. It was only later that I became aware that the opportunities for me in professional football were not the same as my male peers. That's when I trained to become a lawyer, and I pursued my club and international career alongside my studies and later my job. It was the same for all of us at the time, and I don't regret my path. It made me a more rounded person and it has opened up opportunities for me during and since my career as a professional player. Regardless of how much money there is in the game, I believe the football industry should do more to ensure that all professional footballers develop and grow away from the game. Becoming more socially conscious goes hand in hand with that.

Women's football is at an incredibly exciting time, and I'm proud that I was able to play a part in working towards this during my career on the pitch.

Inequality and discrimination exist. Fact. But we can change things. When I was playing, I aimed, alongside many others, to shine a light on these issues and to engage people in a way that was productive and respectful. We were listened to, and things have improved. There is much more we can and need to do, and by acting collaboratively and collectively we can aim high. The response of the football world in coming together against racism after Euro 2020 has shown us that. So too has the #MeToo movement, and so too has Common Goal.

As the women's game continues to evolve, I believe we should explore new ways of doing things, as well as keeping what has made the men's game successful, without being dependent on it. There is an opportunity to make football more inclusive, with a more diverse fan base, and to challenge some of the toxic and abusive behaviours and attitudes that are entrenched in men's football. We can also achieve a fairer distribution of wealth by reinvesting more in the grassroots of women's football, at the same time creating a more sustainable financial model.

At Angel City FC we are aiming to rewrite how women's sports clubs are organised. We are, uniquely, fully owned and fully led by women, and we hope to show that women's football clubs can be commercially viable as well as being purpose-driven. Without a ball being kicked, we have already secured partnerships with a number of global brands, and we have introduced a ten per cent contribution of funds towards social and community development that will be applied to all of our sponsorships. We also want to create a global impact, and to explore how the Angel City FC model could be applied in other parts of the world, including countries where gender inequality is most deep-rooted, and where women's football is in the earliest stages of development.

I believe, however, that we also need to continue thinking of football as one whole. It is the same game after all. This can help to create a more equitable sport, and in the same way that women's tennis has benefitted enormously from combined tournaments, women's and men's football could also be more integrated. Matches could be played back-to-back at the same stadium, widening exposure and encouraging fans to support both of their teams. Just like Wimbledon and the Olympics, football tournaments such as the World Cup could also be held at the same time. This would have all-round benefits, increasing audiences for women's football and allowing the environment of the women's game to positively influence the mentality of men's football, helping to create a more inclusive and respectful game.

At a governance level, we also need to push for more progressive and radical action to tackle discrimination and prejudice. Despite the solidarity of most people and fans to challenge racism, the governing bodies are not doing enough to address the issue, with token fines and measures that do little to incentivise real change. The response to the European Super League showed us that with a collective voice, we can make a difference – quickly and decisively; and FIFA's response to dealing with match-fixing shows us that when properly motivated, the governing bodies can act with resolve.

I joined Common Goal because I believe passionately in the power of football to directly assist some of the world's most disadvantaged people and communities. But I also believe that together we can do more to drive change in the game, and to send out a powerful message to the rest of society, by raising awareness of issues and injustices, and by lobbying for greater social responsibility in all areas of the sport. As the Common Goal movement grows, and as more players, clubs and fans join, our voice will become stronger, and our ability to influence the powerful institutions and decision makers within football will increase. The bigger the team, the bigger the impact, and by acting and speaking together, we can change the game, and the world, for the better.

61

Embedding 'Purpose' within a Football Club – by Preeti Shetty

Preeti has worked in Football for Good for over a decade, notably at the Football Foundation, a charity established by the Premier League, the FA and the UK government. She is founder of tech start-up Upshot, an impact measurement system used by more than 1,000 organisations globally. In 2021, Preeti took a position as a non-executive director at Brentford FC, becoming the only South Asian woman on the board of a Premier League club.

IF YOU asked me a few years ago all the different ways I saw myself making tangible change in football, sitting on the board of a football club would not have been one of them, much less a Premier League football club. But that is where I find myself and it's made me rethink my purpose in a whole new way.

I grew up in Dubai, without football playing a big part in my life. I am Indian and so cricket was the religion in my family, and I don't remember local football clubs being visible to us locally. I was a bit of a 'third culture' kid with quite a confused sense of identity. But then I moved to London when I was 19 and I got to choose – really decide for the first time who my football team would be and why. Who was playing well? Who was local to where I lived? Who had the best stadium? But I realised it only came down to one thing: where would I feel that I belonged? That is when I realised how closely football and values are intertwined.

I have worked in the world of football for 15 years – in the media, in grassroots, for corporates and in Football for Good NGOs. I started my career at BBC Sport at a project called BBC Your Game which gave me my first taste of Football for Good. I worked with numerous NGOs all over the world seeing the difference they made on the ground. I spent eight years at the Football Foundation learning how large funders and charities operate and I now run a tech start-up called Upshot that helps thousands of organisations collect good data and measure their impact. Outside of my day job, I also sit on the board of London Sport Trading, Street Child United, and, as of the summer of 2021, Brentford FC – coinciding with the first time Brentford has played top-flight football in 74 years. What a time I picked!

But this time is unique for other reasons also. Over the last decade I have seen numerous iterations of the word 'purpose'. Value-led, community-focused, Corporate Social Responsibility/opportunity, they all touched on 'your why' in some way. A whole bunch of new initiatives with great intention but often little impact. And trust me, if it isn't having any impact, we shouldn't be doing it. For me your purpose isn't something you can just decide. Hire a consultant, hold a workshop, and then pick a purpose that feels 'okay'. It needs to come from an innate sense of community or identity. It needs to come from looking within and understanding why you are here, understanding the role you play in your community or with your fans, the value you are adding by what you do.

So how does a football club embed purpose? When I reflect on this question, I consider that I am halfway through a five-step journey, and I can use the story of that journey to explain.

Football clubs get their legitimacy from their fan base and historically football was built for working-class communities. This is still reflected in many clubs around the world who still listen to, and cater for, their local fans and community. But it feels to me like this connection is threatened; in the big leagues anyway. Local has become global and clubs are starting to reinvent what their purpose is – to a more convenient model that fits nicely with their marketing and sponsorship requirements.

Brentford FC has always had a strong connection with its fans. Once run by the supporters' trust, our fans still own a golden share giving them a seat on the board and the right to veto certain decisions. Our owner, being a true fan himself, aligns with the values of the club but this golden share effectively protects the club's purpose, and enshrines it legally. What is amazing is that Brentford's real strength lies not in publicising that fact; instead, it comes from choosing to put its community first. It comes from genuinely wanting to be representative of our community and adding value to the local area. Just like me when I first moved here.

For the club this means more than funding another community programme or celebrating its amazing community trust or shouting on social media about religious holidays. Our purpose is forward-thinking football – inclusive, innovative and humble – on and off the pitch.

Building a genuine sense of togetherness with our players, our staff, our fans and our community and adding real value to our local area and to the Premier League.

So, knowing your purpose is step one. Now what? What's step two? The next stage is taking tangible, measurable strides to embed and achieve it. This is where Brentford and I cross paths.

In early 2021, Brentford FC did something no club has done – they went to an open advert to hire a new non-executive director for their board. This showed me their commitment to inclusivity, and I applied because I saw my values, and my purpose, reflected in them. In short, I applied because I could: I was welcome to. It was an open and transparent process at the highest levels of the game that gave an opportunity to anyone. And I got it! A woman, a person of colour, and a millennial. Brentford FC makes me feel like I belong, not just part of the club but immediately part of the family and the community. A respected addition whose voice is being heard. Good thing I have plenty to say!

Now to step three. If we're to give this third stage a name it's this, 'With great power comes great responsibility.'

I'm told I'm the only South Asian woman on a Premier League board. And that's great but so what? It's what I do next that counts: how am I listening to the voices of my community, ensuring they have a say, holding the door open for others like me? The club has given me the platform to try.

So, we have purpose, and action, followed by a recognition of the power and responsibility that comes with this.

Step four. How will we know we have succeeded? Well, there is no such thing as enough when it comes to these things. You can always do more. But how will we know we are making a difference? For me, the answer is data. My day job with Upshot is helping organisations measure their impact, understanding their why and their 'so what', using data to help inform their decision-making. The same applies here – in order to know whether we are really being purposeful, we need to measure change: with whom we engage, in attitudes and behaviours, in changes to recruitment and policies. We need to be data-driven and evidence-led. We need metrics and targets. This is not easy because often change is slow and it's easier to run a PR campaign than it is to change your structure or your culture.

But it's very important to do this. To take the hard path. Football, in my opinion, has never been in a worse place – morally, fiscally and emotionally. The data is telling us that younger generations are disillusioned by football, and our communities are feeling isolated. Our politics are polarised, and this is reflected in our game. Whatever successes we see on an individual club basis, this is not the time for us to be looking back and congratulating ourselves. The work is not even close to being done. The last year of exacerbated inequalities, increased racism and more social isolation has shown us that. This is just the beginning and my vision for football is that football looks within itself, understands where it adds value and how it can have the most impact and then lives by this everyday – authentically, openly, transparently. Even when it's difficult.

Step five. If we aren't looking ahead, we are looking behind. The world is changing every day, quicker than we ever knew possible. The rapid adoption of alternative technologies such as blockchains and cryptocurrencies – especially among young people – is a telling sign that the future of football will be very different from now. And if we don't embed our purpose authentically, football will just be left behind. The world is more connected than ever before and if we want to achieve real impact, another CSR programme will not cut it. We need to be giving people a seat at the table and a chance for their voices to be heard, the opportunity to co-create what they want themselves.

Football, as the most viewed sport in the world, is one of the most important battlegrounds for purpose. We've all seen what happens when a club like Lewes FC or an athlete like Marcus Rashford takes a stand on an issue. So, what we – the decision makers in the game – do next matters. We need to be actively creating the future of football we believe in. A football that is values-based, that understands its reason to be, and its role in its community; a football that is one with fans. A football that makes people proud on the pitch as well as off it. This may seem radical now but the future of football depends on it. And, after all, it's just good business.

62

A New Democracy Must Put Our Human Needs First
– by Jonas Baer-Hoffmann

Jonas has been general secretary of FIFPRO, the international professional football players' union, since 1 January 2020. FIFPRO, based in Amsterdam, represents more than 65,000 professionals worldwide across 65 member associations. Prior to several roles at FIFPRO, Jonas was general secretary of Spin, the German professional basketball players' union, and previously worked for EU Athletes, a multi–sport federation of athlete and player associations.

FOOTBALL IS stuck in a crisis of leadership. The institutions who once charged themselves to govern the sport are turned inwards, detached from the people they serve, trapped inside endless battles over territory, bickering over who organises which competitions and where. They offer little vision of how our sport might sustainably and inclusively evolve into its potential in the decades to come. Endless growth, for its own sake, seems to be the only goal.

The millions of individuals who live football – players, professional and amateur, supporters, coaches, referees – can hardly recognise themselves in the boards that manage our game. The path forward must go far beyond any set of technical reforms: we have come too far. Instead, we need new thinking, a new sense of purpose, leadership by genuine values. How might we start afresh, and what should be the founding principles of a better path?

Let us start by looking at ourselves. In 2022, our societies embrace their diversity more than ever before. People have understood this; they demand to be heard. Democracy is being asked to renew one of its oldest missions: to build open institutions that reflect who we are, and what we value. How could football or any other human activity escape such a call? The world's most popular sport must face a simple truth: the millions of people who play and watch football want to shape its future.

Why, in the world of football, should our most basic human concerns – our desire to learn and flourish, to compete and win, but also to be part of something bigger, a collective – not be the central mission of our democracy? And so the question we must ask is this: can we invent a collective governing culture and model, built on a new set of principles, which would allow all players to reach their full potential – as athletes and humans, respectful of their physical and mental health, mindful not only of their community of fellow players but of the sport's vital role within our local, national and international communities?

Athletes are humans in all our complexity: powerful and vulnerable, capable of excellence and prone to error, uniquely outstanding and one small part of a wider group. They have never been and will never become resources or assets or costs; they cannot be bought and sold; their true value lies not in any statistics or percentages but in the human relations and shared experiences that bind them to each other, to their clubs and their supporters. For the governance of football, this should be our point of departure.

What does democratic football look and feel like when we put human needs at the centre?

- We see players as humans who enjoy all fundamental rights, and who seek dignity and fulfilment in their work, free to offer their skills as part of a fair and transparent contract.
- We see human relations at the centre of life in a club, where individual players, coaches and administrators have chosen to commit to a common endeavour, making their own contribution to a shared history, embedded in a local community of supporters.
- We see our stadiums as a shared home, where everyone is welcome except those who seek violence and hate. Places where football brings out our brightest passion but not our darkest instincts.
- We create environments that respect the physical and emotional integrity of all, free of sexual, physical and emotional abuse, exploitation or harassment, and where we ensure protection, support and remedy for those who are harmed.
- We put the physical and mental health of all players first, and treat serious injuries, like concussions, as an urgent priority because we learn to balance the responsibility for long-term well-being with short-term gain.

The democratic institutions to express such a vision would grow naturally out of the communities that make football work, starting with the people who devote their lives to the game. But they deserve and require accountability, shared responsibility, inclusive democracy, selfless leadership.

Democracy, at its core, is our continuous human endeavour to peel away the layers of power, ideology and prejudice, which serve only those who seek dominance and commercial gain. To put our human needs at the centre of democracy is to allow every individual to flourish: to develop our natural abilities and to learn new skills, to find dignity in our work and a sense of belonging in our community. By focusing on what makes us human, we might take up once again the centuries-old endeavour to govern ourselves freely, rooted in our values, so that together we find the true purpose in our lives.

This is the new ground for collective governance in football: where human rights, the rule of law and the right to democratic representation become our new foundation, a set of values that underpin every part of our industry. Where players and their employers around the globe, in clubs and leagues of every size, shape their world of work as part of an inclusive, sustainable vision for the sport. Where a new social contract of employment embodies these values, because it is fair, transparent and protected by the law. A world in which we share the stewardship of the game and therefore share in the responsibility to govern it, grow it, protect it and evolve it.

This is no revolution – it's a world that already exists, in the dreams of young players and in the minds of those who see the need for change. Our path is clear if we find the will to follow it.

63

Radical Teamplay
– by Jürgen Griesbeck

DURING THE entire experience of pulling together this book, I had all kinds of feelings. From gratitude and pride for so many people giving their all over the years, to slight shame thinking about why my story should be told while countless others remain unwritten, to surprise at how all the pieces finally seem to fall into their place with only this inner voice and absolutely no strategic plan when this whole journey started nearly 30 years ago, to disappointment about myself because now I could see clearly the many wrong choices that had taken their toll and sad about all the moments I had missed with my loved ones, to extreme joy about where we've landed with our collective effort and finally to renewed motivation for how much more we still need to do.

The good news is that we've never been so many. That despite the magnitude of the challenges, we have never had this wealth of solutions at our disposal, which brings it all down to one very simple question: do we really want change?

Do we really want to fix the planet and save our people? Or do we have to be honest with ourselves and accept that we actually don't want it enough?

This is why we talk about Radical Football, about unearthing its full potential and magic in a moment where both football and the world need it, desperately. Commercialised football can't live for much longer in this bubble, entrenched in its inner workings, wildly disconnected from fans, athletes and the world's reality, reducing itself to yet another entertainment industry and a playground for the capital of a few, while ignoring or exploiting a social dimension.

It has always been wrong, but now it starts to be dangerous, negligent. Despite all the wrongdoings of the past, football is maybe the only remaining unifying force of a universal nature. It connects all corners of the world, from backyards to living rooms, from streets to stadiums, from pubs and bars to boardrooms and corner offices, across all kinds of divides. It connects to the heart of people.

The Sustainable Development Goals represent a consensus regarding what needs to be fixed by 2030. To achieve it all, hardly anything needs to be invented. Most, if not all, solutions are readily available and striving to scale up. But we are not making progress fast enough mainly because of two gaps: a financial gap and a collaboration gap. There is a lot of conversation about the need for massive financial injection or redistribution, but hardly a word on the need to radically collaborate.

So, we have a collective agenda and we understand the challenges, but our mindset is still dominated by an interpretation of success that is intimately linked to the concept of individual accumulation. The more I have the more successful I am. Me over we, egosystem over ecosystem.

What if success was equal to contribution, with a focus on stakeholder wellbeing over shareholder value? Jack Sim, another thought leader, founder of the World Toilet

Organization and serial social entrepreneur from Singapore, brings it to the point and says we need to measure success by societal impact and 'redefine a billionaire as someone who has improved the lives of a billion people'.

It's time to make a choice.

For Common Goal we chose 1% because it's achievable – insignificant for most, but a game changer if every person and organisation with a stake in football did it. It's also democratic and symbolic, and only allows for change at scale if we all do it. Game of our Lives makes contribution of our time a valuable currency that, invested in concrete and meaningful tasks, offers the scale and, actually, limitless opportunities to act.

The ideas and endeavours of the Radical XI, and everyone else who wants to make football better and to increase its positive impact on society, hopefully serve as a spark to rally behind a shared vision which is within reach if we embrace radical teamplay.

And, we have a date – 2030 is the deadline for the UN's Global Goals. It is also the 100th anniversary of the men's World Cup. What if, instead of staging just another glamorous football event, the World Cup became a truly global celebration of football's contribution to people and planet? That would be the victory of our lifetime. For the first time in history, it would be a World Cup that rightfully carries its name, in which we all participated and we all had equity in, independently of where we live, who we are, where the event happens, who qualifies and who ends up lifting the trophy. It would be the result of our collective action. As a team we would have won this World Cup before the first whistle is blown.

What can you do to help make this vision a reality?

A lot is already being done by fans and athletes. Athlete activism is only growing, increasingly courageous, starting to reinterpret their platforms in support of the causes they are passionate about. Imagine what could be possible if all these individual efforts were efficiently coordinated, and if fans and athletes teamed up for meaningful and shared action? It doesn't matter how local or global, big or small your contribution is, I urge you to look around and connect yourself to the initiatives and movements that are building; they can help to leverage and magnify your efforts and to amplify and accelerate your impact. Only together can we drive action at a speed of change that is fast enough.

We also need decision makers, rights holders and traditional shareholders in the industry to take on true leadership. A leadership that feels the weight, and honours the privilege of acting in the name of football, at the service of its stakeholder, the people. Leaders who understand the true power of the game, who leverage, with respect and accountability, the love for the game which is shared by more than half of the world's population. Leaders who have the courage to unleash football's unique potential by challenging the comfortable but irresponsible status quo and take the game forward with bold, radical strides.

Let's all choose to be part of this change – it is necessary and it is possible. Football does belong to all of us and we all have our part to play. Each of us in our positions, together as a team.

Whatever your role, and whatever your stake in the game, if you believe in football to inspire humanity to strive for a better version of itself, then we need you on this team, now.

As a young leader who implements the football3 methodology in Colombia with Tiempo de Juego, I try to inspire other kids. Football is more than just people's favourite sport but a great enabler to build understanding, to develop shared goals, to have a space for personal growth and to raise the voice around important topics. From my own experiences, as a participant and as a coach, I know that football is a powerful tool to empower children and entire communities, and to build a common goal among everyone involved.

Katherine, age 18,
Monday, 15 November 2021

About the Author

Steve Fleming is the co-founder of Kick4Life FC, a multi-award-winning charity, social enterprise and football club based in Lesotho in Southern Africa. The organisation has reached more than 100,000 orphans and vulnerable children through health, education, gender and employability programmes, as well as providing structured training and employment opportunities to hundreds of young people via its hospitality enterprises – No.7 Restaurant and the Hokahanya Inn & Conference Centre. In 2020, Kick4Life FC became the first top-flight football club in the world to commit to gender equal pay and budgets, and Steve has worked globally through the organisation's training and consultancy service, Kick4Life Assist.

He is author of *Eleven: Stories of Development through Football*, published in 2010, and was named in the Beyond Sport Inspirational 50 in 2015. Steve lives with his wife and two daughters in Cambridgeshire in the UK.